THE
PRUNER'S
BIBLE

THE
PRUNER'S
BIBLE

A step-by-step guide to pruning
every plant in your garden

Steve Bradley

RODALE

A QUARTO BOOK

Published by Rodale Inc.
33 East Minor Street
Emmaus, PA 18098-0099

Library of Congress CIP Data
Bradley, Steve, date.
 The pruner's bible : a step-by-step guide to pruning every
 plant in your garden / Steve Bradley
   p. cm
 Includes index.
 ISBN-13 978–1–59486–033–1 paperback
 ISBN-10 1–59486–033–5 paperback
 1. Pruning. I. Title
 SB125 B73 2005
 631.5'42—dc22   2004026657

This book was conceived, designed, and produced by
Quarto Publishing plc
The Old Brewery
6 Blundell Street
London N7 9BH

Project editor: Jo Fisher
Art editor and designer: Sheila Volpe
Copy editor: Lydia Derbyshire
Illustrator: John Woodcock and Ann Savage
Photographer: Paul Forrester
Proofreader: Susie May
Indexer: Diana LeCore
Assistant art director: Penny Cobb

Art director: Moira Clinch
Publisher: Piers Spence

Color separation by PICA Digital, Singapore
Printed by Star Standard Industries Pte, Singapore

2 4 6 8 10 9 7 5 3 1 paperback

RODALE
LIVE YOUR WHOLE LIFE™

Contents

How to use this book

This book is laid out to give the maximum amount of information in the clearest possible way. An introductory section (pages 8 to 27) outlines the essential reasons for pruning, with information on tools and equipment, health and safety, and basic pruning techniques. The main part of the book is the plant directory (pages 28 to 175) which features over 70 of the most widely-grown garden plants. Arranged alphabetically by botanical name, each entry includes a general discussion of the plant, along with detailed pruning instructions and illustrations specific to each plant. At the back of the book you will find articles on specialist pruning topics, such as hedges, ground cover, and pruning climbers. In addition, charts and checklists give at-a-glance summaries of information, including a list of no- or low-prune plants.

40

Berberis (deciduous species)

Berberis, barberry

Berberis are good-value shrubs, providing leaf color, flowers, and berries, even in unpromising conditions.

Berberis thunbergii *f.* atropurpurea *is an attractive, deciduous shrub with dark reddish-purple, arching stems that turn brown-gray with age. The small, spoon-shaped leaves are copper-red in spring and summer, turning orange and crimson before falling in the fall. Clusters of small, yellow flowers tinged with red are produced in the spring followed by glossy red fruits.*

The genus contains both deciduous and evergreen species (see pages 42 and 43). The deciduous species have rather thin, spindly stems, which are armed with needle-sharp spines (usually arranged in clusters of three) along their length. These often remain long after the stems have died—so take care when you're handling prunings. The plants will survive in almost any soil as long as it is well drained and not too rich. They have shallow, fibrous root systems, which seem to deter other plants from growing close by. The shrubs will grow in full sun or partial shade, but the displays of fall leaf color and berries are far superior on plants growing in full sun. There is a wide choice of deciduous berberis species and cultivars, but you can usually prune all types in the same way.

The shrubs have broadly oval leaves, which are arranged in clusters close to the spines along the stem. The leaves are usually midgreen, and they often turn vivid shades of orange and red before falling in autumn. The pale-yellow to golden-yellow flowers are borne in small hanging clusters, usually in groups of three to five, along the length of the stems in midspring, and the flowers are often followed by small, red fruits in fall and winter. Plants can vary in height from 2 to 8 feet, and some forms spread to over 8 feet across, often forming a dense, tangled thicket of old, new, and dead stems.

Berberis thunbergii and its cultivars are widely grown, providing a wide range of leaf colors and habits of growth. The cultivars with red, gold, purple, and variegated leaves are the most popular. Be mindful that this species is spread by birds in wild areas and is considered invasive in much of the country.

Formative pruning

Prune young plants to encourage them to develop a bushy habit with strong shoots emerging from ground level.

After planting, cut out any weak or damaged growth. Lightly tip back the remaining shoots to about two-thirds of their length so that the plant will form new shoots from the base.

WHY PRUNE?

To make sure that a supply of new shoots emerges from ground level each year.

PRUNING TIPS

- *Wait until summer to remove dead wood—it's much easier to see then.*

PLANTS PRUNED THIS WAY

Berberis x ottawensis: *in early summer, immediately after flowering*
Berberis x rubrostilla: *in early summer, immediately after flowering*
Berberis thunbergii: *in early summer, immediately after flowering*
Berberis wilsoniae: *in early summer, immediately after flowering*

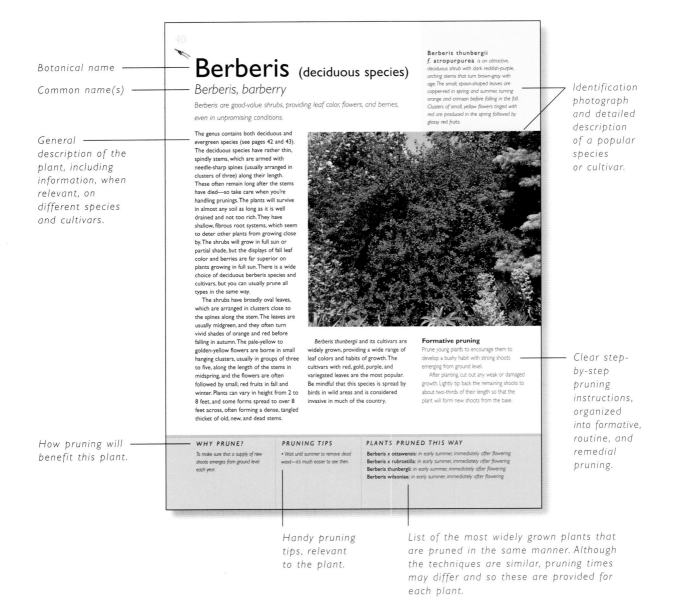

Botanical name

Common name(s)

General description of the plant, including information, when relevant, on different species and cultivars.

How pruning will benefit this plant.

Identification photograph and detailed description of a popular species or cultivar.

Clear step-by-step pruning instructions, organized into formative, routine, and remedial pruning.

Handy pruning tips, relevant to the plant.

List of the most widely grown plants that are pruned in the same manner. Although the techniques are similar, pruning times may differ and so these are provided for each plant.

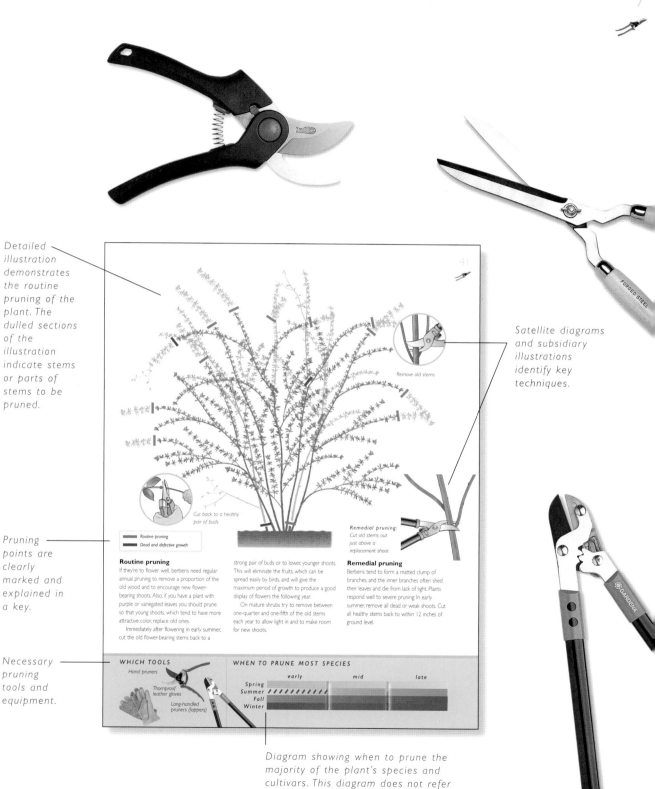

Detailed illustration demonstrates the routine pruning of the plant. The dulled sections of the illustration indicate stems or parts of stems to be pruned.

Satellite diagrams and subsidiary illustrations identify key techniques.

Pruning points are clearly marked and explained in a key.

Necessary pruning tools and equipment.

Diagram showing when to prune the majority of the plant's species and cultivars. This diagram does not refer to all species and cultivars; if you are unsure, refer to your local nursery.

41

Remove old stems

Cut back to a healthy pair of buds

Remedial pruning: Cut old stems out just above a replacement shoot

Routine pruning
Dead and defective growth

Routine pruning

If they're to flower well, berberis need regular annual pruning to remove a proportion of the old wood and to encourage new flower-bearing shoots. Also, if you have a plant with purple or variegated leaves you should prune so that young shoots, which tend to have more attractive color, replace old ones.

Immediately after flowering in early summer, cut the old flower-bearing stems back to a strong pair of buds or to lower, younger shoots. This will eliminate the fruits, which can be spread easily by birds, and will give the maximum period of growth to produce a good display of flowers the following year.

On mature shrubs try to remove between one-quarter and one-fifth of the old stems each year to allow light in and to make room for new shoots.

Remedial pruning

Berberis tend to form a matted clump of branches, and the inner branches often shed their leaves and die from lack of light. Plants respond well to severe pruning. In early summer, remove all dead or weak shoots. Cut all healthy stems back to within 12 inches of ground level.

WHICH TOOLS

Hand pruners

Thornproof leather gloves

Long-handled pruners (loppers)

WHEN TO PRUNE MOST SPECIES

	early	mid	late
Spring			
Summer			
Fall			
Winter			

PRUNING ESSENTIALS

Beginning with a practical discussion of the whys and hows of pruning, this first section contains some general pruning guidance for the home gardener. Basic pruning techniques are outlined and the proper tools and equipment described. This straightforward advice provides a sound starting point to help you prune your plants to their best advantage.

Why prune?

GENERATIONS OF gardeners have been mystified by the art of pruning. Some have even given up on pruning trees and shrubs altogether because they find it so mysterious. Fear of getting it wrong can mean that the unpruned plants don't perform as they should in terms of producing flowers or fruit and that they gradually deteriorate and become susceptible to pests and diseases. On the other hand, there are unknowing pruners who cut because they think it's the thing to do (but don't know how or why). Plants that are hastily and heavily pruned can be as unproductive as unpruned specimens and may bear no resemblance to the original form and habit of the plant. Well-pruned plants will produce more flowers, more fruit, or more colorful stems or leaves.

Look at the plants you have in your own garden. Instead of asking yourself why you should prune, you should ask yourself:

- *When do I prune my plants?*
- *How do I do it?*
- *What result am I hoping to achieve?*

At its simplest, pruning is a means of manipulating a plant's growth, shape, and productivity by cutting and training it to achieve what you want to happen. There are many different reasons for pruning plants, and, there are different reasons for pruning the same plant at different stages in its life. To prune plants well is not so much about knowing how and where to cut but about knowing what you're trying to achieve. Experienced gardeners are able to describe what a plant should look like when they've finished, even before they've taken their hand pruners out of their pocket.

Of course, not all plants have to be pruned regularly. Some are hardly ever touched or are pruned only when they start to spread out beyond the spot in the garden allocated to them. On the other hand, some plants exist in certain forms only because pruning shapes them in a certain way—without pruning, for example, there would be few formal hedges, ornamental or practical, and certainly topiary would never exist. If you grow fruit trees or bushes, pruning becomes an important way to keep the plants healthy and vigorous, and capable of bearing large yields.

It's also possible to prune for the wrong reasons. Gardeners who are determined to manage nature set out to create trees and shrubs that are uniform in size and shape, standing like troops on a parade ground. In these circumstances, gardeners prune plants so that they can exercise control in their neat, tidy gardens. Some municipal authorities savagely chop trees to a standard height and shape, simply to use labor resources efficiently. This shows scant regard for the growth patterns and flowering cycles of the different plants they are dealing with.

Pruning plants into structured, topiary shapes is *labor-intensive (and an art form in itself), but the results can be very rewarding if you desire a formal appearance for your garden.*

Conifers *provide the garden with a structured, formal framework. As long as proper formative pruning is carried out when the plant is young, most of them require little routine pruning.*

REASONS FOR PRUNING

Your reasons for pruning any plant should be specific to the plant and its purpose. You may use different techniques on a single plant over time to manage its growth and performance so that it fulfills a particular function at different stages in its life.

The main reasons for pruning are to train a plant to grow in a particular way; to balance its growth; to control the production of flowers and fruit; to maintain its health; and to restrict its growth. A final type of pruning, remedial or renovation pruning, may also be necessary from time to time.

TRAINING

A plant left to its own devices may not develop the shape and habit of growth you want, and you might need to help the plant along with some training. A type of

A flowering hedge (above) *will provide color as well as shelter and privacy. Time the pruning carefully to get the most out of the flowers.*

Many trees (left) *are pruned to have a clear stem or "leg" to allow light to penetrate to the base of the tree and enable other plants to grow under the tree's canopy.*

Traditional, formal knot gardens (right) *are created by clipping small-leaved plants, such as box, into geometric patterns.*

pruning—often referred to as formative pruning—takes place in the early years of a plant's life to encourage it to produce a framework of strong, well-positioned branches.

Careful pruning in the early years will allow you to create a plant that's well-proportioned, attractive, and that carries flowers or fruits where they are visible and easily reached for picking. A tree or shrub with well-spaced stems and branches with good angles—which will reduce the risk of breakage and stem splitting. Plants pruned correctly while they're young are easier to care for in later years. Time spent on training and pruning young plants should be regarded as an investment in their future and as a time-saving, long-term benefit for the gardener.

No amount of training, however, will achieve the impossible. A plant with an erect habit can not be trained to grow as a groundcover!

Buddleia is an excellent choice for a garden shrub, but it must be pruned regularly to prevent it from smothering the surrounding plants with its vigorous growth and long, arching branches.

BALANCING GROWTH

A healthy plant should show signs of vigorous, active growth, especially when it's young and establishing itself in the soil or growing medium and producing its framework of stems and branches. Any pruning in the early years should encourage the plant to develop into the shape you want.

Most plants will start to flower earlier in their lives if they are allowed to grow naturally. Pruning in the early stages can delay flowering. Young woody plants will often produce only a few flowers until they are established. As plants mature and begin to flower and fruit on a regular basis, the production of shoots will gradually slow down, so that fewer new shoots are produced each year and individual shoots are shorter. As plants age, there is less annual growth. While leaves are produced on older and on younger wood, it's often the younger wood that produces the flowers.

From the gardener's point of view, it's important that a plant's shoot growth and flower production are going on at the same time. Pruning should strike a balance, allowing woody plants to continue producing young woody stems while providing a regular display of flowers and fruits. Often, regulating the timing of pruning can maintain this balance. Pruning plants in late winter and early spring, for example, often encourages the plant to produce large quantities of new shoots, whereas pruning in midsummer can induce a plant to produce more flower or fruit buds for the following year. Even the simple process of removing old flowerheads (also known as deadheading) to prevent plants from producing seeds, will help to extend the flowering season, as plants continue to produce flowers if their energy is not devoted to producing seeds. A plant that has produced seeds will gradually stop flowering, as the previous flowers have served the intended purpose. Seed equals survival of the species.

CONTROLLING FLOWER AND FRUIT QUALITY

As plants develop a cycle of flowering and fruiting regularly, they often slip into overproduction. You have only to look at a rose or crabapple that has been left unpruned for a number of years to see that the more flowers and fruit a plant produces, the smaller they become. Often, too, the flowers and fruits on the inner sections of the branches are not only small but of poor quality.

Pruning away some sections of stems and branches allows you to remove some of the poorer stems altogether. Pruning weak stems also diverts energy into the production of larger, though fewer, flowers and fruit. A good example of this is the butterfly bush (*Buddleja davidii*). On an unpruned bush there may be profuse quantities of flower spikes, each about 4 inches long. A plant that's pruned

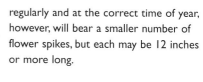

Dogwoods and willows (left and far left) *are often grown for their new growth, which provides beautiful color during the winter months. To achieve this, plants must be pruned hard annually.*

Many hollies (below left) *have a natural cone-shaped habit, which requires little pruning. However, they will also respond to being clipped into formal shapes.*

regularly and at the correct time of year, however, will bear a smaller number of flower spikes, but each may be 12 inches or more long.

CREATING A PATTERN OF GROWTH

Some plants don't have particularly nice-looking flowers—in fact, some plants produce flowers that are barely noticeable—but other characteristics do make them attractive garden plants. A number of deciduous shrubs, including dogwoods (*Cornus* spp.) and willows (*Salix* spp.), have colored bark that's especially bright in winter, and other plants, such as some hazels (*Corylus* spp.) and elders (*Sambucus* spp.), have large, colorful leaves in spring and summer. These colored stems and large leaves are produced only from the current season's growth, and the more vigorous this growth is, the better the effect will be. In both instances, the vigorous growth can be achieved only by severe pruning, often cutting down whole plants to within 4 to 6 inches of ground level each year.

MAINTAINING PLANT HEALTH

Combating pests and diseases is a vital part of gardening. Often the best method of control is prevention, either before a problem becomes established or, even better, before it begins. Pruning is an effective way to achieve this. Often, good pruning can preempt some serious problems, and good formative pruning to encourage strong stems and wide angles where branches join the main trunk will reduce the chance of branches splitting or breaking and providing a site where pests and diseases can take hold.

Many of the diseases that attack woody plants damage the wood and hence the whole structure of the plant. Disease often enters through dead tissue, such as a wound or injury, and is spread throughout the live, healthy parts of the plant. Canker is a classic example. This fungal disease kills bark and the underlying wood of trees. This is why the first part of any pruning process should be removing dead, dying, diseased, or damaged wood (the four Ds) before the real pruning begins.

Certainly, if there's any suspicion of disease, it's best to look for telltale signs, such as a brown staining in the wood on or just under the bark. Always cut back to healthy sections of branch or stem where there's no staining. Pruning to create a good, open structure will allow a free flow of air around the branches. This reduces the chance of diseases, including mildew, and helps to reduce hospitable areas for pests such as aphids that find shelter and become established in weakened and sheltered sites on plants.

Simply changing the time of year that you prune your plants can combat certain diseases. Oak wilt can kill strong, healthy oaks within a few years if it gains a foothold. The beetles that carry the oak wilt disease are active from late April through June in most parts of the country, so it's best to prune oaks in winter, when the beetles are not active. Cutting down tall roses to half their height in an exposed garden will prevent them from rocking in the wind and suffering root damage through the winter.

RESTRICTING GROWTH

Perhaps the ultimate example of restrictive pruning is the practice of bonsai, but in a garden the most common use of clipping and pruning is to make

Restrict the growth of a row of plants so that they form a hedge, as seen in this tapestry hedge. This is an attractive way to achieve shelter or a screen in your garden.

rows of plants form a dense shelter or screen—a hedge.

Many plants will keep getting larger if they are left to develop naturally. In gardens and along pathways this can be a problem if space is restricted. In a natural setting it's often survival of the fittest and biggest, so large plants often crowd out smaller ones. Most gardeners face this at some stage and need to prune routinely to keep plants within their allotted area as well as encourage balanced growth and production of flowers and fruit.

REMEDIAL PRUNING

This type of pruning is also referred to as renovation pruning, and it's usually used to gain control of a plant that's not growing in a desirable way or one that has been neglected and becomes misshapen or unsightly.

Remedial pruning varies in effectiveness. Some plants respond well and often recover, growing for many more years after getting a new lease on life. Unfortunately, other plants, such as brooms and many conifers, won't respond to this treatment and often die after severe pruning instead of regenerating themselves.

Even if plants respond positively, problems sometimes arise if they've been budded or grafted on to a rootstock (a healthy plant used as a root system for a grafted plant base), because the rootstock may grow as vigorously as the cultivar that has been grafted onto it. Also, if you're doing remedial pruning on a grafted plant it's important to discover exactly where the rootstock and scion (a young shoot from the desired plant) are joined together. If the plant is cut below

this union, the cultivar will be removed and only sucker growth from the rootstock will emerge.

Remedial pruning can improve the plants in your garden, but don't expect miracles! Years of neglect can't be rectified in one season.

Remedial pruning is not recommended for conifers, as they are unable to produce new growth from old, bare wood. It is best to dig up any neglected or damaged conifers and replace them.

Equipment

PRUNING CAN BE hard work, and it can be even more difficult if you have poor-quality or blunt tools that have not been regularly sharpened and oiled to stay in good condition.

The most important rule to remember is that you should match your tool to the task at hand. You can not expect any piece of equipment to handle a job that really requires a larger tool. Hand pruners, long-handled pruners (loppers), saws (fixed blade and folding), pole saws, and shears are all designed to do specific jobs and to cut through wood up to a certain thickness. Shears are used for shaping and trimming.

HAND PRUNERS

Most pruning will be done with hand pruners, and the type you choose will be largely a matter of personal preference. When you're buying a pair, hold them in your hand to make sure they feel comfortable. Some of the better makes are available in a range of sizes, and you can even find models that are specially designed for left-handed people.

The cutting mechanisms of different models vary slightly, but there are two groups: those that have cutting blades that meet together and those with cutting blades that pass.

PRUNING KNIVES

Pruning knives have a curved blade which makes it easier for them to cut through thin stems and branches. The knife handle is usually fairly thick to provide extra grip.

LOPPERS AND LONG-ARM PRUNERS

Long-handled pruners, often called loppers, are heavy-duty hand pruners for tackling thicker stems or branches. The long handles are for extra reach and leverage. They are available with both anvil and bypass cutting mechanisms.

You can use long-arm pruners to prune high branches so that you don't need a ladder. They consist of a pole some 6 to 10 feet long with a heavy-duty pruner at the tip. The blade is operated by pulling on a cable attached to the bottom end of the pole. A model with shears fitted to the top is available for cutting high hedges.

Bypass hand pruners

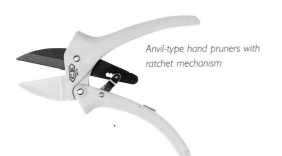

Anvil-type hand pruners

Anvil-type hand pruners with ratchet mechanism

TYPES OF HAND PRUNERS
Those with cutting blades that meet together can be further subdivided into two types:
• **Anvil-type** hand pruners have a single, straight-edged cutting blade, which closes down onto an anvil, a bar of softer metal or plastic. Some of these models are fitted with a ratchet mechanism, which makes it possible to cut through wood in stages, but this type of cutting action is slower than with conventional models. The anvil action isn't ideal in some situations; it has a tendency to crush stems and split bark.
• **Bypass** hand pruners have cutting blades that pass one another and are the most popular pruning tool for small jobs. The scissor action of bypass pruners makes a clean cut and won't splinter the remaining branch edge.

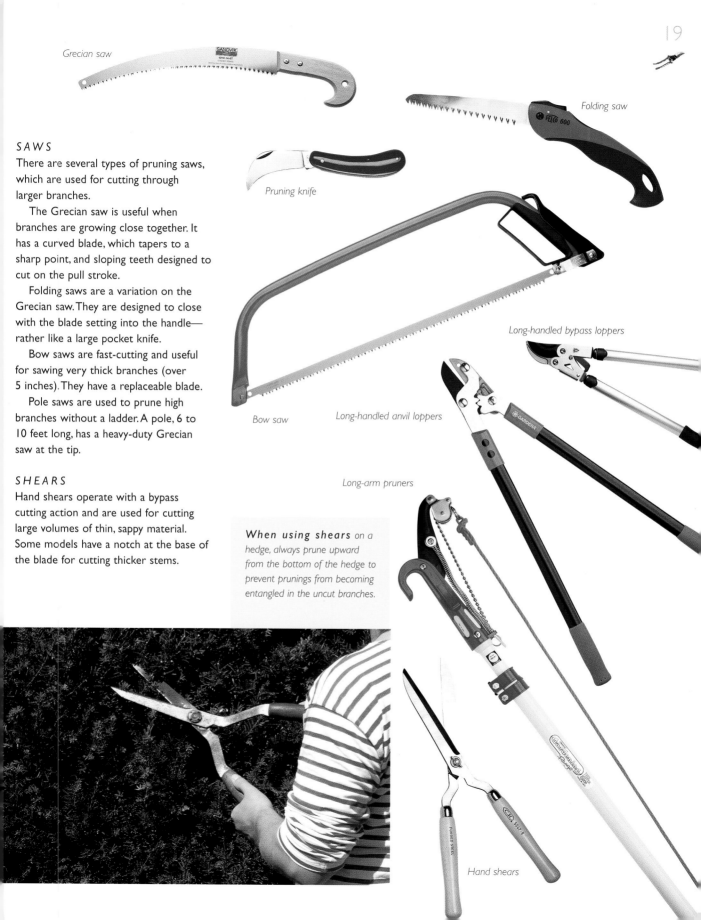

Grecian saw

Folding saw

Pruning knife

SAWS

There are several types of pruning saws, which are used for cutting through larger branches.

The Grecian saw is useful when branches are growing close together. It has a curved blade, which tapers to a sharp point, and sloping teeth designed to cut on the pull stroke.

Folding saws are a variation on the Grecian saw. They are designed to close with the blade setting into the handle— rather like a large pocket knife.

Bow saws are fast-cutting and useful for sawing very thick branches (over 5 inches). They have a replaceable blade.

Pole saws are used to prune high branches without a ladder. A pole, 6 to 10 feet long, has a heavy-duty Grecian saw at the tip.

SHEARS

Hand shears operate with a bypass cutting action and are used for cutting large volumes of thin, sappy material. Some models have a notch at the base of the blade for cutting thicker stems.

Long-handled bypass loppers

Bow saw

Long-handled anvil loppers

Long-arm pruners

When using shears on a hedge, always prune upward from the bottom of the hedge to prevent prunings from becoming entangled in the uncut branches.

Hand shears

Health and safety

ALWAYS TAKE precautions in the garden, especially when you're using powered tools. Some gardening tasks can be hazardous, and there are occasions when you should wear protective clothing. Tough leather gloves or gauntlets are a wise choice when pruning, especially when you're handling plants that have spines or thorns. If you have sensitive skin, wear gloves when you're pruning plants such as euphorbias, which exude an irritating sap, or rue (*Ruta* spp.), which can cause phytodermatitis, to avoid triggering an allergic reaction.

It's often advisable to wear safety goggles or glasses, particularly when you're using powered tools or cutting implements. When you're engaged in jobs that are likely to create large amounts of dust or fumes, wear a face mask to protect your mouth and nose.

Many accidents occur while gardeners use mowers, string trimmers, hedge trimmers, spades, forks, and pruners. Whenever you use garden machinery and tools, especially electric- or gasoline-driven items, always wear appropriate safety clothing, including gloves, ear and eye protectors, and sturdy footwear. If you're uncertain about the clothing you should wear, look on the machine itself, because most models have safety symbols to indicate the minimum protective clothing to be worn. Never wear loose, flapping clothing, which could become caught in the moving parts of machinery.

Another potential hazard, and one that's often overlooked, is the debris you create as you prune. Always drag large pieces clear of the area where you're working so that you don't get tangled in them and fall. It's quite useful to have a shredder nearby—possibly in the center of the lawn—so that the prunings can be piled next to the shredder. After you have a few shrubs pruned, take a break from pruning and shred the accumulated bits and put them on the compost pile.

TOOL CARE

Tools can't function properly if they are dirty, rusty, or damaged. Clean all garden tools after using them, and wipe the

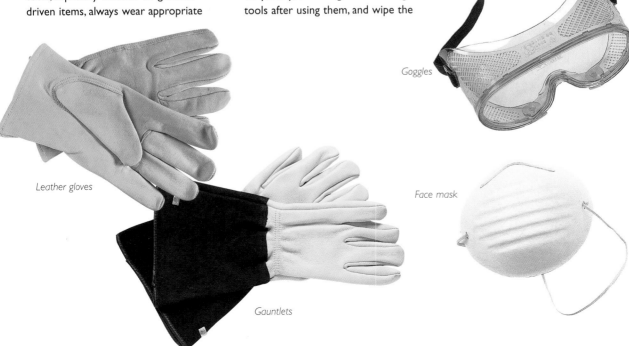

Goggles

Leather gloves

Face mask

Gauntlets

When pruning large, thick branches with a saw (left), *always make a cut on the underside of the branch first to prevent the branch from tearing the bark as it falls.*

Always wear thick gloves (below) *when pruning plants with thorns or irritating sap.*

exposed metal surfaces with an oily cloth. Mechanized equipment will need regular oiling and sharpening. Electrically powered tools should be wiped dry and cleaned before being stored. Large equipment should be professionally serviced every year or two. All tools should be stored in a cool, dry place to stay in good condition.

USING LADDERS

When you're pruning trees, large shrubs, and hedges, the dilemma is often how high to go and still prune safely. This will largely depend on whether you feel comfortable working off the ground. As long as you're in good health, working from a supported stepladder or platform won't cause any problems. For pruning jobs that require you to lean away from your ladder or platform or for tall plants and trees, consider calling a pro, such as a landscaping contractor, for hedges and shrubs or a qualified arborist for pruning or removing large trees or heavy branches.

Basic techniques

TO SOME EXTENT you can determine the amount of basic pruning you will need to do by choosing good-quality plants that have no obvious signs of pests and diseases, damage, or injury and that are growing well (although that's not easy to tell during the dormant season).

When you're buying climbers, roses, and shrubs for your garden, select plants that have several healthy stems emerging from close to ground level. Trees with a vigorous single stem and sideshoots emerging at regular intervals almost at right angles to the main stem or trunk of the tree will form strong branches and a good framework as they mature.

MAKING A START

Before you prune any plant, it will help to have a basic idea of how that plant grows. You don't need to be a botanist, but you should have an idea of the plant's natural habit of growth—whether it should be erect, bushy, spreading, and so on—and when it flowers. This knowledge will give you some idea of the plant's likely reaction when you prune it, although you should bear in mind that most plants will react differently to pruning at different times of the year.

A quick examination of the plant you want to prune will show that at the tip of each shoot there's a terminal (apical) bud, which is often called the growing point. Below this bud on the stem are arranged other smaller side buds, called lateral (axillary) buds. These are arranged in a particular way, which varies from plant to plant. They get their name from the place where they form on the shoot—the leaf axil (or the angle where a leaf is attached to the stem of the plant). The position of these buds will determine where the future side (lateral) branches or flowering shoots are likely to develop.

The apical bud in the tip of the shoot influences the growth and development of

the axillary buds by producing chemicals that discourage their growth, a characteristic known as apical dominance. If the apical bud is damaged or removed, its control is lost and the axillary buds or shoots respond by growing rapidly to form laterals or sideshoots. Apical dominance seems to be much stronger in younger plants and is often more significant when plants are undergoing some type of formative pruning.

It is useful to understand how a plant will respond when you have to decide just where to make a pruning cut. Don't make the mistake of thinking that severe pruning is the best way to control vigorous growth in plants—in fact, severe pruning usually provokes the plant to grow even more vigorously.

POSITIONING PRUNING CUTS

On most of the plants you're likely to prune, the buds will be arranged along the stem at regular intervals in one of two ways: either alternately (one on one side of the stem, one farther up on the other side, and so on) or in opposite pairs (one on each side of the stem, directly opposite from one another). The buds are usually closer together at the base of the stem and slightly wider apart as you progress upward.

Always cut to strong, healthy buds (left) *to encourage new growth and promote the rapid healing of the pruning wound.*

Once they have reached their intended size (right), *some plants will require only an annual trim with shears or a hedge trimmer.*

If a plant has an alternate arrangement of buds, look from the tip of the stem downward and you may notice that the buds run in a spiral pattern down the stem. Where the buds are arranged in opposite pairs, look from the tip of the stem downward and you may notice that the pairs of buds are arranged roughly at right angles to one another. These bud (and leaf and stem) arrangements are

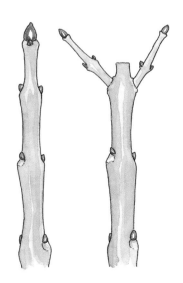

Plants with buds in opposite pairs will naturally produce a pair of shoots after the stem has been pruned.

designed to give each leaf the maximum
amount of space and light.

On plants with the buds arranged
alternately, any pruning cut should be at an
angle, about an inch above a bud, with the
bud itself near the uppermost point of the
cut. This is important because the healing
of any cut is greatly influenced by the
proximity of these growth buds. Usually,
cuts are made to an outward-pointing bud
to encourage an open structure of stems
and branches. On plants with buds
arranged in opposite pairs, any pruning cut
should be about an inch above a pair of
buds, but at a right angle: this will leave a
flat cut across the top of the shoot, so
that both buds are left undamaged.

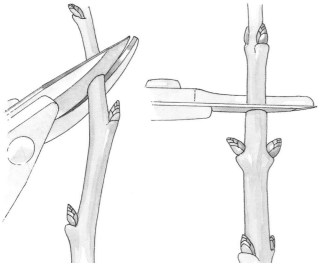

Pruning cuts: Alternate buds Make
a sloping cut angled up toward the bud.

Pruning cuts: Opposite buds Make a
flat cut at right angles to the stem, just above a
pair of buds.

Prune plants grown for attractive fruits (left) *in late winter—once the birds have eaten the fruits.*

Prevent disease in Japanese maples (right) *by pruning in summer while they are actively growing. This will reduce the chance of fungal spores entering the open cuts.*

such as birch (*Betula* spp.), buckeye or horse chestnut (*Aesculus* spp.), maple (*Acer* spp.), poplar (*Populus* spp.) and walnut (*Juglans* spp.) are pruned in summer, when they are in full leaf, to protect them from bleeding copious quantities of sap. The leaves draw sap past the pruning wounds, keeping them relatively dry and reducing the chance of stems dying back.

Some plants are pruned at a particular time of year to protect them from specific pests or diseases. If fungal and bacterial plant diseases are common in your area, you'll need to schedule pruning when the weather is dry. Dogwood anthrancnose and fire blight on crab apples (*Malus* spp.) can spread easily during wet spring weather.

AVOIDING DAMAGE

Pruning a plant creates wounds. Some will be quite small, but sometimes, as when branches are removed from a tree, they may be quite large. How quickly the wound heals over is a good measure of how healthy the plant is. However, it's a fact that pruning wounds, like any other injuries a plant might receive, are potential entry points for fungal or bacterial spores. Although the risk of diseases taking hold can never be wholly eliminated, you can reduce the risk by using sharp cutting tools to make clean, well-placed cuts.

TIMING

Pruning is often done in winter because it's convenient for the gardener rather than ideal for the plant. Pruning is a good way to keep warm in the garden when the weather is chilly and the ground is wet or frozen, making it impossible to dig or cultivate the soil. At times like this, we rely on other gardening tasks, such as pruning, to keep us busy until the soil conditions improve.

As a rule, most deciduous plants are best pruned either after they've finished flowering or in the fall, winter, and early spring when they are dormant. However, as with most rules, there are exceptions for practical reasons. Plants that are grown for their attractive fruit will be left unpruned for several years to get a good display of hips or berries. Some plants don't respond well to pruning when they are dormant, especially in late winter or early spring, and pruning at the wrong time can kill a large section of the plant or, in extreme cases, the whole plant. For this reason some plants,

For thousands of years, gardeners "helped" plants recover by smothering the wounds with paints and preparations to protect them. In recent years, however, research has shown that covering a wound can actually seal in disease spores and encourage fungal rot.

Woody plants naturally produce chemical and physical barriers that resist the invasion of rot-causing organisms. The correct positioning of a clean cut offers more protection than any wound covering. On many plants, the natural barrier point is visible—it's the slightly swollen area where the lateral shoot or branch joins the main stem or trunk—and pruning at precisely this point improves the chances of the pruning wound healing quickly. For the same reason, any pruning cut on a branch should be about an inch above a bud, because buds can produce chemicals that encourage wounds to heal quickly.

The only reason for painting over pruning cuts is purely cosmetic: to cover a large, pale wound that contrasts with the darker color of the surrounding bark.

Fan-training *against a wall is an excellent way to grow larger plants in a confined space. It is important to allow younger, more productive shoots to replace older branches when you prune.*

Removing dead or diseased flower heads (left) *will prevent fungal infections from spreading and allow the development of new shoots and flowers.*

Deadhead on a regular basis (below) *to prevent the spent flowers from producing seeds. Deadheading will prolong the flowering period by encouraging a later flush of flowers.*

PRUNING AND TRAINING

With many pruning techniques, making a good clean cut at the correct place on the plant is only part of the story. Often pruning is carried out in conjunction with some form of training, which can take the form of tying growths into a particular position, or trimming away shoots that are trying to grow in a certain direction. The use of canes or stakes to guide a plant's stems or shoots to grow in an upright position or the use of wires, trellis, and frames to steer growths in an angled or horizontal direction is usually practiced as the pruning is carried out.

It's important to remember that pruning can't be carried out in isolation of other cultural practices when you're growing plants. Don't neglect your plants' nutritional needs, because removing large areas of leaf from growing plants (especially with summer pruning) can have a debilitating effect on them. Feeding, watering, and mulching are essential to maintain balanced, healthy growth and to help the plants to respond quickly after pruning is complete.

PINCHING

One of the main techniques you can use to shape a young plant is pinching. This involves removing the plant's growing point to encourage the sideshoots to develop. Since young shoots are often soft and sappy, you can snap off this growth with your thumb and pointer finger.

DEADHEADING

Plants flower to produce seeds. Once a flower is pollinated, it will gradually develop fruits with seeds inside, while an unpollinated flower will linger on the plant for much longer. As soon as seed is set, the plant will gradually produce fewer flowers and the garden display will look less impressive. So removing fading flowers from a plant will stimulate the rapid development of another flush of flowers, as happens with repeat-flowering roses.

This aspect of pruning is less important with plants such as species roses that flower only once. But deadheading may still keep the plant tidy and improve its appearance. For many plants, the best approach to deadheading the flowers is to remove only the flower and a short section of its supporting flower stalk, leaving as many leaves and sections of soft young stem as possible. These parts of the plant can still manufacture food to support the rest of the plant while it's growing.

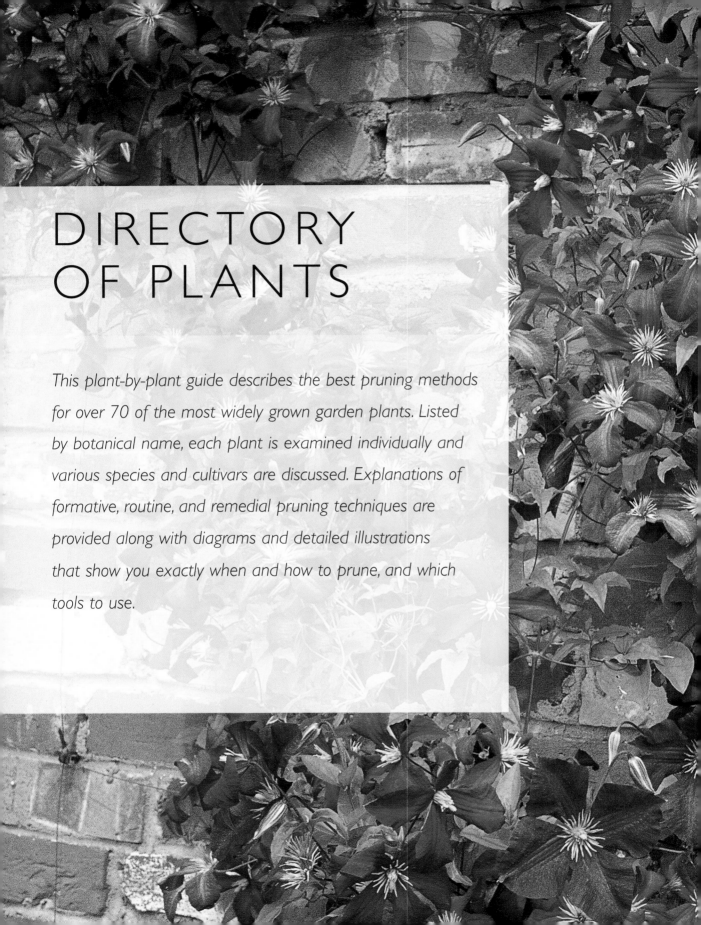

DIRECTORY
OF PLANTS

This plant-by-plant guide describes the best pruning methods for over 70 of the most widely grown garden plants. Listed by botanical name, each plant is examined individually and various species and cultivars are discussed. Explanations of formative, routine, and remedial pruning techniques are provided along with diagrams and detailed illustrations that show you exactly when and how to prune, and which tools to use.

Abelia

Abelia

The glossy, dark-green leaves and pretty flowers make abelias attractive additions to a mixed border or a sheltered wall or fence.

Abelias are grown for their attractive foliage and plentiful flowers. The species are deciduous, evergreen, or semievergreen, although evergreen forms may behave like deciduous shrubs and lose their leaves in very cold winters. They are only borderline hardy and grow best in a sunny, well-drained position, preferring to have some shelter, especially from cold winds that may cause frost damage in exposed gardens. The range of species and cultivars available makes it possible in some gardening zones to have plants in flower from early summer (the evergreen *A. floribunda*) until late fall (the deciduous *A. schumannii*). Early-flowering species sometimes produce a second, later flush of flowers on the current season's shoots.

Abelias have oval, glossy, dark-green leaves—paler green when they first emerge—arranged in opposite pairs along reddish-brown stems, which mature to dark-brown. The bark becomes cracked and flaky as it ages. Abelias form dense, bushy thickets, with branches emerging from the base of the plant, almost erect to begin with but often arching over as they increase in length.

Masses of small, tubular flowers up to ¾ inch long are produced on the shoot tips and from the leaf joints along the stems. Flower colors range from white

with pink markings to lilac-pink and deep-pink. The pink to bronze-red calyces remain long after the flowers have faded. Several forms have variegated leaves, including some cultivars of *A. x grandiflora*, such as 'Francis Mason', 'Gold Spot', and 'Sunrise'.

The natural habit of this plant means that it needs regular annual pruning to make room for new young shoots to develop and to replace older shoots.

Abelia schumannii is a vigorous shrub with an upright, spreading habit. As the stems age, the bark becomes deeply fissured and flakes away. The deciduous leaves are broadly oval in shape with a pointed tip and are held on slender stems in opposite pairs. They are bronze when young and turn glossy green as they mature. In summer, small, star-shaped, highly-scented flowers are produced, which are lilac-pink in bud and pinkish-white inside when open.

WHY PRUNE?

To encourage annual production and development of new shoots and to remove old, nonflowering wood.

PRUNING TIPS

• *Don't prune late-flowering plants immediately after flowering, or the resultant new growth will be severely damaged by the winter frosts.*

PLANTS PRUNED THIS WAY

Abelia floribunda: *in late spring and summer, after flowering*
Abelia chinensis: *in early spring*
Abelia x grandiflora *and cvs.*: *in early spring*
Abelia schumannii: *in early spring*

Cut back to a healthy pair of buds

Routine pruning
Dead and defective growth

Remove thin, weak shoots

Formative pruning

Prune young plants to encourage them to develop a bushy habit with strong shoots emerging from ground level.

After planting, cut out any weak or damaged growth. Cut the remaining shoots back to about one-third of their length. This will encourage new shoots to develop from the plant's base as it becomes established.

Routine pruning

Abelias usually produce new shoots from the base or low down on existing stems. Regular annual pruning to remove some of the oldest stems will give these new shoots room to grow.

After flowering, cut out about one-quarter of the existing stems (choose the ones that look the oldest). Either cut them back to a healthy pair of buds or down to ground level. Remove any thin, weak shoots to avoid overcrowding. Cut out any frost-damaged shoots in late spring.

Remedial pruning

If abelias are left unpruned for several years, they will produce large numbers of weak, short, thin stems and much poorer flowers, in terms of both size and quantity.

In spring, cut all the stems back to within 6 to 8 inches of ground level.

In summer, remove up to one-third of the weakest and thinnest shoots to prevent overcrowding.

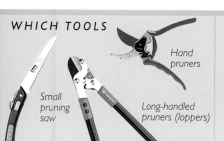

WHICH TOOLS

Hand pruners

Small pruning saw

Long-handled pruners (loppers)

WHEN TO PRUNE MOST SPECIES

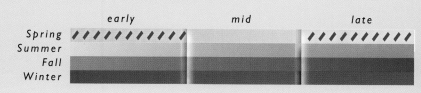

	early	mid	late
Spring	/////		/////
Summer			
Fall			
Winter			

Actinidia
Chinese tara vine

This is a perfect climber for a sunny south- or southeast-facing wall close to a door or window—it will let you catch the full benefit of the delicately fragrant flowers in early summer.

These vigorous vines, which are grown for both their fruits and their attractive foliage, have twining stems and can grow more than 25 feet high. They grow well in a moist, well-drained, fertile soil. For the best leaf color, they need a bright, sunny position that is sheltered from cold winds. The oval to oblong leaves of most species are dark-green, but *Actinidia kolomikta* has green, pink, and white foliage, and *A. polygama* (silver vine) has green and silver-white leaves. The foliage of most species turns dull yellow before dropping in fall.

Small, white, lightly scented flowers are produced in early to midsummer, and if there are both male and female plants, they are often followed by golden-yellow fruits.

Actinidia kolomikta *is a vigorous, deciduous climber with rich-brown, twining stems; these have a hairy surface when young. The leaves are oval- to heart-shaped and dark green. They may have pink and white markings in broad bands toward the tip of each leaf, especially if grown in a bright, sunny position. In fall, the foliage turns a dull yellow before it falls. Small, white, delicately fragrant flowers are produced in early summer, sometimes followed by small, yellowish-green, insignificant fruits.*

Formative pruning

Prune young plants to encourage them to develop a framework of strong shoots emerging from the base.

In the first spring after planting, cut out any weak or damaged growth. Cut all remaining stems back to a strong, healthy bud about 12 inches above ground level. As the new shoots develop, select about six of the strongest ones for training onto the supporting structure.

In the second spring, cut all sideshoots back by two-thirds, cut back any thin shoots to one or two buds, and remove any weak shoots altogether.

Formative pruning: First spring

WHY PRUNE?

To produce balanced growth and to control vigor.

PRUNING TIPS

• *Prune before growth starts.*

PLANTS PRUNED THIS WAY

Actinidia arguta *and cvs.: in late winter or early spring*
Actinidia deliciosa (chinensis) *and cvs.: in late winter or early spring*
Actinidia kolomikta *and cvs.: in late winter or early spring*
Actinidia polygama *and cvs.: in late winter or early spring*
Vitis *spp. and cvs.: in late winter or when plants are in full leaf*

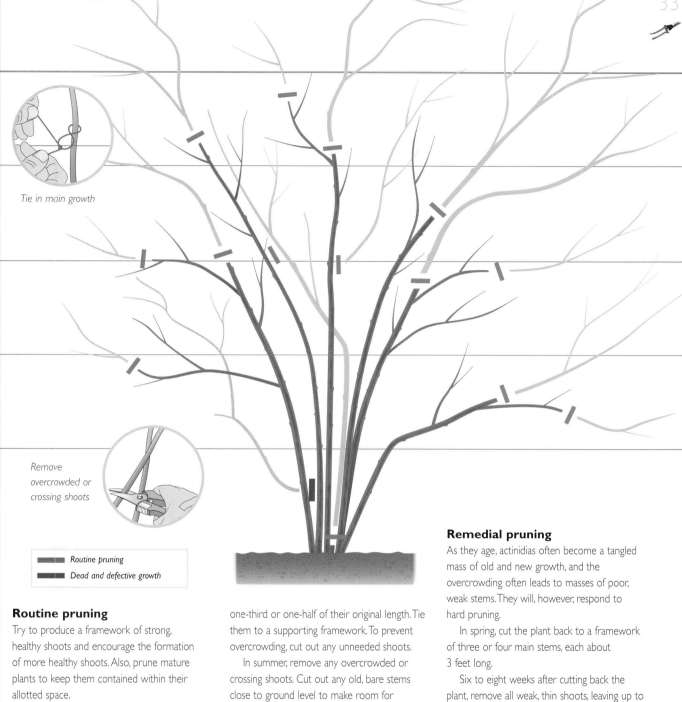

Tie in main growth

Remove
overcrowded or
crossing shoots

Routine pruning
Dead and defective growth

Routine pruning

Try to produce a framework of strong, healthy shoots and encourage the formation of more healthy shoots. Also, prune mature plants to keep them contained within their allotted space.

In late winter or early spring, shorten the main growths by cutting them back to about one-third or one-half of their original length. Tie them to a supporting framework. To prevent overcrowding, cut out any unneeded shoots.

In summer, remove any overcrowded or crossing shoots. Cut out any old, bare stems close to ground level to make room for new growths.

Remedial pruning

As they age, actinidias often become a tangled mass of old and new growth, and the overcrowding often leads to masses of poor, weak stems. They will, however, respond to hard pruning.

In spring, cut the plant back to a framework of three or four main stems, each about 3 feet long.

Six to eight weeks after cutting back the plant, remove all weak, thin shoots, leaving up to six of the strongest, healthiest shoots to form a new framework. Train these into position.

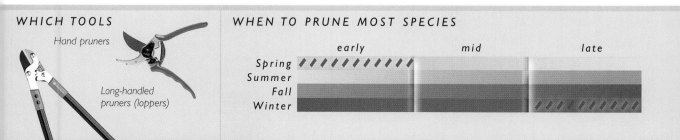

WHICH TOOLS

Hand pruners

Long-handled pruners (loppers)

WHEN TO PRUNE MOST SPECIES

	early	mid	late
Spring	/////////		
Summer			
Fall			
Winter			/////////

Amelanchier
Juneberry, shadbush

There can be few more stunning sights than a mature amelanchier in full flower in midspring, when it foams with white blooms that emerge just as the leaves are beginning to unfurl.

Amelanchiers need moist, well-drained, fertile soil. They do best in acidic soil—that is, soil that does not have lime in it—although *Amelanchier asiatica* is lime tolerant. They also need a position in full sun or partial shade. In spring, small, white, star-shaped flowers are produced in clusters along the slender, brown-black stems, and small, blue-black fruits follow these from summer onward. The oval leaves are bronze-green when young, turning dark green as they mature and later changing to vivid shades of red and orange just before dropping in fall.

Young plants often have an erect habit, but as they mature they usually spread, often forming dense thickets up to 18 feet high and 25 feet across as suckers are produced around the parent plant.

Amelanchier canadensis *is a large, suckering shrub grown for its spring flowers and attractive leaf colors in fall. When young, the plant has an upright habit but forms a dense, spreading thicket of brownish-black stems and branches as it ages. In spring, the oval-shaped leaves are bronze-green and later dark green. In fall, they turn bright red and orange before dropping. In the spring, before the leaves emerge, small, white flowers are produced, followed by small, black fruits.*

Formative pruning: After planting

Formative pruning

Prune young plants to encourage them to grow bushy, with strong shoots emerging from soil level.

After planting, cut out any damaged growth. Cut the weaker shoots back to one or two buds above ground level to encourage new shoots to develop from the base of the plant as it becomes established.

WHY PRUNE?

To produce new growth and to improve flowering.

PRUNING TIPS

• *Always prune lightly to avoid overproduction of suckers.*

PLANTS PRUNED THIS WAY

Amelanchier asiatica: *in late spring, after flowering*
Amelanchier arborea: *in late spring, after flowering*
Amelanchier canadensis: *in late spring, after flowering*
Amelanchier laevis: *in late spring, after flowering*
Amelanchier lamarckii: *in late spring, after flowering*

Remove old stems

*Remove overcrowded
or crossing stems*

▰▰ ▰	Routine pruning
▰▰▰	Dead and defective growth

Routine pruning

These plants are usually grown as large, multistemmed shrubs. They generally produce new shoots from the base or low down on existing stems. Removing any overcrowded stems will encourage new shoots to form and give them space to grow.

After flowering, thin out any congested or rubbing stems (choose the ones that look the oldest). Cut them back either to a healthy bud or to ground level. Remove any thin, weak shoots to avoid overcrowding.

Alternatively, some species can be trained as trees. In this case, it is important to remove suckers growing around the trunk.

Remedial pruning

If these plants are left unpruned for a number of years, they will produce large numbers of weak, thin stems, creating a thicket of overcrowded stems that can twist around one another.

In spring, cut all stems back to within 3 to 10 inches of ground level. In summer, remove up to one-third of the weakest and thinnest shoots to prevent overcrowding.

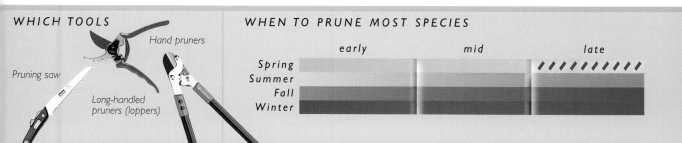

WHICH TOOLS

Hand pruners

Pruning saw

Long-handled
pruners (loppers)

WHEN TO PRUNE MOST SPECIES

	early	mid	late
Spring			/////////
Summer			
Fall			
Winter			

Aronia
Chokeberry

This spring-flowering shrub makes an excellent feature when it is grown as a freestanding plant. The plentiful berries are an ornamental feature throughout the summer.

Aronias are large, hardy, suckering shrubs that will grow up to 10 feet high and across. They will grow in most moist but well-drained soils—but not in shallow soil overlying chalk—and they need a position in full sun or partial shade. The pale-brown stems turn dark gray as they age. The oval, dark-green, deciduous leaves have a matte finish on the upper surface and are covered with a gray, felty layer on the underside. In fall, just before they drop, the leaves turn to shades of yellow, orange, and rich red. Small, white, pink-tinged flowers are produced in clusters on the tips of shoots and branches in spring, and small red or purple-black fruits follow these from summer onward.

Aronia melanocarpa *produces masses of small, white, pink-tinged flowers on the tips of shoots and branches in spring, followed by small, purple-black fruits. This large, spreading, deciduous shrub often produces large quantities of sucker growth. The pale-brown stems turn a deep gray as they age. It has dark-green leaves that are oval shaped with a gray, downy underside. These turn yellow, orange, and red in fall.*

Formative pruning

Prune young plants to encourage them to grow bushy, with strong, suckering shoots emerging from around ground level.

After planting, cut out any damaged growth. Cut the weaker shoots back to one or two buds above ground level to encourage new shoots to develop from the base of the plant as it becomes established.

WHY PRUNE?

To produce new growth and to improve flowering.

PRUNING TIPS

• *Be prepared to replace an old, overgrown plant rather than attempting remedial pruning.*

PLANTS PRUNED THIS WAY

Aronia arbutifolia *and cvs.: in late spring, after flowering*
Aronia melanocarpa *and cvs.: in late spring, after flowering*
Aronia prunifolia *and cvs.: in late spring, after flowering*

Remove thin, weak growth

Cut back to a healthy bud

Routine pruning
Dead and defective growth

Remove old stems

Routine pruning

Aronias are often grown as large, multistemmed shrubs, and they usually produce new shoots from the base or close to ground level on existing stems. Annual pruning to remove some of the oldest stems will not only encourage new shoots to develop but will also give them room to grow.

After flowering in spring, cut out about one-quarter of the existing stems, selecting the ones that look the oldest. Cut them back either to a healthy bud or down to ground level. Remove any thin, weak shoots to avoid overcrowding.

Remedial pruning

Aronias do not always respond to severe pruning, and plants often fail to regrow after remedial pruning. Although it might be worth cutting back an old plant to ground level to see if it will reshoot, replacing it is likely to be a better course of action.

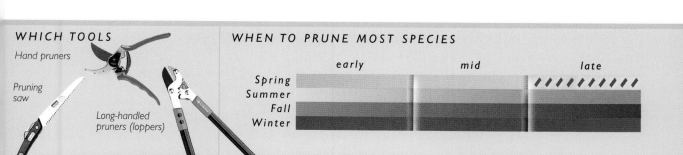

WHICH TOOLS

Hand pruners

Pruning saw

Long-handled pruners (loppers)

WHEN TO PRUNE MOST SPECIES

	early	mid	late
Spring			/////////
Summer			
Fall			
Winter			

Aucuba japonica
Spotted laurel

*Guaranteed to brighten a shady corner where little else will grow, spotted
laurel has handsome, glossy leaves and a neat, rounded shape.*

Despite its common name, *Aucuba japonica* is not related to the true laurel.
The genus actually contains three species; by far the most widely grown species is
the hardy and reliable *A. japonica* or one of its many excellent cultivars. Aucubas do
not take much looking after and will grow in a wide range of soil types as long as the
ground is well drained. Although they are usually grown as freestanding shrubs,
aucubas make a good hedge. They are also ideal plants for a city garden because the
evergreen leaves tolerate not only dense or partial shade but also atmospheric
pollution. Even though the leaves can be covered in a layer of dirt and grime, as
soon as it rains they look fresh and glossy all over again.

In fall, female forms bear bright-red berries, up to ½ inch across, and these
often remain on the plant until late winter or early spring. To be certain of a good
display of fruit, it's best to plant one male form with four or five female plants.

The leathery, glossy green leaves are broadly oval. They have slightly toothed
margins and are arranged in pairs on thick, green stems, which turn gray-green
with age. The shrub will form a broad, dome-shaped plant, 10 to 12 feet high and
about the same width across. Small, reddish-purple flowers are borne on the
tips of the shoots in spring, and these are followed by green berries that turn red in
fall. The most sought-after plants are those with variegated leaves, such as the
female *A. japonica* 'Crotonifolia', which has golden-yellow spots scattered over the
bright-green background, and another female form, *A. japonica* 'Picturata', which
has especially attractive foliage, with a conspicuous gold-colored flash in the
center of each leaf. The variegated forms lose their colored markings if they are
grown in deep shade.

Aucuba japonica *is a tough shrub
with a stocky, rounded habit and thick, green
stems that turn grayish green with age. The
glossy, dark-green leaves, often with yellow
markings, are broadly oval shaped with a
slightly toothed margin. In spring, small,
reddish-purple flowers are produced on the
tips of the shoots. These are often followed
by red berries in the fall.*

WHY PRUNE?

*To keep a well-balanced and rounded
shape and to prevent the plants
from becoming bare and straggly at
the base.*

PRUNING TIPS

• *Prune in spring after the risk of
frost has passed to reduce the
chances of late frosts damaging
new growth.*

PLANTS PRUNED THIS WAY

Aucuba japonica *and cvs.:* *in midspring, after the berries have faded*
Daphne odora *and cvs.:* *in late spring, after the flowers have faded*
Enkianthus chinensis: *in midspring, after the flowers have faded*
Skimmia japonica: *in midspring, after the berries have faded*

Remove dead or damaged stems

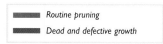

> Routine pruning
> Dead and defective growth

Remove overvigorous stems

Formative pruning

Prune young plants to encourage them to develop a bushy habit with strong shoots emerging from 6 to 8 inches of ground level.

After planting, cut out any weak or damaged growth. Cut the remaining shoots back by about one-third to encourage new shoots to develop from the base of the plant as it becomes established.

Routine pruning

Prune lightly in spring after the brightly colored berries have finished their display and after the risk of severe frost has passed. Try to maintain a well-balanced overall shape with healthy, glossy foliage.

Cut any excessively vigorous shoots back to help the plant retain its natural shape. Remove any all-green shoots that have developed on variegated plants to prevent them from reverting back to the all-green characteristics of the parent plants.

Prune back to healthy growth any shoots that show signs of frost damage or dieback.

Remedial pruning

Aucubas have a natural tendency to produce long, bare shoots with only a few leaves on the ends, and they often become bare at the base, revealing dull-green stems.

In the first year, remove half of the main shoots to within 6 to 8 inches of ground level. Cut down to ground level any thin, weak shoots.

In the second year, cut the remaining old stems down to 6 to 8 inches above ground level. Remove any thin, spindly growth that developed as a result of the previous year's pruning.

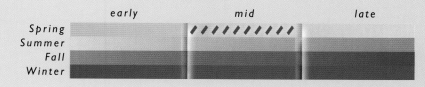

WHICH TOOLS

Hand pruners

Long-handled pruners (loppers)

WHEN TO PRUNE MOST SPECIES

	early	mid	late
Spring		/////////	
Summer			
Fall			
Winter			

Berberis (deciduous species)
Berberis, barberry

Berberis are good-value shrubs, providing leaf color, flowers, and berries, even in unpromising conditions.

The genus contains both deciduous and evergreen species (see pages 42 and 43). The deciduous species have rather thin, spindly stems, which are armed with needle-sharp spines (usually arranged in clusters of three) along their length. These often remain long after the stems have died—so take care when you're handling prunings. The plants will survive in almost any soil as long as it is well drained and not too rich. They have shallow, fibrous root systems, which seem to deter other plants from growing close by. The shrubs will grow in full sun or partial shade, but the displays of fall leaf color and berries are far superior on plants growing in full sun. There is a wide choice of deciduous berberis species and cultivars, but you can usually prune all types in the same way.

The shrubs have broadly oval leaves, which are arranged in clusters close to the spines along the stem. The leaves are usually midgreen, and they often turn vivid shades of orange and red before falling in autumn. The pale-yellow to golden-yellow flowers are borne in small hanging clusters, usually in groups of three to five, along the length of the stems in midspring, and the flowers are often followed by small, red fruits in fall and winter. Plants can vary in height from 2 to 8 feet, and some forms spread to over 8 feet across, often forming a dense, tangled thicket of old, new, and dead stems.

Berberis thunbergii f. atropurpurea *is an attractive, deciduous shrub with dark reddish-purple, arching stems that turn brown-gray with age. The small, spoon-shaped leaves are copper-red in spring and summer, turning orange and crimson before falling in the fall. Clusters of small, yellow flowers tinged with red are produced in the spring followed by glossy red fruits.*

Berberis thunbergii and its cultivars are widely grown, providing a wide range of leaf colors and habits of growth. The cultivars with red, gold, purple, and variegated leaves are the most popular. Be mindful that this species is spread by birds in wild areas and is considered invasive in much of the country.

Formative pruning

Prune young plants to encourage them to develop a bushy habit with strong shoots emerging from ground level.

After planting, cut out any weak or damaged growth. Lightly tip back the remaining shoots to about two-thirds of their length so that the plant will form new shoots from the base.

WHY PRUNE?

To make sure that a supply of new shoots emerges from ground level each year.

PRUNING TIPS

• *Wait until summer to remove dead wood—it's much easier to see then.*

PLANTS PRUNED THIS WAY

Berberis x ottawensis: *in early summer, immediately after flowering*
Berberis x rubrostilla: *in early summer, immediately after flowering*
Berberis thunbergii: *in early summer, immediately after flowering*
Berberis wilsoniae: *in early summer, immediately after flowering*

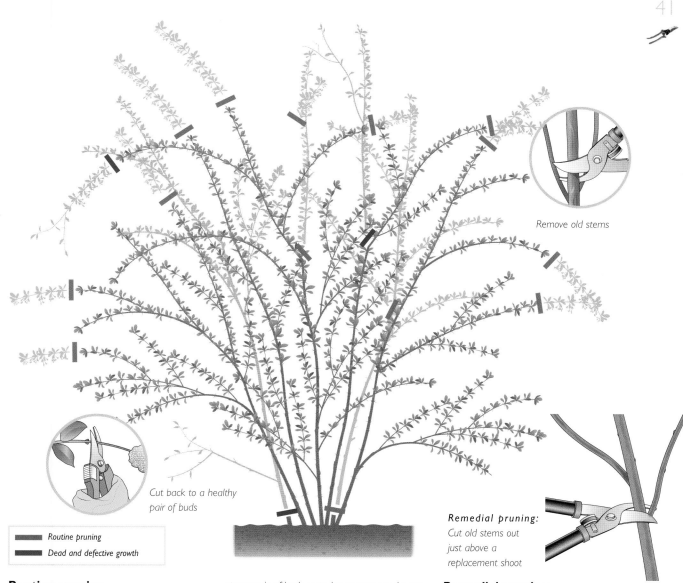

Remove old stems

Cut back to a healthy
pair of buds

Routine pruning
Dead and defective growth

Remedial pruning:
Cut old stems out
just above a
replacement shoot

Routine pruning

If they're to flower well, berberis need regular annual pruning to remove a proportion of the old wood and to encourage new flower-bearing shoots. Also, if you have a plant with purple or variegated leaves you should prune so that young shoots, which tend to have more attractive color, replace old ones.

Immediately after flowering in early summer, cut the old flower-bearing stems back to a strong pair of buds or to lower, younger shoots. This will eliminate the fruits, which can be spread easily by birds, and will give the maximum period of growth to produce a good display of flowers the following year.

On mature shrubs try to remove between one-quarter and one-fifth of the old stems each year to allow light in and to make room for new shoots.

Remedial pruning

Berberis tend to form a matted clump of branches, and the inner branches often shed their leaves and die from lack of light. Plants respond well to severe pruning: In early summer, remove all dead or weak shoots. Cut all healthy stems back to within 12 inches of ground level.

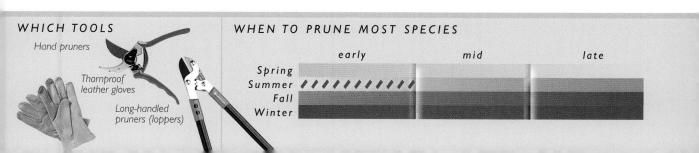

WHICH TOOLS

Hand pruners

Thornproof
leather gloves

Long-handled
pruners (loppers)

WHEN TO PRUNE MOST SPECIES

	early	mid	late
Spring			
Summer			
Fall			
Winter			

Berberis (evergreen species)
Berberis, barberry

*These useful shrubs provide year-round foliage as well as good
flower and berry color.*

Like deciduous berberis (see pages 40
and 41), evergreen berberis are versatile
shrubs that range in size from prostrate
and dwarf forms to large bushes, almost
developing into small trees. They are easy
to grow and provide excellent displays of
flowers, berries, and foliage. Many are well
defended with spines on the leaves as
well as on the stems. They make excellent
screens or barriers, but you must wear
gloves to handle the stems. They will
grow in full sun or partial shade, but the
flower quantity and quality will be poorer
in shady conditions even though the plant
itself will grow well.

Most evergreen berberis have broadly
oval leaves arranged in clusters close to
the spines along the stem. The leaves are
usually glossy, dark-green, paler on the
undersides, and often armed with spines
on the tips or margins. From mid- to late
spring, the orange-yellow to golden-
yellow flowers are produced in
abundance in small, pendent clusters
containing 3 to 15 blooms. These flowers
are usually followed in fall and winter by
small, oval fruits, which may be purple or
bluish black. Plants can vary in height
from 12 inches to 9 feet, and some forms
spread to over 15 feet across, often
forming a dense, tangled thicket of old,
new, and dead stems.

Berberis x *stenophylla* and its cultivars
are the most common, offering a wide
range of flower colors and growth habits.

Formative pruning

Prune young plants to encourage them to
develop a bushy habit with strong shoots
emerging from ground level.

After planting, cut out any weak or damaged
growth. Leave the plant to become established
for 1 year. In its second year, remove all the old
shoots, leaving only the young, vigorous growth
that developed in the first year.

Berberis x stenophylla *is an
evergreen, vigorous shrub with long, arching
branches that are light-brown when young
and turn grayish brown with age. The narrow,
dark-green leaves have a tough, leathery
texture and carry sharp spines on their tips.
In late spring, small, hanging clusters of
deep-yellow flowers are produced along the
stems; these are followed by a profusion of
small, bluish-black berries in the fall.*

WHY PRUNE?

*To make sure a supply of new shoots
emerges from ground level each year.*

PRUNING TIPS

• *Wait until summer to remove dead
wood—it's much easier to see then.*

PLANTS PRUNED THIS WAY

Berberis buxifolia: *in summer, after flowering*
Berberis x gladwynensis: *in summer, after flowering*
Berberis darwinii: *in summer, after flowering*
Berberis julianae: *in summer, after flowering*
Berberis linearifolia: *in summer, after flowering*

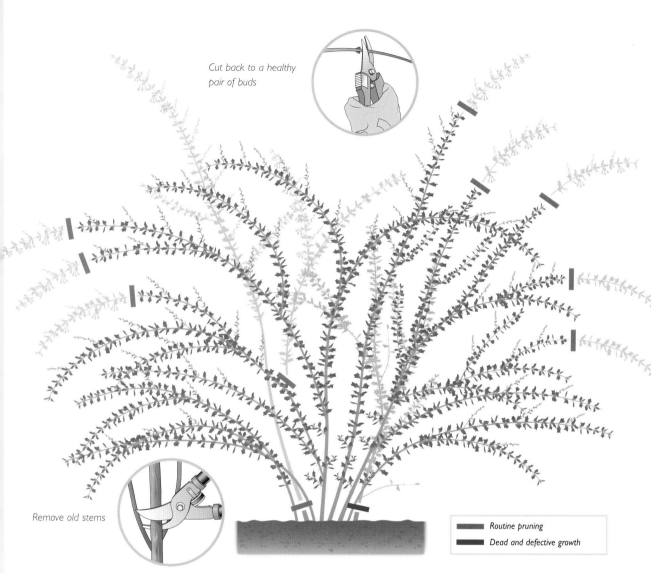

Cut back to a healthy pair of buds

Remove old stems

	Routine pruning
	Dead and defective growth

Routine pruning

These plants need regular annual pruning to replace the old stems, which would gradually accumulate and clog up the center of the shrub, and to encourage new flower-bearing shoots.

Immediately after flowering or in early summer, cut the old flower-bearing stems back to a strong pair of buds or cut down to lower, younger shoots. This will sacrifice the berries but will give the maximum period of growth for a good display of flowers the following year.

On mature shrubs, try to remove from one-quarter to one-fifth of the old stems each year to allow light in and make room for new shoots to develop.

Remedial pruning

Berberis tend to form a matted clump of branches, and the inner branches often shed their leaves and die from lack of light. In these circumstances, the only growth that occurs is around the edges of the plant. Plants respond well to severe pruning: In early summer, remove all dead or weak shoots. Cut all healthy stems back to within 12 inches of ground level.

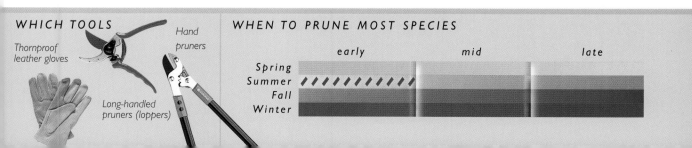

WHICH TOOLS

Thornproof leather gloves

Hand pruners

Long-handled pruners (loppers)

WHEN TO PRUNE MOST SPECIES

	early	mid	late
Spring			
Summer			
Fall			
Winter			

Bignonia capreolata
Cross vine

This attractive climber produces a mass of flame-orange flowers in summer. It is perfect for training into a tree or over a large structure, to provide extra color and interest in the garden.

Bignonia capreolata is a vigorous climber that supports itself with twining tendrils found at the tips of the leaves. The evergreen leaves are broadly oval in shape and mid- to dark green. The leaflets are arranged in pairs, with a tendril between them, and each has a wavy margin. In summer, orange-red, trumpet-shaped flowers are produced in clusters along the stems.

Bignonia capreolata, the only species in the genus, is a vigorous climber once it is established, often reaching up to 30 feet high if it can find suitable supports to cling to with its twining tendrils. The evergreen leaves are broadly oval to lance shaped, and the leaflets, which are carried on slender, supple stems, have wavy margins. The trumpet-shaped flowers are about 2 inches long, orange-red in color, and are produced in clusters of up to five along the stems in summer. This vine will grow well in moist, well-drained, fertile soil, and it needs a bright, sunny position that is sheltered from frosts and chilly winter winds. In colder climates, it should be grown as a cold greenhouse or conservatory plant.

Formative pruning

Prune young plants to encourage them to develop a framework of strong shoots emerging from the base of the plant.

In the first spring after planting, cut out any weak or damaged growth. Select and tie in the strongest two or three shoots to form a framework for the plant's future growth. As the new shoots develop, train the strongest ones against the supporting structure.

Routine pruning

Try to produce a framework of strong, healthy shoots and encourage the formation of flower-bearing spurs. Also, prune mature plants to keep them within their allotted space.

Cut all lateral shoots back to two-thirds of their original length; these are the shoots that will bear the current season's flowers. At the same time, remove any weak or straggly growths.

Cut any vigorous shoots that outgrow their allotted space back to a strong bud to encourage branching.

WHY PRUNE?

To encourage the production of new shoots that will replace the old ones and to promote regular flowering.

PRUNING TIPS

• *Prune in spring, before growth starts.*

PLANTS PRUNED THIS WAY

Bignonia capreolata *and cvs.: in spring, before growth starts*
Lonicera japonica: *in spring*
Macfadyena unguis-cati: *in spring, before growth starts*
Passiflora caerulea: *in spring*
Smilax aspera: *in spring*
Tecoma capensis *and cvs.: in spring, before growth starts*

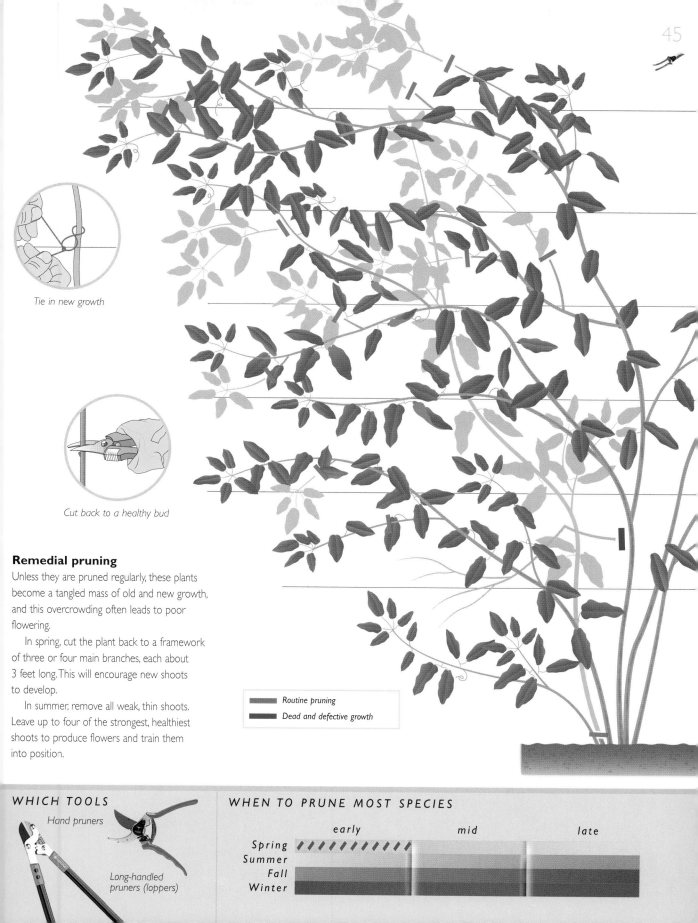

Tie in new growth

Cut back to a healthy bud

Remedial pruning

Unless they are pruned regularly, these plants become a tangled mass of old and new growth, and this overcrowding often leads to poor flowering.

In spring, cut the plant back to a framework of three or four main branches, each about 3 feet long. This will encourage new shoots to develop.

In summer, remove all weak, thin shoots. Leave up to four of the strongest, healthiest shoots to produce flowers and train them into position.

	Routine pruning
	Dead and defective growth

WHICH TOOLS

Hand pruners

Long-handled pruners (loppers)

WHEN TO PRUNE MOST SPECIES

	early	mid	late
Spring	/////////////		
Summer			
Fall			
Winter			

Bougainvillea

Bougainvillea, paper flower

The vividly colored flowers, so prolifically borne that they almost obscure the foliage, are a spectacular sight from summer into fall.

Bougainvilleas are frost-tender plants that should be grown in a sunroom or container and moved into a greenhouse for the winter in all but reliably frost-free gardens. They need warmth and plenty of sun. They are vigorous, semievergreen scramblers; in the wild, their thorns hook the stems over surrounding plants and objects to provide support; in a garden or sunroom, you will have to provide a sturdy support and tie the stems as they grow.

They are grown for their attractive blooms, but the flowers themselves are small, tubular, and quite insignificant. They are, however, surrounded by three colorful petaloid bracts (modified leaves), which provide the eye-catching display. Colors range from white to shades of yellow and apricot through to reds, mauves, and purples.

Bougainvilleas have broadly spear-shaped, mid- to deep-green leaves, although some forms have been developed with variegated foliage. The leaves are arranged alternately along midgreen stems, which turn a dull green-brown as they age. Sharp thorns are arranged along the stems between the leaves. The attractive bracts are produced (along with the flowers) in summer and fall, and they often retain their color for several months after the flowers have

Bougainvillea glabra is a vigorous, evergreen climber with broad, pale-green leaves held on thin branches, often with partially hidden spines. This plant is grown for its brightly colored, papery bracts, which surround the small, white flowers produced from summer until early fall. This plant will scramble over any support it can find. B. glabra 'Scarlet O'Hara' (pictured right), has stunning red bracts.

finished, gradually fading to resemble the color and texture of paper—hence the common name.

Most bougainvilleas will grow to a height of 25 feet and spread to about 40 feet across, but this will depend on the amount and size of the support provided for them. They flower on the current season's wood, and the best time to prune them is soon after the color or the bracts have faded.

Formative pruning

Prune young plants to encourage a framework of strong shoots emerging from the base of the plant.

In the first spring after planting, cut out any weak or damaged growth. Then cut all strong, healthy stems back to 12 inches above ground level. As new shoots develop, tie the strongest ones onto the supporting structure.

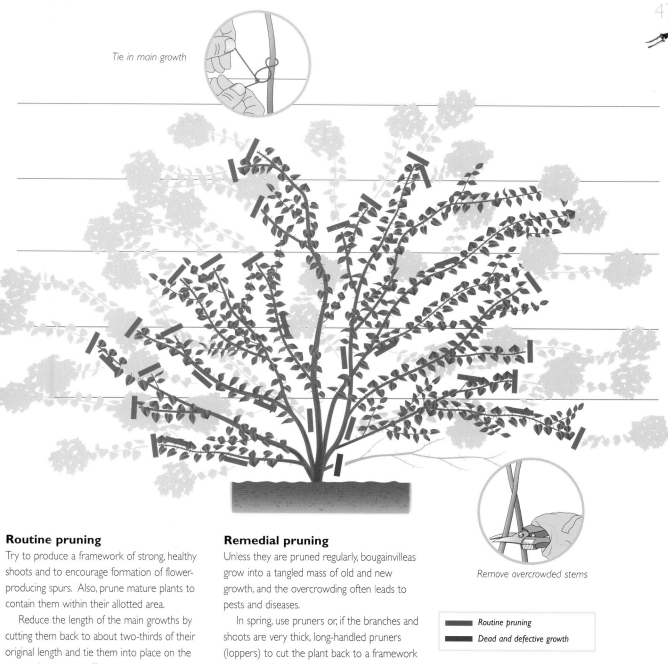

Tie in main growth

Remove overcrowded stems

Routine pruning

Try to produce a framework of strong, healthy shoots and to encourage formation of flower-producing spurs. Also, prune mature plants to contain them within their allotted area.

Reduce the length of the main growths by cutting them back to about two-thirds of their original length and tie them into place on the supporting structure. To prevent overcrowding, cut out any unneeded shoots.

Cut all lateral shoots back to within two or three buds of the main stems—these will bear the current season's flowers and bracts.

Remedial pruning

Unless they are pruned regularly, bougainvilleas grow into a tangled mass of old and new growth, and the overcrowding often leads to pests and diseases.

In spring, use pruners or, if the branches and shoots are very thick, long-handled pruners (loppers) to cut the plant back to a framework of three or four main branches, each about 3 feet long. This will encourage new shoots.

Six to eight weeks after cutting back the branches, remove all weak, thin shoots. Leaving

▬▬	Routine pruning
▬▬	Dead and defective growth

up to about six of the strongest, healthiest shoots to produce flowers, remove three or four of the oldest stems and train replacements into position.

WHICH TOOLS

Hand pruners

Thornproof leather gloves

Long-handled pruners (loppers)

WHEN TO PRUNE MOST SPECIES

	early	mid	late
Spring	/////////		
Summer			
Fall			
Winter			

Buddleja davidii
Buddleia, butterfly bush

This tough, reliable, and showy shrub is always popular with new gardeners, simply because few plants are easier to grow.

Commonly called the butterfly bush because its fragrant, nectar-rich flowers attract many types of butterflies, in mid- to late summer this shrub can be covered with an eye-catching display of long, arching spikes (panicles) of hundreds of tiny flowers carried at the tips of shoots. Often a secondary flush of slightly smaller flower spikes, which develop on the sideshoots, follows this display. There are many cultivars available, with flower colors ranging from deep blackish purple through blues and mauves to pure white.

It's a hardy, deciduous shrub, with deep-green, broadly spear-shaped leaves, which are often silvery on the underside. The light-brown stems mature to dark brown and eventually become dull gray, and the older bark becomes cracked and deeply fissured. The shrub will grow in a wide range of soils, ultimately reaching to 18 feet high and 15 feet across in warmer climes and developing into a generally dome-shaped shrub with a narrow base. The flower spikes are borne on the tips of long, arching shoots formed in the current growing season.

Eventually, especially if left unpruned, the plant will form a dense, bushy thicket, with masses of small flower spikes. The shrub's natural habit of growth means that it needs regular annual pruning to make sure that it produces larger, stronger shoots and bigger, more attractive flower spikes.

Buddleja davidii 'Empire Blue' is a vigorous shrub with strong, arching stems and pale-green branches that become dull-gray as they age. These stems carry opposite pairs of long, straplike, gray-green leaves, often covered by a downy felt on the underside. The long, tapering flower heads are borne on the tips of the stems and branches from midsummer through early fall.

Formative pruning

Young plants should be pruned to encourage a bushy shape with strong shoots emerging from about 12 inches above soil level.

In spring, just as the new growth starts, cut out any thin, weak growth or damaged shoots. Cut back the remaining stems to three or four pairs of buds to develop a framework of new shoots from 12 inches above the base of the plant so that a short trunk or leg forms as it becomes established.

Routine pruning

If it's to flower well, buddleia needs regular annual pruning not only to remove the old flowering wood, which would gradually accumulate and cause overcrowding, but also to encourage the production of new, flower-bearing shoots.

In spring, cut back all the old flower-bearing stems to two or three pairs of buds or shoots to allow the maximum period of growth for a good display of flowers in summer and fall.

WHY PRUNE?

To encourage strong growth and production of larger, more attractive flower spikes.

PRUNING TIPS

• *Use bypass pruners because anvil-type pruners will easy crush the stems.*

PLANTS PRUNED THIS WAY

Buddleja crispa *and cvs.: in midspring, after the risk of frost has passed*
Buddleja fallowiana *and cvs.: in midspring, after the risk of frost has passed*
Buddleja globosa *and cvs.: late winter, before fresh growth appears*

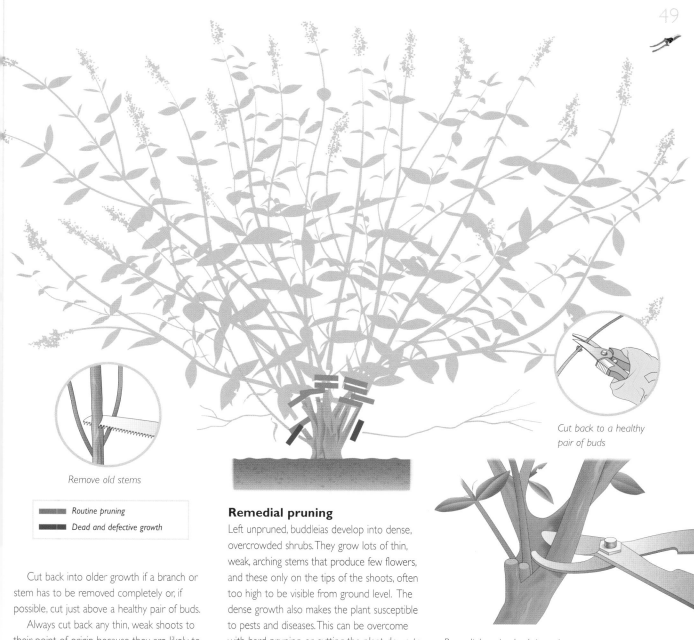

Remove old stems

Routine pruning	
Dead and defective growth	

Cut back to a healthy pair of buds

Cut back into older growth if a branch or stem has to be removed completely or, if possible, cut just above a healthy pair of buds.

Always cut back any thin, weak shoots to their point of origin because they are likely to succumb to pests and diseases and rarely produce good flowers.

Remedial pruning

Left unpruned, buddleias develop into dense, overcrowded shrubs. They grow lots of thin, weak, arching stems that produce few flowers, and these only on the tips of the shoots, often too high to be visible from ground level. The dense growth also makes the plant susceptible to pests and diseases. This can be overcome with hard pruning, or cutting the plant down to its original stem or leg.

In spring, depending on the thickness of the branches and shoots, use a saw or long-handled pruners (loppers) to cut the plant back to its original framework, encouraging new growth to replace the old shoots.

Remedial cutting back in spring

A month after the initial pruning, remove all the weak, thin, sappy young shoots and leave up to eight of the strongest, healthiest shoots to produce flowers and form a new framework for future years.

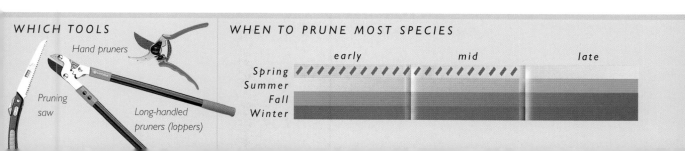

WHICH TOOLS

Hand pruners

Pruning saw

Long-handled pruners (loppers)

WHEN TO PRUNE MOST SPECIES

	early	mid	late
Spring	/////	/////	
Summer			
Fall			
Winter			

Callicarpa
Callicarpa, beautyberry

Callicarpas are grown for their small, round, brightly colored fruits, which are borne in generous clusters after a long, hot summer and last well into the winter.

Callicarpa bodinieri var. giraldii 'Profusion' *is a shrub with an open, upright habit and medium-size, broadly oval-shaped leaves that are a glossy green in the spring and summer and turn orange and purple tinted before dropping in the fall. Clusters of small, lilac flowers are produced in late summer followed by glossy, violet-purple fruits that last well into the winter.*

They are borderline hardy to tender shrubs with a bushy habit, and they prefer fertile, well-drained soil. They do best in full sun or partial shade. *Callicarpa japonica* 'Leucocarpa' needs some winter shelter or it may be cut to the ground by hard frosts, although it usually recovers well. All callicarpas benefit from regular mulches of organic matter. Apart from the need for shelter from biting cold winds, they are easy to grow and often produce such large quantities of berries, there is a risk that the branches will break under the weight.

Most callicarpas have broadly elliptical, dark-green leaves, often ending in a sharp point at the tip. They are arranged in opposite pairs on greenish-purple stems, which turn dull green as they mature. The leaves of *C. bodinieri* var. *giraldii* 'Profusion' are bronze when young, turning dark green with age. Most callicarpas are deciduous, but *C. rubella* has pale yellow-green, evergreen leaves.

In summer, clusters of small, pink flowers are produced from the leaf axis, on the tips of the shoots, and these are followed by dense clusters of small, beadlike, bright purplish-pink berries in fall and winter. An exception is *C. japonica* 'Leucocarpa', which has small, white flowers followed by white berries that become translucent with age.

WHY PRUNE?

To replace the older stems with new ones and to remove frost-damaged shoots.

PRUNING TIPS

• Cut frost-damaged stems down to ground level, and they will shoot again from the base.

PLANTS PRUNED THIS WAY

Callicarpa bodinieri *and cvs.: in early spring*
Callicarpa japonica *and cvs.: in midspring*
Callicarpa rubella *and cvs.: in midspring*

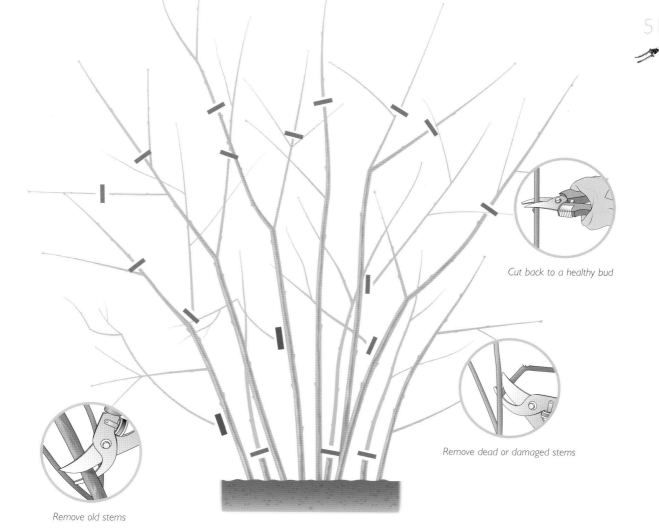

Cut back to a healthy bud

Remove dead or damaged stems

Remove old stems

▬▬▬	Routine pruning
▬▬▬	Dead and defective growth

Formative pruning

Prune young plants to encourage them to develop a bushy habit with strong shoots emerging from just above ground level.

In spring, just as the new growth starts, cut out any weak or damaged growth. Then cut the remaining shoots back to three or four buds above ground level

Routine pruning

If they are to flower well, callicarpas need regular annual pruning to remove the old wood and to encourage new flower-bearing shoots.

In midspring after the risk of frost has passed, cut the oldest shoots down to ground level. Aim to take out between one-fifth and one-quarter of the growth each year, always selecting the oldest wood or any damaged or broken shoots for pruning.

Cut the previous year's flower-bearing stems back by at least half, pruning just above a healthy bud or a well-placed new sideshoot.

Remedial pruning

These shrubs will naturally become thick and overcrowded as they age, producing fewer flowers and fruits and becoming increasingly susceptible to pests and diseases, especially if the pruning has been neglected.

In spring, leave just three or four strong stems and cut the remaining shoots back to within 2 to 3 inches of ground level to encourage new shoots that will replace the old ones.

The following year, completely remove any thin or weak shoots. Cut out the three or four remaining old stems close to ground level.

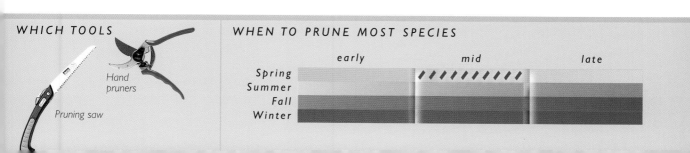

WHICH TOOLS

Hand pruners

Pruning saw

WHEN TO PRUNE MOST SPECIES

	early	mid	late
Spring			
Summer			
Fall			
Winter			

Callistemon

Bottlebrush

Callistemons are grown for their fantastic displays of bristlelike blooms.
They often make the plant look as if it has caught fire, especially when the
branches are swaying in the wind.

These evergreen shrubs are native to
Australia. They do best in moist, well-
drained, fertile soil that does not have
too much lime in it, and they need a
bright, sunny position, sheltered from
cold winds. They will often grow to 12
feet high (taller if grown against a wall)
and 15 feet across. The long, narrow,
dark-green leaves are held on long,
arching branches and are light brown in
color and often turn gray-brown and
develop a slightly corky surface as they
age. In late spring and summer, clusters of
bristlelike flowers are produced on the
tips of the shoots. They are followed by
small, acornlike seed cases, which can
linger on the stems for several seasons.

Prune *Callistemon citrinus* (crimson
bottlebrush) and its cultivars and
C. rigidus (stiff bottlebrush) in summer,
after flowering. *C. sieberi* (alpine
bottlebrush) requires only minimal
pruning.

Callistemon citrinus *is an evergreen*
shrub with long, slender, arching branches that
are light brown in colour and turn grayish brown
as they age. The leaves are long, narrow, dark
green, and spear shaped. In late spring and
early summer, clusters of bright-red, bristlelike
flowers are produced on the tips of the previous
year's shoots and followed by small, acornlike
seed cases.

WHY PRUNE?

To prevent the plant from
becoming straggly and untidy.

PRUNING TIPS

• *Cut back to strong, healthy buds.*

PLANTS PRUNED THIS WAY

Callistemon citrinus *and cvs.: in late summer, after flowering*
Callistemon rigidus *in late summer, after flowering*

Cut back to a healthy bud

_Remove thin,
straggling growth_

▬▬▬	Routine pruning
▬▬▬	Dead and defective growth

Formative pruning

Prune young plants to encourage them to grow bushy, with strong shoots emerging from low down on the stems.

After planting, cut out any weak or damaged growth. Lightly tip the remaining shoots back to about two-thirds of their length to encourage new shoots to develop from the base of the plant as it becomes established.

Routine pruning

These plants do not need regular annual pruning to flower well. However, they are pruned to avoid long, straggly stems with lots of bare wood and to encourage the production of new flower-bearing shoots.

Immediately after flowering, cut the old flower-bearing stems back to a healthy bud. This will allow the maximum period of growth to produce a good display of flowers the following year.

Remedial pruning

Callistemons naturally produce long, straggly stems, and plants can look open and untidy, especially if the pruning has been neglected. This can be overcome with hard pruning, which must be done in stages over 2 or 3 years rather than just cutting the plant down completely.

Each year, remove one or two stems after flowering, cutting them back to within 2 to 3 inches of ground level to encourage new shoots to replace the old ones.

WHICH TOOLS

Hand pruners

Long-handled pruners (loppers)

WHEN TO PRUNE MOST SPECIES

	early	mid	late
Spring			
Summer			/////////
Fall			
Winter			

Calluna
Heather, Scots heather, ling

Heathers are hardy, compact, evergreen shrubs available in a wide range of foliage and flower colors, providing interest in the garden all year round.

Calluna vulgaris *is a bushy shrub with a low, spreading habit. The stems are dull green, turning light brown with age and later becoming gray and woody with flaking bark. The leaves are narrow, short, and tufted. They closely overlap to give a coniferlike appearance along slender stems. From midsummer until late fall, small, white, bell-shaped flowers are borne on short, erect spikes, often remaining on the plant long after they have died.*

The hundreds of named cultivars of *Calluna vulgaris* are ideal for gardens with acidic soil, where you may be limited in your choice of flowering groundcover plants. Some of the smaller cultivars are suitable for rock gardens, while larger ones can be used as specimen or feature plants. They grow well in sandy or poor to moderately fertile, moisture-retentive but free-draining soil and will actually flower more prolifically in poor soil. Heathers need a position in full sun but will not tolerate drought. They do not suffer from any pests, but they are susceptible to fungal diseases in warm, wet growing conditions, and the roots may rot in heavy clay or waterlogged soils.

The plants form compact, bushy shrubs with a low, spreading habit. The tallest cultivars grow to about 2 feet high and about 3 feet across, giving a low mound or mat-like profile. The smallest cultivars grow to about 10 inches high and no more than 20 inches across. The foliage can vary from shades of green, yellow, orange, and red to silver-gray. The individual leaves are narrow, straplike, and 1/8 inch long, and they often closely overlap, giving a coniferlike appearance. The leaves are arranged along thin, yellow-green stems, which turn light brown as they age, later becoming woody with flaking bark.

From midsummer until late fall, small, bell-shaped flowers are held on short, erect spikes, each with 30 to 50 blooms. The colors range from white through every imaginable shade of pink, purple, and red.

Formative pruning

Prune young plants to encourage them to form a bushy shape with many shoots emerging from ground level.

After planting, cut out any weak or damaged growth. Cut the remaining shoots back to one-third of their original length.

WHY PRUNE?

To promote new flower-bearing shoots and keep the plant tidy.

PRUNING TIPS

• *Calluna vulgaris can be pruned just after flowering in milder climates.*

PLANTS PRUNED THIS WAY

Calluna vulgaris: *in late winter or early spring, after flowering*
Erica carnea *and cvs.: in midspring, after flowering but before new growth starts*
Erica cinerea *and cvs.: in early spring, after flowering*
Erica x darleyensis *and cvs.: in midspring, after flowering but before new growth starts*

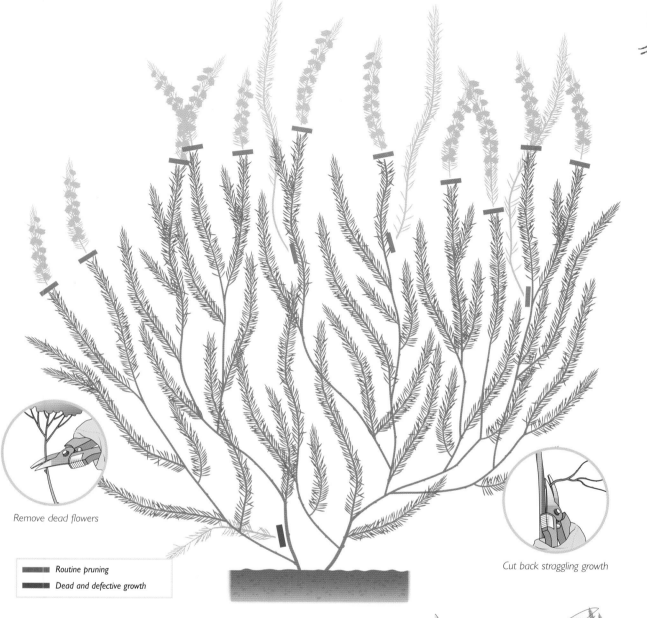

Remove dead flowers

Routine pruning
Dead and defective growth

Cut back straggling growth

Routine pruning

Try to prevent the plant from becoming too straggly and open in the center.

In late winter or early spring, trim back all old flower-bearing shoots to just below the dead flowers. Use hand pruners to cut back any long, straggling growths to make them branch.

Remedial pruning

These low-growing shrubs often become open and bare in the center. They do respond to severe pruning, but it is usually better to remove and replace old, straggly plants.

Dig up and dispose of old, overgrown plants.

Use shears to cut the plant back hard (by a third or a half) every 5 years

WHICH TOOLS

Hand pruners

Pruning shears

WHEN TO PRUNE MOST SPECIES

	early	mid	late
Spring	/////////		
Summer			
Fall			
Winter			/////////

Camellia

Camellia

In late winter and early spring, the beautiful flowers of camellias are a welcome promise that warmer weather is on the way.

Camellia *'Black Lace'* is a slow-growing, dense, upright, evergreen shrub with pale-brown shoots that turn deep grayish brown with age. The broadly oval-shaped, glossy, very dark-green leaves usually end in a sharp point at the tip and often have a serrated pattern around the margins. From early to late spring, large, black-red, double flowers are produced from large, pale-green, swollen buds. These are occasionally followed by greenish-brown fruits with a corky texture in late fall.

These popular evergreen plants are grown for their attractive, roselike flowers and handsome, glossy green leaves. Once established, they are generally trouble free, but they must be grown in an acidic soil or in containers of ericaceous growing mix (a growing mix formulated for acid-loving plants). They prefer moist, well-drained soil with a mulch of bark or leaf mold to keep the surface roots moist and the protection of partial or dappled shade. Hybrids of *Camellia japonica* are hardy, although the flowers may be damaged by harsh frosts, but *C. sasanqua* camellias are not fully hardy and must be protected from frost. Some named cultivars are unstable and may revert—that is, produce flowers of a different color, often resembling that of an original parent plant.

Camellias usually develop into large shrubs—even small trees—reaching up to 28 feet high and to 25 feet across. The evergreen, dark-green leaves are broadly elliptical, often ending in a sharp point at the tip and with a slight toothing around the margins.

There are a huge number of cultivars, flowering from late winter to midspring and in a vast range of colors, including shades of red, pink, white, and yellow. There are even a few with white-, pink-, and red-variegated blooms. The flower types range from singles, with only about

seven petals, to formal doubles with more than 60 petals.

Many camellias will do quite well without any pruning at all, but they can develop an open, leggy habit and begin to produce smaller flowers.

Formative pruning

Prune young plants to create a bushy, well-structured shrub with plenty of branches growing close to ground level.

In spring, cut any weak, leggy shoots back to about two or three buds. Remove the top one-third of any long, straggling shoots.

WHY PRUNE?

To develop a healthy, bushy, free-flowering plant.

PRUNING TIPS

• Prune soon after flowering, just before the plant begins its main growing period.

PLANTS PRUNED THIS WAY

Camellia japonica *and cvs.:* in spring, after flowering
Camellia reticulata *and cvs.:* in spring, after flowering
Camellia sasanqua *and cvs.:* in spring, before new growth starts
Camellia x williamsii *and cvs.:* in spring, after flowering

After flowering,
cut back old
flower-bearing
stems

Shorten overvigorous stems

Routine pruning

Dead and defective growth

Routine pruning

Camellias grow quite happily for many years
with little or no pruning. However, if you
shorten the previous season's growth by cutting
close to the old wood immediately after
flowering, you are more likely to have a bushy,
free-flowering plant. This is also a good way to
keep the plant from getting too bare and leggy.

In spring, immediately after the flowers have
fallen, cut the flower-bearing shoots back to
within three to five buds of the old wood. This
will encourage the plant to develop many
short, flowering stems for the following year.

In summer, shorten by one-third any overly
vigorous shoots to prevent the plant from
becoming unbalanced and lopsided.

Remedial pruning

In time, camellias often become bare and leggy
at the base. They respond well to remedial
pruning, but this should be phased over 2 years.
Do not cut the plant back in one operation.

In spring after flowering, cut the thickest
branches down to 2 feet above ground level.
The following year, cut any remaining old
branches down to the same height. If necessary,
thin some of the new shoots to prevent
overcrowding.

WHICH TOOLS

Pruning
saw

Hand
pruners

Long-handled
pruners (loppers)

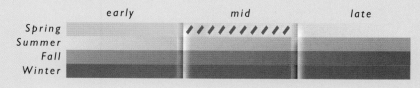

WHEN TO PRUNE MOST SPECIES

	early	mid	late
Spring			
Summer			
Fall			
Winter			

Campsis

Trumpet creeper, trumpet vine

If you need a good climber for a hot, sunny wall or a dry position, this is the plant for you. It produces an amazing display of trumpet-shaped flowers from late summer until the first fall frosts.

Campsis grandiflora *is a vigorous, deciduous climber that clings onto supports with its aerial roots or trails over structures. The long, trailing stems are pale, golden brown. The large leaves are divided into oval-shaped leaflets, arranged along a central main stalk attached to the stems and branches. Large, trumpet-shaped, orange-red flowers are carried in clusters on the tips of the shoots. Podlike fruits are sometimes produced in the fall.*

The plants in this genus are vigorous, deciduous climbers that cling to supports by means of aerial roots that emerge from the stems. Plants can reach 30 feet high and about 18 feet across. *Campsis grandiflora* (Chinese trumpet creeper, Chinese trumpet vine) is rarely self-supporting, however, and must be tied into a supporting framework.

The long, trailing stems are green, turning to pale golden-brown as they age, and the large leaves are divided into about nine oval, midgreen leaflets, with toothed margins and often a coating of fine hairs on the underside. They are arranged along a central main stalk attached to the stems and branches. The trumpet-shaped flowers, in shades of red, orange, or yellow, are carried in clusters of up to 12 on the tips of the shoots and are sometimes followed by slender, woody, podlike fruits in fall. The most widely grown cultivar is *C. tagliabuana* 'Madame Galen', which has large, orange-red flowers up to 3 inches long.

Formative pruning

Prune young plants to encourage them to develop a framework of four or five vigorous shoots emerging from the base of the plant.

In the first spring after planting, cut out any weak or damaged growth. Cut all healthy stems back to 6 inches above ground level.

As new shoots develop, tie the strongest ones into the supporting structure. Cut smaller, thinner shoots back to a single bud.

WHY PRUNE?

To encourage the production of flower-bearing spurs and to control vigor.

PRUNING TIPS

• *Use sharp tools, because the stems are brittle.*

PLANTS PRUNED THIS WAY

Campsis grandiflora *and cvs.: in late winter or early spring*
Campsis radicans *and cvs.: in late winter or early spring*
Campsis x tagliabuana *and cvs.: in late winter or early spring*

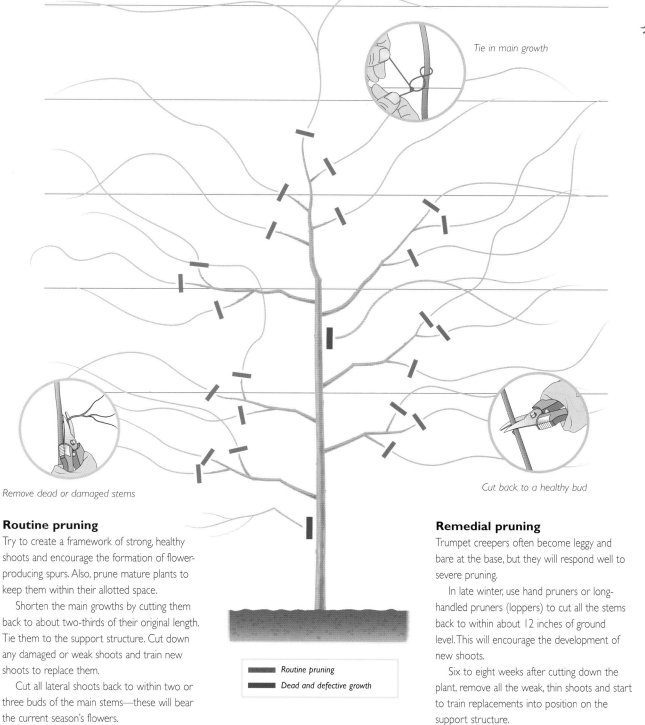

Tie in main growth

Remove dead or damaged stems

Cut back to a healthy bud

Routine pruning

Try to create a framework of strong, healthy shoots and encourage the formation of flower-producing spurs. Also, prune mature plants to keep them within their allotted space.

Shorten the main growths by cutting them back to about two-thirds of their original length. Tie them to the support structure. Cut down any damaged or weak shoots and train new shoots to replace them.

Cut all lateral shoots back to within two or three buds of the main stems—these will bear the current season's flowers.

▬	*Routine pruning*
▬	*Dead and defective growth*

Remedial pruning

Trumpet creepers often become leggy and bare at the base, but they will respond well to severe pruning.

In late winter, use hand pruners or long-handled pruners (loppers) to cut all the stems back to within about 12 inches of ground level. This will encourage the development of new shoots.

Six to eight weeks after cutting down the plant, remove all the weak, thin shoots and start to train replacements into position on the support structure.

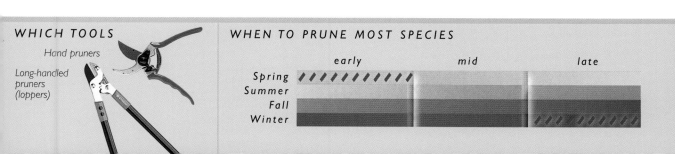

WHICH TOOLS

Hand pruners

Long-handled pruners (loppers)

WHEN TO PRUNE MOST SPECIES

	early	mid	late
Spring			
Summer			
Fall			
Winter			

Ceanothus (deciduous species)
Ceanothus, California lilac

Blue ceanothus is a wonderful sight in a summer garden, as are the rarer pink-flowered species, which flower as abundantly.

Ceanothus x pallidus 'Marie Simon' is a spreading shrub with a dense, bushy habit. Its slender, green stems are tinted pinkish red when young and turn grayish brown with age. The leaves are oval shaped, dark-green, and have a finely toothed margin. From midsummer to fall, small, flesh-pink flowers are grouped together to form large dense clusters on the tips of shoots and sideshoots on the current season's growth.

Of the 55 species in the genus, several are evergreen (see pages 62 and 63). The deciduous plants are relatively hardy shrubs that produce cascades of mainly blue flowers, although some pink-flowered forms are also available. They make attractive freestanding shrubs, but in colder areas they are often grown as wall shrubs. They can benefit from the added shelter of a wall or fence, but they may reach twice the height of a freestanding plant. They prefer a position in full sun in well-drained, fertile soil. Ceanothus will tolerate lime in the soil, but the foliage may turn pale green or even yellow if the soil is excessively alkaline.

Plants will usually grow to 5 to 6 feet high and about 6 feet wide. The oval, dark-green leaves have finely toothed margins and are carried on reddish-brown stems, which turn gray-brown with age. Deciduous *Ceanothus* plants will flower in midsummer and through into fall on the current season's growth. The small flowers, $\frac{1}{8}$ inch across, are grouped together to form large clusters on the tips of shoots and, in some cases, the sideshoots. New growth is susceptible to scorch damage from late spring frosts. The plants usually recover, although they may flower slightly later as a result.

WHY PRUNE?
To keep the plant growing well and producing new growth and flowers.

PRUNING TIPS
• *Use sharp tools that will cut cleanly through the stems, because crushed or bruised tissue tends to dieback.*

PLANTS PRUNED THIS WAY
Ceanothus *'Gloire de Versailles':* in early spring, before new growth starts
Ceanothus x delileanus *and cvs.:* in midspring, before new growth starts
Ceanothus x pallidus *and cvs.:* in midspring, before new growth starts

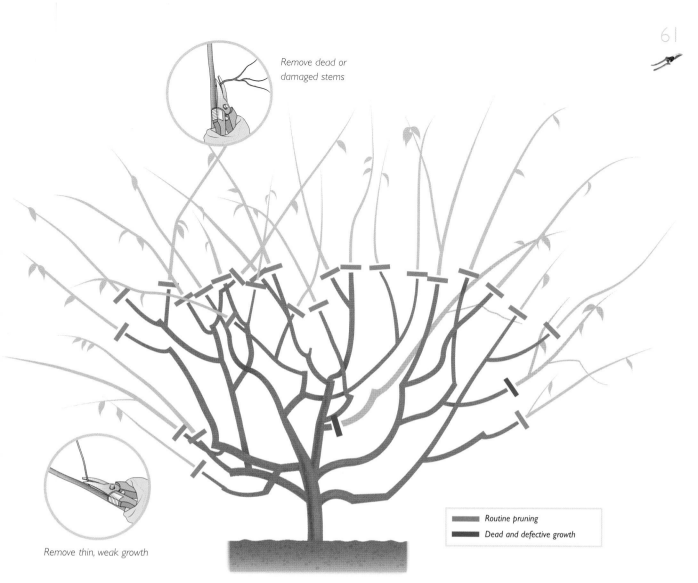

Remove dead or damaged stems

Remove thin, weak growth

	Routine pruning
	Dead and defective growth

Formative pruning

Prune young plants to encourage them to develop a bushy habit with strong shoots emerging from just above ground level.

In the first spring after planting, cut out any weak or damaged growth. Then cut all strong, healthy stems back to about one-third of their original length.

The following spring, cut all the main stems back to one-third of their original length. Shorten all sideshoots to within 6 inches of the main stems.

Routine pruning

Established plants often become large, open, and rather straggly. To avoid this, prune them annually when they reach 3 to 4 feet high. In addition, remove any weak shoots, which can cause overcrowding.

In spring before new growth starts, cut all shoots back to within three or four buds of the previous season's growth. Remove any dead stems from the center of the plant.

Remedial pruning

Left unpruned, ceanothus will develop into open, sprawling shrubs, often with splitting and breaking branches. Hard pruning can overcome this, as can cutting the plant down to its original stem about 12 inches above ground level.

In spring, cut the plant back to its original framework to encourage new shoots to develop. Depending on the thickness of the branches and shoots, use a pruning saw or long-handled pruners (loppers).

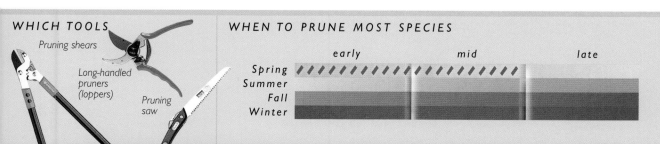

WHICH TOOLS

Pruning shears

Long-handled pruners (loppers)

Pruning saw

WHEN TO PRUNE MOST SPECIES

	early	mid	late
Spring			
Summer			
Fall			
Winter			

Ceanothus (evergreen species)

Ceanothus, California lilac

Few shrubs bear blue flowers, and evergreen ceanothus are doubly valued—for their year-round foliage and for their beautiful blooms.

Like the deciduous species (see pages 60 and 61), the relatively hardy evergreen shrubs can be grown as freestanding shrubs or as wall shrubs. In colder areas, they benefit from the added shelter of a wall or fence, as they are prone to wind-chill damage and don't thrive in exposed positions. Indeed, when they are grown as wall shrubs they may reach twice the height of freestanding plants. However, they must be tied securely to a supporting framework or they tend to fall over because of their brittle root systems. They do best when they grow in full sun in well-drained, fertile soil; although they prefer soil with lime in it, they may turn pale green or even yellow in soil that is excessively alkaline.

Evergreen ceanothus species are diverse in terms of shape and habit, ranging from treelike forms growing to 18 feet high and about 25 feet across to the low, spreading cultivars of *Ceanothus gloriosus*, which are only 12 inches high but may spread to 12 feet across. Most have roughly oval leaves, which are glossy and deep-green, usually paler on the underside, with deep veins and toothed margins. The leaves are held on green-brown stems, which turn gray-brown with age. Small blue or white flowers, ⅛ inch across, are grouped together to form large clusters on the tips of shoots and sideshoots in late spring and early summer. *C.* 'Autumnal Blue' often produces a second, smaller flush in fall.

Ceanothus arboreus 'Trewithen Blue' *is a vigorous, evergreen shrub or small tree with erect, greenish-brown stems and glossy green leaves. The oval leaves have a shallow-toothed margin and downy felt on the underside. In spring and early summer, large, pyramid-shaped spikes of light- to medium-blue flowers appear on the tips of the main stems and side branches.*

Formative pruning

Prune young plants to encourage them to develop a bushy habit with strong shoots emerging from just above ground level.

In the first spring after planting, cut out any weak or damaged growth. Pinch off the tips of the main shoots by removing about one-third of each shoot.

WHY PRUNE?

To keep the plant growing well and producing new growth and flowers.

PRUNING TIPS

• *Do not prune back into old, bare wood because it rarely produces new shoots.*

PLANTS PRUNED THIS WAY

Ceanothus arboreus and cvs.: *in midsummer, after flowering*
Ceanothus impressus and cvs.: *in midsummer, after flowering*
Ceanothus thyrsiflorus and cvs.: *in midsummer, after flowering*
Ceanothus 'Burkwoodii': *in early spring, before new growth starts*

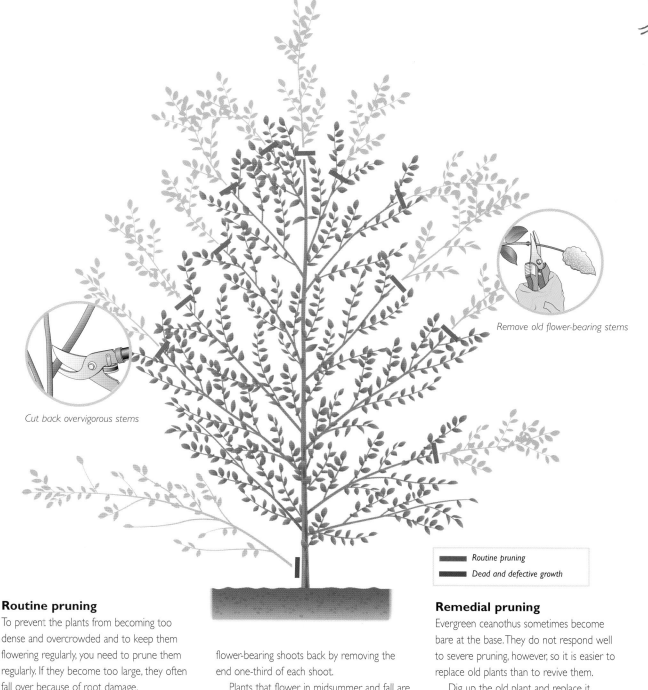

Cut back overvigorous stems

Remove old flower-bearing stems

| | Routine pruning |
| | Dead and defective growth |

Routine pruning

To prevent the plants from becoming too dense and overcrowded and to keep them flowering regularly, you need to prune them regularly. If they become too large, they often fall over because of root damage.

Plants that flower in spring or early summer should be pruned in midsummer: Cut all flower-bearing shoots back by removing the end one-third of each shoot.

Plants that flower in midsummer and fall are pruned in spring: Cut all flower-bearing shoots back by removing the end one-third.

Remedial pruning

Evergreen ceanothus sometimes become bare at the base. They do not respond well to severe pruning, however, so it is easier to replace old plants than to revive them.

Dig up the old plant and replace it. Completely replace the soil in the planting hole when you do so.

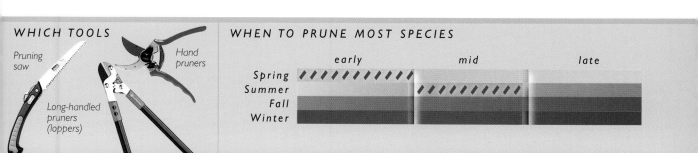

WHICH TOOLS

Pruning saw

Hand pruners

Long-handled pruners (loppers)

WHEN TO PRUNE MOST SPECIES

	early	mid	late
Spring	////////////		
Summer		////////////	
Fall			
Winter			

Cercis

Redbud

*These remarkable trees or shrubs
produce small, pealike flowers on
bare branches (even on the main
trunk) before the leaves emerge in
spring. Before they drop in fall, the
leaves turn a pretty buttery yellow.*

The thin, twiggy branches of redbuds
bear round to heart-shaped leaves, often
tinged bronze before opening to a bright
green; there are also purple-leaved forms.
The flowers are carried in tight clusters
along the bare branches. They may be
white, deep red, purple, and shades of
pink, and they are often followed by
green-black, flattened, podlike fruits that
remain on the plant long into winter. The
plants naturally have a rounded shape,
and they will grow up to 30 feet high,
spreading to 18 feet across.

Cercis is the perfect choice for a hot,
dry site because it does well on poor,
light soils, but it is prone to weak forks
that can split as the tree ages.

Prune *Cercis canadensis* (eastern
redbud) and its cultivars and hybrids,
including *C. canadensis* var. *occidentalis*
(California redbud, western redbud), and
C. siliquastrum (Judas tree) and its cultivars
in early summer, after flowering.

*Cercis siliquastrum is a small
tree with thin, twiggy branches and a
bent, twisting stem. It has dark-gray,
almost black, bark that cracks and splits
with age. The leaves are round to heart
shaped, often tinted bronze before
opening to become bright green. They
turn yellow before dropping in fall. The
small, pealike flowers are deep pinkish
purple and are carried in tight clusters on
bare branches before the leaves emerge
in spring.*

Formative pruning

Prune young plants to encourage them to grow
bushy, with strong shoots emerging 2 to 3 feet
above soil level.

After planting, cut out any damaged growth.
Cut the main stem back to about 3 feet above
ground level to encourage the development of
new shoots that will create a multistemmed
tree as it becomes established.

WHY PRUNE?

*To remove damaged or
overcrowded growth and to
develop a strong structure.*

PRUNING TIPS

• *Wait until the new growth starts
before pruning.*

PLANTS PRUNED THIS WAY

Cercis canadensis *and cvs.: in early summer, after flowering*
Cercis siliquastrum *and cvs.: in early summer, after flowering*

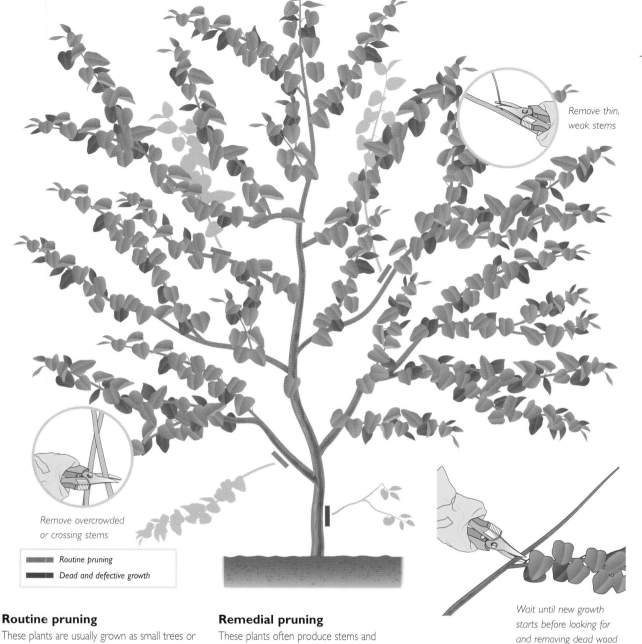

Remove thin,
weak stems

Remove overcrowded
or crossing stems

- Routine pruning
- Dead and defective growth

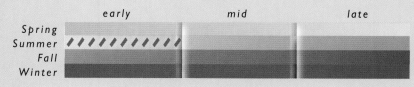

Wait until new growth
starts before looking for
and removing dead wood

Routine pruning

These plants are usually grown as small trees or multistemmed shrubs and are pruned to remove overcrowded or damaged stems, or to lift the canopy when drooping branches are a problem.

After flowering, remove any broken, frost-damaged, or rubbing stems, cutting them back to a healthy bud. Remove any thin, weak shoots to avoid overcrowding.

Remedial pruning

These plants often produce stems and branches with sharply angled crotches, which can split in strong, gusting winds. Plants will, however, respond well to severe pruning.

In late spring or early summer, use a saw or long-handled pruners (loppers), depending on the thickness of the branches and shoots, to cut the plant back to a framework of branches 2 to

3 feet above soil level. This will encourage new shoots to develop.

Six to eight weeks after cutting down the plant, remove all the weak, thin shoots, leaving up to six of the strongest, healthiest shoots.

WHICH TOOLS

Pruning saw

Hand pruners

Long-handled pruners (loppers)

WHEN TO PRUNE MOST SPECIES

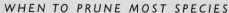

	early	mid	late
Spring			
Summer			
Fall			
Winter			

Chaenomeles

Flowering quince, Japanese quince

This is one of the most popular early-flowering shrubs and an excellent freestanding shrub, wall shrub, or flowering hedge.

These deciduous, rather spiny shrubs can cope with a wide range of growing conditions, ranging from full sun to a partially shaded or shaded wall; they do flower and fruit best, however, when they are grown in full sun. They will grow in almost any well-drained soil but tend to develop yellow leaves if the soil is shallow and chalky. They are often pruned after flowering, but if you cut off old flowering wood you will remove the embryo fruits, which can be attractive and highly fragrant in late summer and early fall.

The early spring flowers appear on bare stems and branches, which are a pale-brown when young but turn almost black as they age. The flowers are saucer shaped, with five or more petals, and borne singly or in clusters. The colors range from flame red to orange, pink, and white, and they are followed by pale-orange, applelike fruits in fall and winter. The leaves are round to oval in shape with toothed margins and are carried on robust, thorny stems. Plants vary in habit from the strong, erect growth of *Chaenomeles cathayensis*, which will get to 10 feet high, to the low-growing *C. speciosa* 'Geisha Girl', which will grow to about 3 feet high.

*Chaenomeles x superba **'Crimson and Gold'** is a versatile deciduous shrub, ideal as a hedge plant or wall shrub. It has a compact habit with thorny, spreading, light-brown young shoots that turn almost black as they age. The broadly oval leaves are mid- to dark green in color and emerge as the plant finishes flowering. The dark-red flowers are carried directly on the branches and open in mid- to late spring, often followed by green, applelike fruits which turn yellow as they ripen.*

Formative pruning

Freestanding and wall-trained shrubs are grown as multistemmed plants, with strong shoots emerging from just above ground level.

In the first spring after planting, as the new growth starts, cut out any thin, weak growth or damaged shoots. Cut the remaining shoots back to about two-thirds of their existing length.

WHY PRUNE?

To replace old growth with new flower-bearing shoots.

PRUNING TIPS

• *Prune plants in alternate years if you want a display of fruits.*

PLANTS PRUNED THIS WAY

Chaenomeles x californica *cvs.: after flowering*
Chaenomeles cathayensis: *after flowering*
Chaenomeles japonica *cvs.: after flowering*
Chaenomeles speciosa *cvs.: after flowering*
Chaenomeles x superba *cvs.: after flowering*

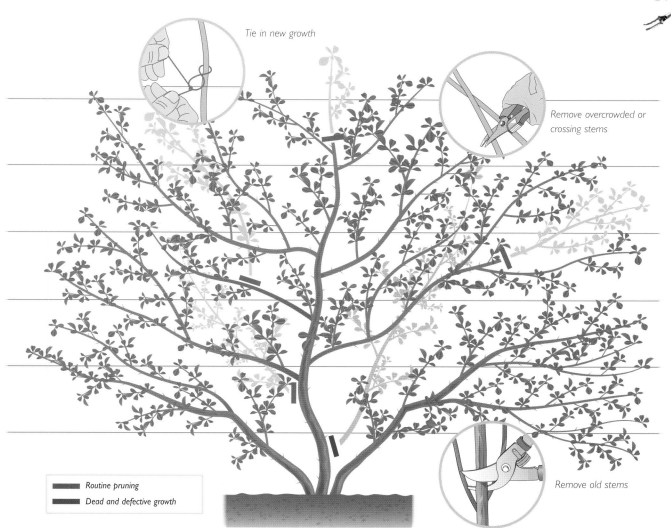

Tie in new growth

Remove overcrowded or crossing stems

Remove old stems

■ Routine pruning
■ Dead and defective growth

Routine pruning

Flowering quinces will grow quite well with little or no pruning, but they tend to become congested, which leads to smaller and fewer flowers and invites disease. Regular pruning will encourage the plant to replace old, nonproductive growth with new, flower-bearing shoots and will improve air circulation within the plant.

After flowering, in late spring or early summer, remove any crossing or rubbing branches and thin out congested shoots. Cut out one or two of the very old stems each year to make room for replacement branches.

Cut any sideshoots back to three or four leaves, which will form next year's flowering spurs.

On wall-trained shrubs, tie the new growth to form a fan-shaped plant after pruning, leaving 6 to 8 inches between stems.

Remedial pruning

When plants are allowed to become congested, the inner branches will often shed their leaves and die from lack of light, so that the only growth is around the edges. These plants respond well to severe pruning, but it should be done in stages over 2 or 3 years.

Cut about one-third of the stems back to within 6 inches of ground level. Repeat this process over the next 2 or 3 years until the old growth has been removed and replaced.

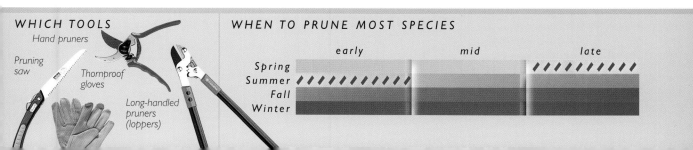

WHICH TOOLS

Hand pruners

Pruning saw

Thornproof gloves

Long-handled pruners (loppers)

WHEN TO PRUNE MOST SPECIES

	early	mid	late
Spring			
Summer			
Fall			
Winter			

Choisya
Mexican orange blossom

This popular evergreen shrub has aromatic leaves and bears fragrant flowers twice a year. Plant close to a path or house window to get maximum benefit from the flowers.

Choisya ternata is a medium-size, evergreen shrub with a dense, compact habit and dull-green stems that become grayish green as they age. The glossy, dark-green leaves are arranged in clusters of three leaflets, each narrowly oval in shape. In late spring, and again in late summer and fall, white, fragrant, star-shaped flowers are produced on the tips of the stems and branches in clusters of up to six blooms.

Choisyas can grow up to 8 feet high and often 6 to 10 feet across. They prefer fertile, well-drained soil and a position in full sun that is sheltered from cold winds. The glossy, dark-green leaves are arranged in clusters of three leaflets, each narrowly oval in shape and carried on dull-green stems, which turn gray-green as they age.

The star-shaped flowers are white, occasionally tinged pink, and are held on the tips of the stems and branches in clusters of up to six blooms in late spring and again in late summer and fall. The golden-leaved form, *Choisya ternata* 'Sundance', rarely produces flowers. C. 'Aztec Pearl', which bears dainty white flowers, has attractive narrow, dark-green leaves, but it is not fully hardy and may be damaged by frost unless it is grown in a sheltered position.

Prune all the species and their cultivars, including those of *C. arizonica* and *C. ternata*, in spring, after flowering.

WHY PRUNE?

To keep the plant growing well and producing new growth and flowers.

PRUNING TIPS

• *Prune in late spring so that the new shoots aren't unduly damaged by frost.*

PLANTS PRUNED THIS WAY

Choisya arizonica *and cvs.: in late spring, after flowering*
Choisya ternata *and cvs.: in late spring, after flowering*

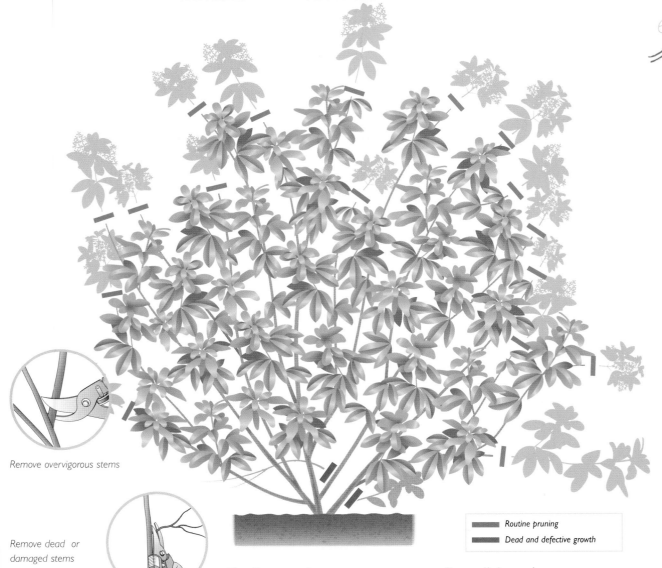

Remove overvigorous stems

Remove dead or damaged stems

Routine pruning
Dead and defective growth

Formative pruning

Prune young plants to encourage them to grow bushy, with strong shoots emerging 6 to 8 inches above soil level.

After planting, cut out any weak or damaged growth, and cut the remaining shoots back by about one-third to encourage the development of new shoots from the base of the plant.

Routine pruning

Prune in spring, immediately after flowering and after the risk of severe frost has passed. Try to encourage the plant to develop and maintain a well-balanced shape and encourage the production of a second flush of blooms.

Prune back any excessively vigorous shoots to help the plant retain its natural shape. Cut the old flower-bearing stems back by 8 to 12 inches.

Prune any shoots that show signs of frost damage or dieback.

Remedial pruning

These shrubs often develop bare stems at the base and open, straggly growth. Fortunately, they respond well to remedial pruning.

In spring, cut all of the main shoots back to within 6 to 8 inches of soil level. Cut down to ground level any thin, weak shoots.

During the second year, remove any thin, spindly growths that have developed as a result of the previous year's pruning.

WHICH TOOLS

Hand pruners

Long-handled pruners (loppers)

WHEN TO PRUNE MOST SPECIES

	early	mid	late
Spring			//////////
Summer			
Fall			
Winter			

Clematis
Early-flowering clematis

If you choose carefully, it's possible to have a clematis in flower in your garden just about every month of the year, even in the depths of winter.

The early-flowering clematis are the evergreen species and cultivars. The group also includes some deciduous types, such as the *alpina*, *macropetala*, and *montana* groups and their respective cultivars. These clematis flower early in the year—indeed, some are in bloom late in the year as they flower from early winter into spring. Many have small, cup- or bell-shaped flowers, which are usually found in clusters of two or more on each stem, on shoots that developed in the previous growing season. The midgreen leaves are subdivided into leaflets and are carried on thin, tough stems. The young stems are green, but they turn light brown and eventually gray with age. The colorful parts of the flowers are modified leaves (not petals), and some of the blooms are fragrant, making them especially welcome in winter.

Most clematis are true climbing plants because they can cling to other plants or structures for support. The climbing mechanism is actually a part of the leaf that's modified to twine around any object it contacts.

The clematis in this group begin to develop new shoots only after flowering has just about finished, which is when they are usually pruned.

Clematis montana var. rubens *is a vigorous, early-flowering climber with purple young stems that age to brownish gray. The leaves, borne on the branches in opposite pairs, are tinged purple when young and become deep green as they mature. The fragrant, pale mauve-pink, four-petaled flowers are produced in late spring and early summer.*

Formative pruning

Young plants should be pruned to encourage a bushy habit with strong shoots emerging from soil level.

In the first spring after planting, cut out any weak or damaged growth. Then cut back all strong, healthy stems to 12 inches above ground level. The following spring cut back all shoots to 3 feet above ground level.

Formative pruning: First spring

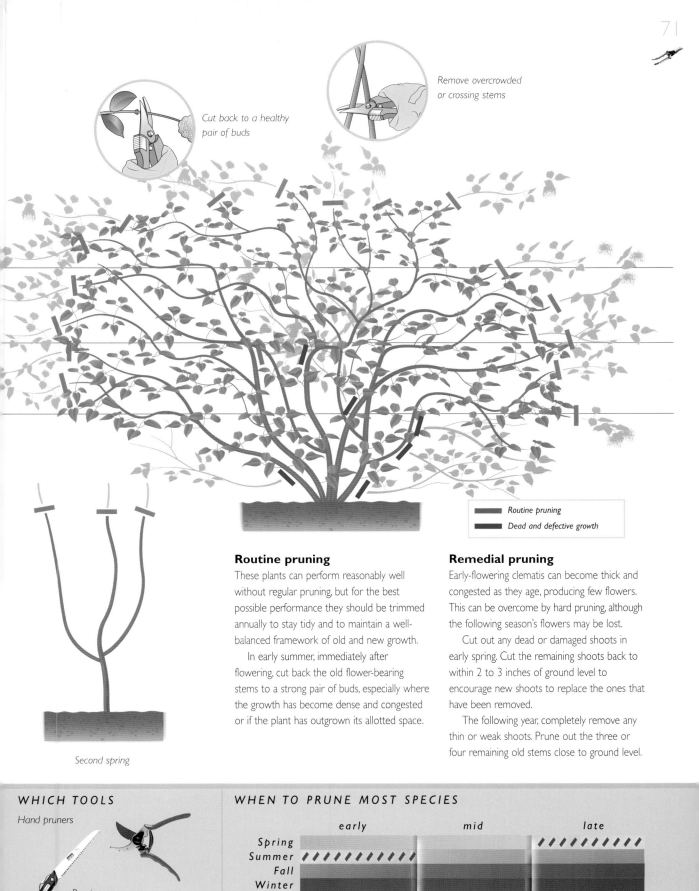

Cut back to a healthy pair of buds

Remove overcrowded or crossing stems

Routine pruning
Dead and defective growth

Second spring

Routine pruning

These plants can perform reasonably well without regular pruning, but for the best possible performance they should be trimmed annually to stay tidy and to maintain a well-balanced framework of old and new growth.

In early summer, immediately after flowering, cut back the old flower-bearing stems to a strong pair of buds, especially where the growth has become dense and congested or if the plant has outgrown its allotted space.

Remedial pruning

Early-flowering clematis can become thick and congested as they age, producing few flowers. This can be overcome by hard pruning, although the following season's flowers may be lost.

Cut out any dead or damaged shoots in early spring. Cut the remaining shoots back to within 2 to 3 inches of ground level to encourage new shoots to replace the ones that have been removed.

The following year, completely remove any thin or weak shoots. Prune out the three or four remaining old stems close to ground level.

WHICH TOOLS

Hand pruners

Pruning saw

WHEN TO PRUNE MOST SPECIES

	early	mid	late
Spring			///////////
Summer	///////////		
Fall			
Winter			

Clematis

Midseason-flowering clematis

It's this group of plants—the large-flowered hybrids with their big, decorative blooms covering fences, walls, and other structures—that has helped earn clematis the title "Queen of Climbers."

Clematis 'Nelly Moser' is a compact, flowering climber with twining leaf stalks and broad, oval, midgreen leaves carried on slender, reddish-brown stems. The large, single flowers, produced in early to midsummer, are pinkish mauve with darker bands of mauve in the center of each sepal. Often a second flush of blooms is produced in late summer, but these are smaller and paler in color than the first flush.

The group consists of cultivars that flower from early summer through late summer. All the plants in this group flower first on the previous year's shoots and again, later in the season, on the current year's growth, producing a single flower on each stem. The midgreen leaves are subdivided into leaflets and are carried on thin, tough stems. The young stems are green, but they turn light brown and eventually gray as they age. The colorful parts of the flowers are modified leaves (not petals), and only the center of each bloom is a true flower. Some of these hybrids are fragrant.

Like other climbing clematis, these plants can cling to other plants or structures for support. The climbing mechanism is actually a part of the leaf that's modified to twine around any object it contacts.

By pruning the previous year's stems to slightly different lengths, it's possible to delay or stagger the development of flowers. The stems that are cut back most severely produce flowers several weeks later than those that are pruned lightly, and this technique can extend the flowering period of individual plants.

Formative pruning

Young plants should be pruned to encourage formation of a multistemmed plant with strong shoots emerging from soil level.

In the first spring after planting, cut out any weak or damaged growth. Then cut back all strong, healthy stems to 12 inches above ground level. The following spring, cut back all shoots to 3 feet above ground level.

Formative pruning: First spring

WHY PRUNE?	PRUNING TIPS	PLANTS PRUNED THIS WAY
To encourage the formation of replacement shoots and to extend the flowering period.	*• Start pruning before the new shoots form to avoid losing next year's flowers.* *• Remove older shoots with a pair of long-handled pruners (loppers).*	Clematis *'Proteus': in early spring, as the buds swell* Clematis *'Nelly Moser': in early spring, as the buds swell* Clematis *'Vyvyan Pennell': in early spring, as the buds swell* Clematis *'H.F.Young': in early spring, as the buds swell*

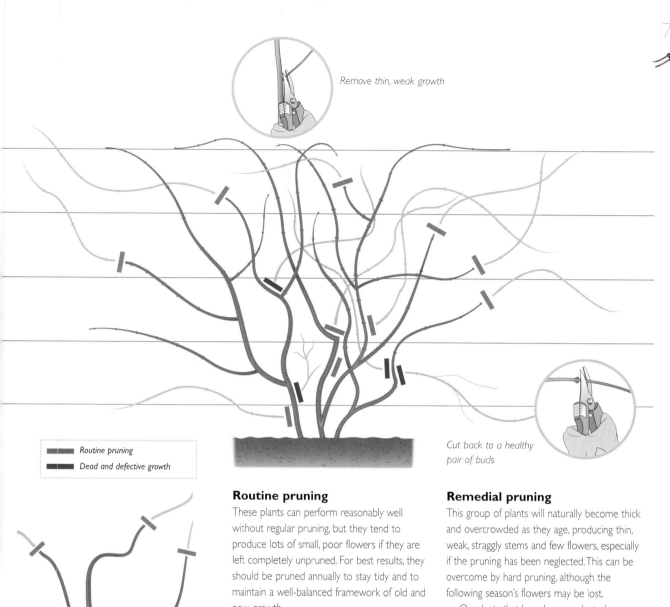

Remove thin, weak growth

Routine pruning
Dead and defective growth

Cut back to a healthy
pair of buds

Second spring

Routine pruning

These plants can perform reasonably well without regular pruning, but they tend to produce lots of small, poor flowers if they are left completely unpruned. For best results, they should be pruned annually to stay tidy and to maintain a well-balanced framework of old and new growth.

In late winter or early spring, remove any dead and weak stems. Shorten the remaining stems by 6 to 10 inches, cutting back to a pair of strong, healthy buds. Cutting some of these remaining shoots back by about 18 inches from the tip will slightly delay their growth, and they will flower later, extending the flowering period.

Tie in all remaining growths after the pruning is finished.

Remedial pruning

This group of plants will naturally become thick and overcrowded as they age, producing thin, weak, straggly stems and few flowers, especially if the pruning has been neglected. This can be overcome by hard pruning, although the following season's flowers may be lost.

On plants that have been neglected, remove any old, damaged, or diseased stems. Cut back the remaining shoots to a healthy pair of buds within 6 inches of soil level.

The following year, completely remove any thin or weak shoots. Shorten the remaining stems by 6 to 10 inches, cutting back to a pair of strong, healthy buds.

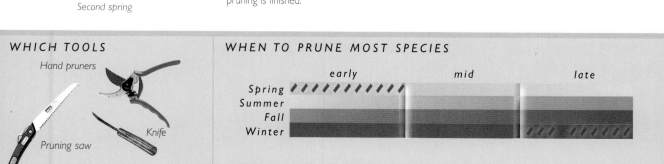

WHICH TOOLS

Hand pruners

Pruning saw

Knife

WHEN TO PRUNE MOST SPECIES

	early	mid	late
Spring			
Summer			
Fall			
Winter			

Clematis
Late-flowering clematis

This group includes some large-flowered cultivars as well as late-flowering species and their related cultivars.

Clematis 'Jackmanii' *is a vigorous, late-flowering climber with pale-brown young stems that turn brownish gray with age. The deep-green leaves are carried on the branches in opposite pairs and are supported by twining leaf stalks. The large, deep-violet, four-sepaled flowers have greenish-brown anthers and are produced from midsummer to fall.*

The species in this group include *Clematis texensis*, *C. viticella*, and *C. terniflora* and related cultivars that flower late in the year—from midsummer into early fall. Late-flowering clematis have a variety of flower types—from the very large to small, tulip-shaped flowers, which nod gently in the breeze. The blooms are produced on shoots from the current year's growth, usually with several flowers borne individually or in clusters on each stem. The flowers are often followed by seedheads, which look like round, silky tassels. The midgreen leaves are subdivided into leaflets and are carried on thin, tough stems. The young stems are green, but they turn light brown and eventually gray with age. The colorful sepals (not petals) vary in size, and some blooms are fragrant.

Like other climbing clematis, these plants can cling to other plants or structures for support. The climbing mechanism is actually a part of the leaf that's modified to twine around any object it contacts.

New shoots on the clematis in this group only start developing in spring. One of the main reasons for pruning these plants is to prevent the base from becoming old, woody, and leafless.

WHY PRUNE?

To restrict the plant's height and to encourage it to develop more flowers lower down.

PRUNING TIPS

• *Start pruning before the new shoots form to avoid losing the current year's flowers.*
• *Remove older shoots with a pair of long-handled pruners (loppers).*

PLANTS PRUNED THIS WAY

Clematis 'Ville de Lyon': *in late winter or early spring, as the buds swell*
Clematis 'Jackmanii': *in late winter or early spring, as the buds swell*
Clematis viticella *and cvs.: in late winter or early spring, as the buds swell*
Clematis texensis *and cvs.: in late winter or early spring, as the buds swell*

Tie in new growth

Remove dead or damaged stems

| | Routine pruning |
| | Dead and defective growth |

Formative pruning: First spring

Formative pruning

Young plants should be pruned to encourage a bushy shape with strong shoots emerging from soil level.

In the first spring after planting, prune any weak or damaged growth and cut back all strong, healthy stems to 12 inches above ground level.

Routine pruning

If they are to flower well, these clematis need regular annual pruning to remove the old wood that would otherwise gradually develop and to encourage production of new flower-bearing shoots.

In early spring, completely remove any dead or damaged stems. Cut back the old flower-bearing stems to a pair of strong, healthy buds 6 to 8 inches above ground level.

Carefully tie in the new shoots (they are brittle) when they are about 12 inches long.

Remedial pruning

These plants should be pruned annually if they are to grow well. If they are neglected, they develop into a thicket of thin, weak, straggly stems, which produce few flowers and make the plant susceptible to pests and diseases. If they've been neglected for a long time, it's usually easier to replace the plant altogether.

Cut back plants that have been left unpruned for a few years to a healthy pair of buds within 6 inches of ground level.

Completely remove the old plant in late winter or early spring, and take care to replace the surrounding soil before planting a new, young plant. Cut the shoots back to within 2 to 3 inches of ground level to encourage strong, healthy shoots.

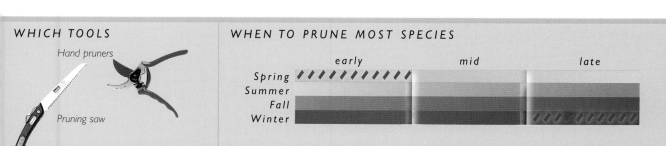

WHICH TOOLS

Hand pruners

Pruning saw

WHEN TO PRUNE MOST SPECIES

	early	mid	late
Spring	///////////		
Summer			
Fall			
Winter			///////////

Cornus alba, Cornus sericea

Dogwood, redtwig dogwood, red-osier dogwood

The dogwoods are among the easiest garden shrubs you can grow—and their stems, leaves, and flowers provide year-round interest.

Dogwoods are tolerant plants, and they will happily grow in a wide range of conditions and soils, including wet—but not waterlogged—ground. They will also put up with a fair amount of neglect, but they need an open, sunny position to show their best colors.

They are hardy, resilient, and adaptable shrubs, usually grown for their attractive and brightly colored stems, which provide welcome interest in winter and early spring. Some cultivars have the added attraction of colorful, golden, or variegated foliage, and they tend to be larger and more vivid when the plants are pruned annually. Dogwoods provide the best display when they are planted in groups to display their depth of color, although some forms are vigorous and need plenty of room to grow.

Dogwoods have a spreading, suckering habit, with new stems emerging from the soil. The oval leaves are carried in opposite pairs on strong, vigorous stems, which are often pale green when young, turning red, orange, yellow, lime green, or blue-black as they mature through the year. If they are pruned regularly, most plants will reach about 6 feet high and across in one growing season. For a limited space, *Cornus sericea* 'Kelseyi' grows to a maximum height of 30 inches.

Cornus alba **'Sibirica'** *is a hardy, suckering shrub grown for its attractive, young, upright stems. These carry midgreen leaves arranged in opposite pairs. In the fall, these leaves turn a soft butter yellow before falling to reveal bright coral-pink stems. These turn a deeper crimson as the weather gets colder. In late spring, small, star-shaped, pale greenish-white flowers are produced, followed by bluish berries.*

Formative pruning

Prune to form a multistemmed plant, with strong shoots emerging close to ground level.

Plants can be cut back hard—to within 6 inches—after planting in winter or early spring to encourage development of new shoots from the base.

WHY PRUNE?

To promote the production of new, brightly colored shoots.

PRUNING TIPS

• *Cut close to the buds to prevent dieback.*

PLANTS PRUNED THIS WAY

Cornus alba **and cvs.:** *in early to midspring*
Cornus sericea **and cvs.:** *in early to midspring*
Cornus sanguinea **and cvs.:** *in early to midspring*

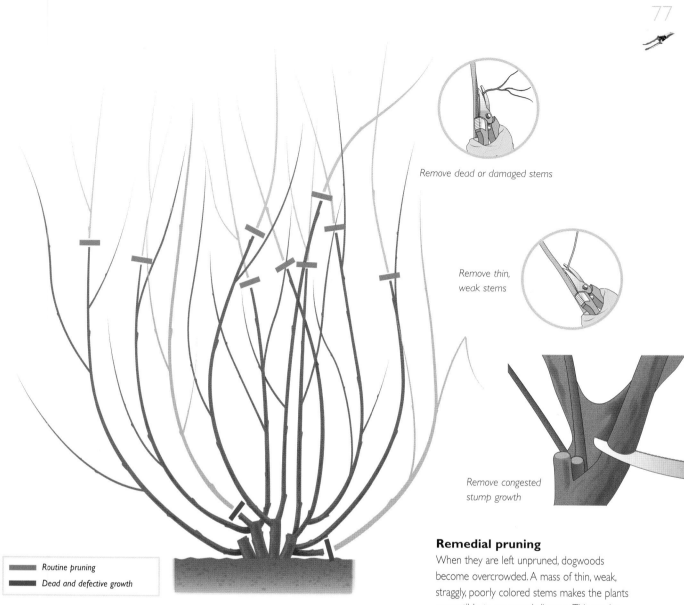

Remove dead or damaged stems

Remove thin, weak stems

Remove congested stump growth

Routine pruning
Dead and defective growth

Routine pruning

For the most attractive winter colors, dogwoods need regular annual pruning to remove the older wood and encourage production of new shoots. At the same time, weak, thin, and diseased shoots should be removed.

In early to midspring, as new growth begins, cut back one-third of the stems as close to the old branch framework as possible, leaving 1- to 2-inch stubs of growth from which the new shoots will emerge.

When the old stubs of growth become overcrowded, remove them with a small pruning saw.

Remedial pruning

When they are left unpruned, dogwoods become overcrowded. A mass of thin, weak, straggly, poorly colored stems makes the plants susceptible to pests and diseases. This can be overcome with hard pruning.

In winter, cut back all of the old stems as close to the old branch framework as possible, using a saw if necessary and leaving 1- to 2-inch stubs of growth from which the new shoots will emerge.

In late spring, completely remove any thin or weak shoots.

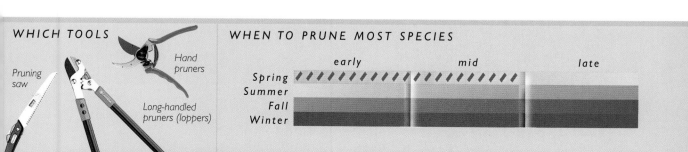

WHICH TOOLS

Pruning saw

Hand pruners

Long-handled pruners (loppers)

WHEN TO PRUNE MOST SPECIES

	early	mid	late
Spring			
Summer			
Fall			
Winter			

Cotinus

Smoke bush, Venetian sumac

The common name smoke bush describes the clusters of tiny flowers that sometimes make you rub your eyes and look at this shrub twice to see if it really does have a fire behind it or if the "smoke" is drifting on the wind.

These are large, attractive shrubs that often have an open, spreading habit. Some forms can grow to 25 feet tall and 25 to 30 feet across, but there are more compact, less rangy cultivars. They have round or oval, midgreen or purple leaves that are borne along the stems. In fall, the leaves turn to shades of yellow, orange, and red before dropping, and the foliage of the purple-leaved forms turns vivid crimson before leaf-fall. In summer, the clusters of pink or purple-pink flowers are produced on the tips of shoots and branches. These turn pale gray as they age and persist on the stems long after the leaves have fallen.

Smoke bushes will grow well in moist, fertile, well-drained soils in full sun or in partial shade, but the purple-leaved forms will turn green if they are grown in deep shade.

None of the most popular species and cultivars, including *Cotinus coggygria* and *C. obovatus*, require regular pruning, but they can be cut back hard every spring and used for foliage effect.

Cotinus coggygria *is a large, attractive shrub with an open, spreading habit and pale green stems that turn grayish brown with age. The rounded, oval-shaped leaves are pale green when young turning mid green with age and carried on the long, slender stems. In the fall, these leaves turn to shades of bright yellow and orange. In the summer, lime green, filament-like flower clusters are produced on the tips of shoots and branches.*

Formative pruning

Prune young plants to encourage them to grow bushy, with strong shoots emerging from just above soil level.

In spring, just before the new growth starts, cut out any thin, weak growth or damaged shoots. Cut the remaining shoots back to three or four buds above ground level.

WHY PRUNE?

No regular pruning is required but cutting the plant back hard for foliage effect is an option.

PRUNING TIPS

• *Regular hard pruning will induce extra large leaves to grow, but plants treated in this manner will not flower.*

PLANTS PRUNED THIS WAY

Cotinus coggygria *and cvs.: in early spring but only if required*
Cotinus obovatus *and cvs.: in early spring but only if required*

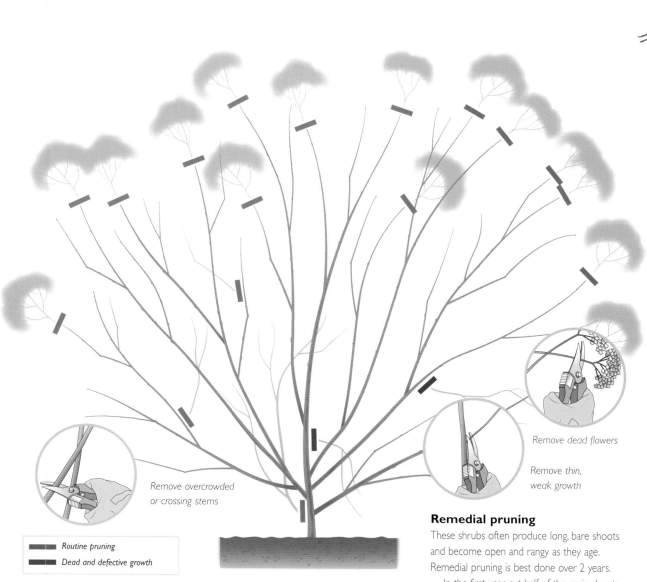

Remove dead flowers

Remove thin,
weak growth

Remove overcrowded
or crossing stems

Routine pruning

Dead and defective growth

Routine pruning

If they are to flower well, these plants are best left unpruned, although you should cut out any overcrowded, damaged, or rubbing shoots to create a multibranched plant and prevent it from becoming too tall, straggly, and unmanageable.

Cut off the old flower stalks in spring, before the new growth starts.

Cut out any thin, straggly growths, because they rarely produce good flowers and often harbor pests and diseases.

An alternative method to promote purple foliage is to cut the entire plant to within a foot of the ground. The leaves will grow in larger, and the plant will act as a colorful foliage accent.

Remedial pruning

These shrubs often produce long, bare shoots and become open and rangy as they age. Remedial pruning is best done over 2 years.

In the first year, cut half of the main shoots back to within 6 to 8 inches of soil level. Cut down to ground level any thin, weak shoots.

In the second year, cut the remaining old stems back to 6 to 8 inches above ground level. Remove any thin, spindly shoots that developed from the previous year's pruning.

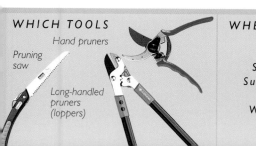

WHICH TOOLS

Hand pruners

Pruning saw

Long-handled pruners (loppers)

WHEN TO PRUNE MOST SPECIES

	early	mid	late
Spring	/////////		
Summer			
Fall			
Winter			

Cotoneaster (deciduous species)

Cotoneaster

Cotoneasters are hardy, adaptable plants, providing structure and form in the garden as well as an excellent display of flowers in spring and summer and small, berrylike fruits throughout fall and long into winter.

This is a large genus, containing both deciduous and evergreen species (see pages 82 and 83). The deciduous forms vary widely in shape and growth habit, from soil-hugging groundcover plants to large, treelike shrubs. They have broadly oval, mid- to dark-green leaves arranged along light-brown stems, which turn almost black as they age. There are also a few cultivars, including *Cotoneaster atropurpureus* 'Variegatus', that have silver-edged leaves, and the leaves of cultivars with large foliage often have deeply marked veins. The small, five-petaled, saucer-shaped flowers, which are either white or white tinged with pink, are borne along the stems in early to midsummer and are followed by berries, which range in color from pale orange to a deep orange-red. The berries will cling to the plants long after leaf-fall. Cotoneasters seem to be able to grow almost anywhere, although they prefer a position in full sun, and many will grow well in fairly dry conditions.

Cotoneaster horizontalis *is a low-growing, deciduous shrub usually grown as ground cover. The stems are pale brown when young and turn almost black as they age. The stems and branches are arranged in a herringbone fashion. The leaves are small, rounded, and glossy green; they turn red and yellow in fall. The small, white flowers, tinged with pink, are produced along the stems in late spring and are followed by bright-red berries long after leaf-fall.*

Formative pruning

Prune young plants to encourage them to become multistemmed, with a framework of about six strong, evenly spaced shoots emerging close to ground level.

In the first spring after planting, remove any dead or damaged shoots. Cut the remaining stems back to 6 to 8 inches above ground level. As these stems develop, remove any branches crossing through the middle of the shrub.

WHY PRUNE?

To maintain even growth and to promote flowering and fruiting.

PRUNING TIPS

• *Prune only when absolutely necessary.*

PLANTS PRUNED THIS WAY

Cotoneaster adpressus *and cvs.: in late winter, before new growth starts*
Cotoneaster apiculatus *and cvs.: in late winter, before new growth starts*
Cotoneaster divaricatus *and cvs.: in late winter, before new growth starts*
Cotoneaster horizontalis *and cvs.: in late winter, before new growth starts*
Cotoneaster multiflorus *and cvs.: in late winter, before new growth starts*
Cotoneaster simonsii *and cvs.: in late winter, before new growth starts*

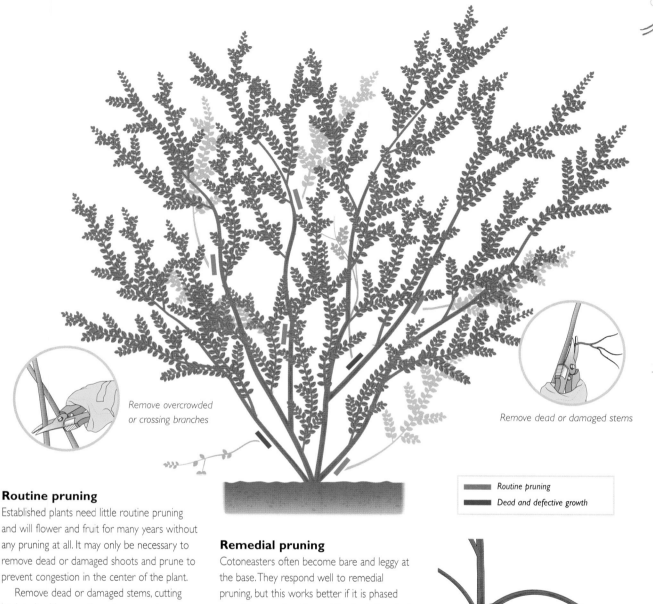

Remove overcrowded or crossing branches

Remove dead or damaged stems

| | Routine pruning |
| | Dead and defective growth |

Routine pruning

Established plants need little routine pruning and will flower and fruit for many years without any pruning at all. It may only be necessary to remove dead or damaged shoots and prune to prevent congestion in the center of the plant.

Remove dead or damaged stems, cutting back to healthy growth, and prune out any branches that cross through the middle of the plant.

Old or nonproductive shoots can be cut down to within 2 to 3 inches of ground level and a new shoot allowed to grow as a replacement.

Remedial pruning

Cotoneasters often become bare and leggy at the base. They respond well to remedial pruning, but this works better if it is phased over 2 years rather than cutting back the plant in one operation.

In winter, before new growth starts, cut the thickest branches down to about 2 feet above ground level. The following year, cut any remaining old branches down to the same height. You may need to thin out new shoots to prevent overcrowding.

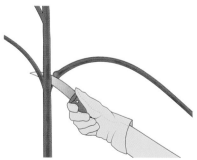

Use a sharp pruning knife to remove torn growth as close to the main stem as possible

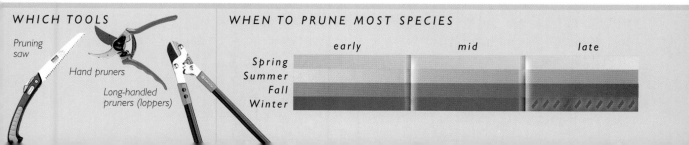

WHICH TOOLS

Pruning saw

Hand pruners

Long-handled pruners (loppers)

WHEN TO PRUNE MOST SPECIES

	early	mid	late
Spring			
Summer			
Fall			
Winter			

Cotoneaster (evergreen species)

Cotoneaster

These hardy, adaptable plants seem to be able to grow almost anywhere and will do equally well in full sun or partial shade. They bring structure and form to a garden as well as an excellent display of flowers in spring and summer and small, berrylike fruits in the fall and long into winter.

The genus contains both evergreen and deciduous species (see pages 80 and 81). The evergreen forms range in shape and growth habit from soil-hugging groundcover plants to large, treelike shrubs. The broadly oval to lance-shaped, glossy dark-green leaves, often with deeply marked veins, are arranged along light-brown stems, which turn almost black as they age. The small, saucer-shaped, five-petaled flowers are white or white tinged with pink and are produced along the stems in early to midsummer. They are followed by berries that range in color from pale orange to deep orange-red and that cling to the plants long after leaf-fall. A few cultivars, such as *Cotoneaster salicifolius* 'Exburyensis' and *C. salicifolius* 'Rothschildianus', have golden-yellow fruits that often remain on the plants for longer than orange or red fruits.

Cotoneaster salicifolius *is a large, vigorous, evergreen shrub with light-brown stems that turn almost black as they age. The leaves are broadly oval to lance shaped, and glossy dark green. They have deeply marked veins and are a paler green on the underside. The small, saucer-shaped flowers are white and carried along the stems in summer. They are followed by deep orange-red berries in winter.*

WHY PRUNE?

To maintain an open habit and to create a framework of strong branches.

PRUNING TIPS

• Look out for fireblight, a serious bacterial disease (symptoms include the death of new shoots and scorched-looking flowers and leaves), and prune out and burn affected growths immediately.

PLANTS PRUNED THIS WAY

Cotoneaster 'Cornubia': *in winter or midspring*
Cotoneaster dammeri and cvs.: *in winter or midspring*
Cotoneaster lacteus and cvs.: *in winter or midspring*
Cotoneaster salicifolius and cvs.: *in winter or midspring*

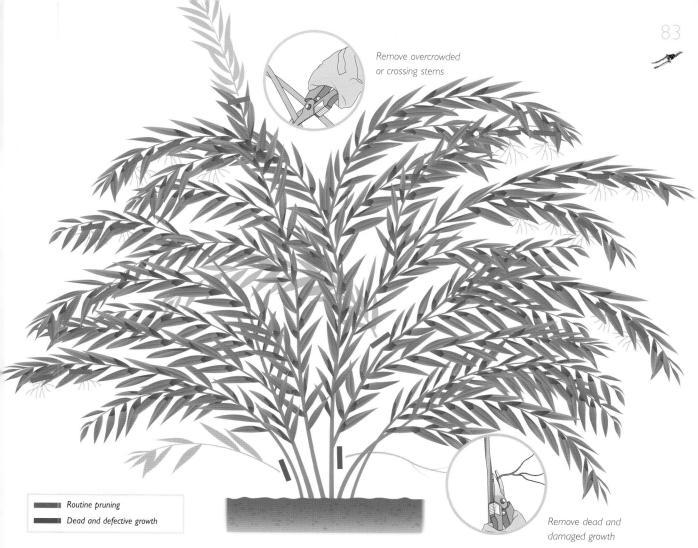

Remove overcrowded
or crossing stems

Remove dead and
damaged growth

■ Routine pruning
■ Dead and defective growth

Formative pruning

Prune young plants to encourage them to become multistemmed, with a framework of about six strong shoots forming close to ground level.

In the first spring after planting, remove any dead or damaged stems. Cut the remaining stems back to 6 to 8 inches above ground level. As these stems develop, cut out any branches that cross through the middle of the shrub.

Routine pruning

Once established, these plants need little routine pruning and will flower and fruit for many years without any pruning at all. Some pruning may be necessary to prevent the plant from becoming congested in the center.

Remove any dead or damaged stems, cutting back to healthy growth. Prune out any branches that cross through the middle of the plant.

Spreading species and cultivars may need yearly pruning to keep them within their alloted space.

Remedial pruning

As they age, these plants often become bare and leggy at the base, particularly if they have been neglected for a number of years, but they will usually respond well to hard pruning.

In winter, cut the plant back to a framework of strong shoots within 12 inches above ground level.

As the new growth develops, remove any thin or weak shoots, cutting back to stronger stems or to ground level.

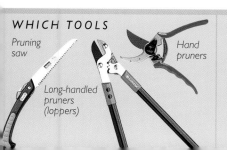

WHICH TOOLS

Pruning saw

Hand pruners

Long-handled pruners (loppers)

WHEN TO PRUNE MOST SPECIES

	early	mid	late
Spring			
Summer			
Fall			
Winter			

Cytisus
Broom

These stunning plants produce a mass of fragrant flowers in late spring and early summer, and from a distance the quantity and color of their flowers make them look as if they are on fire.

Cytisus scoparius f. andreanus *is a shrubby member of the "pea" family, with thin, whippy branches and arching, dull-green stems that bear small, oval, green leaves arranged in groups of three. In late spring and early summer, masses of orange-yellow, pealike flowers are produced in dense clusters along the stems, often followed by small, hairy, grayish-green "pods" that carry four or five small black seeds.*

These plants will tolerate a wide range of soils and are tolerant of lime (although the leaves may turn yellow-green), but they prefer a sunny site with an acidic, moderately fertile, well-drained soil. They are invasive in many parts of the country. The small, pealike flowers vary in color from white through creams and yellows to oranges, pinks, and reds. They are carried on the ends of the slender, arching, green stems either singly or in small clusters, often followed by small, green-black pods in late summer and fall. The small, felt-covered leaves are dull green, arranged singly or in clusters on thin, green stems.

Brooms resent being transplanted and will not tolerate severe pruning, especially if you cut back into older wood. Once they have finished flowering, they go almost unnoticed for the rest of the year, so make sure that you have something else planted nearby to provide late-season interest.

There are several species and cultivars that flower on shoots produced in the previous year, including *Cytisus* x *praecox* and *C. scoparius*, which should be pruned in summer, after flowering. An exception is *C. nigricans*, which flowers later than other species and on shoots produced in the current year; it should be pruned in spring, after the last frosts.

WHY PRUNE?

To encourage regular flowering and to prevent the plant from becoming leggy.

PRUNING TIPS

• *Don't cut into the older wood.*

PLANTS PRUNED THIS WAY

Cytisus nigricans: *in spring*
Cytisus x praecox: *in summer, after flowering*
Cytisus scoparius: *in summer, after flowering*

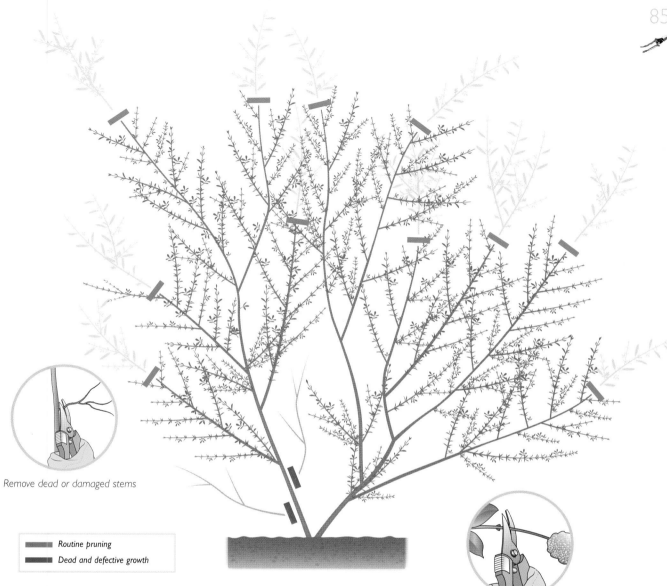

Remove dead or damaged stems

| | Routine pruning |
| | Dead and defective growth |

Remove old flower-bearing stems

Formative pruning

Prune young plants to encourage them to grow bushy, with strong shoots emerging from just above soil level.

In the first spring after planting, cut out any weak or damaged growth. Prune the tips of the main shoots by removing the last one-third to encourage sideshoots to form.

Routine pruning

Prune to keep the plants flowering regularly and to keep them from becoming too open and straggly. If brooms are not pruned regularly and become too large, they often incur root damage and then fall over.

Soon after flowering, cut all flower-bearing shoots back by removing the last one-third of each shoot. Take care that you don't cut back into old wood.

Remedial pruning

Brooms may become bare at the base, but they do not respond well to severe pruning. It's often better to replace an old plant than to attempt to revive it.

Dig up the old plant and replace it.

WHICH TOOLS

Shears

Hand pruners

WHEN TO PRUNE MOST SPECIES

	early	mid	late
Spring			
Summer			
Fall			
Winter			

Euonymus fortunei
Wintercreeper euonymus

This justifiably popular plant is tolerant and easy to grow, reliably providing bright foliage and fall fruits.

Euonymus fortunei *is a bushy, low-growing, evergreen shrub with slender, grayish-green, square stems that root at regular intervals along their length. The tough, leathery leaves are oval shaped with a toothed margin. They are usually dark green in color but can also be variegated gold or white. Small, insignificant flowers are produced in the spring and are followed by small, white fruits that contain orange seed casings.*

This hardy, evergreen species—from which numerous cultivars have been developed—is one of the most widely grown in the large genus *Euonymus*. The shrubs have a range of uses and can be grown as groundcover, low hedges, wall shrubs, and even climbers. They can be grown in a wide range of soil types and situations. They prefer a position in full sun or partial shade, but they can do well in shade, too, as long as it's not too dense (in a very shady site, the variegated forms will lose their attractive color and revert to all-green foliage). Their ability to grow in a range of conditions makes them useful for city gardens, where they will tolerate soot and grime. It simply washes off the leaves the next time it rains. They will grow in most well-drained soils, although they do need shelter from freezing winds.

The plants are mainly prostrate with a low, mound-forming habit, but they can also climb against a wall or fence or even into a tree, where they will grow even though the soil is impoverished. The leaves are broadly oval with toothed, curling margins and a tough, leathery texture. The species has glossy, dark-green foliage with a paler underside, although the silver-, white-, and gold-variegated forms are more popular. The two most widely grown cultivars are *Euonymus fortunei* 'Emerald 'n' Gold', which has bright-yellow leaf margins, and

'Silver Queen', which has dark-green leaves edged with white, later tinted with pink. Small, insignificant flowers, white or green in color, are produced in late spring or summer and followed by white fruits that split to show orange seedcases in fall.

Formative pruning

Prune young plants to encourage them to develop a bushy habit, with many shoots emerging from ground level.

After planting, cut out any weak or damaged growth. Cut the remaining shoots back to one-third of their original length.

WHY PRUNE?

To keep plants neat and tidy and to maintain variegation.

PRUNING TIPS

• *Use hand pruners; use shears only for ground cover Euonymus species.*
• *Do not cut through leaves, or they will turn brown and die.*

PLANTS PRUNED THIS WAY

Euonymus fortunei: *in midsummer, after flowering*
Syringa x prestoniae: *in midsummer, after flowering*
Viburnum tinus: *in early summer, after flowering*

Remove dead or damaged stems

Trim long, straggling stems

▬	Routine pruning
▬	Dead and defective growth

Routine pruning

Regular pruning should stop the plant from becoming too straggly and untidy after flowering. To prevent reversion, remove all-green shoots on variegated plants at their point of origin as soon as you seen them.

After flowering, use pruners to trim back any long, straggling growth. Pinch off the tips to make them branch.

Remedial pruning

These shrubs sometimes spread and may break to reveal an open, bare center.

In spring, cut plants down to 6 to 12 inches above ground level. At the same time, completely remove any broken or damaged shoots.

Euonymus *may produce aerial roots if grown against a support—pull pruned stems gently away from the support*

WHICH TOOLS

Hand pruners

WHEN TO PRUNE MOST SPECIES

	early	mid	late
Spring			
Summer			
Fall			
Winter			

Ficus

Ornamental fig

These attractive evergreens, with their bold, glossy leaves, make excellent specimen plants in a container or border. Where hardy, they provide useful structure in the winter garden when other plants are bare.

Ornamental figs can vary greatly in size, from handsome trees up to 150 feet high to shrubs up to 10 feet high and with a wide, spreading habit. They are usually grown for their large, attractive leaves, which have a thick, leathery texture, often with pronounced veins, arranged alternately along the stems and branches. A number of cultivars have variegated leaves, often with silver-white margins, or mottled gray-green leaves with creamy-yellow markings. The petal-less flowers are carried in the leaf joints and are followed by small, egg-shaped fruits, which may be orange, yellow, green, or purple.

Ornamental figs grow best in moist, well-drained soils containing plenty of organic matter. They will grow in full sun or partial shade, but they must be protected from cold winds, especially when they are young.

Ficus elastica 'Variegata' *will eventually form a large tree with an open, spreading habit. Its green shoots turn gray-green as they age and eventually become red-brown with a corky texture. The large, glossy leaves are thick and leathery with pronounced veins and mottled gray-green and creamy-yellow markings. Small, petal-less flowers are carried in the leaf joints and produce small, oblong, yellow figs.*

WHY PRUNE?

To maintain shape and to keep the plant within its allotted space.

PRUNING TIPS

• *Take care not to get sap on exposed skin; some people may suffer a phytochemical reaction in hot, humid weather, and blisters may occur.*

PLANTS PRUNED THIS WAY

Ficus benjamina: *in late winter or early spring*
Ficus elastica: *in late winter or early spring*
Ficus lyrata: *in late winter or early spring*
Ficus macrophylla: *in late winter or early spring*

Shorten overvigorous stems

Remove dead or damaged stems

| Routine pruning |
| Dead and defective growth |

Formative pruning

Prune young plants to encourage them to become bushy and well-structured, with a central main stem and plenty of branches originating from it.

Remove the top 4 to 6 inches of the main stem to encourage branching along its length.

In spring, cut any weak, leggy shoots back to about two-thirds. Remove the end one-third of any long, straggly shoots.

Routine pruning

Ornamental figs will grow well for many years with little or no pruning, but shortening the previous season's growth by about one-quarter in late winter or early spring will encourage the development of a bushy, balanced plant with a good framework of branches. This is also a good way of keeping the plant from getting too leggy.

In spring, shorten by one-third any overly vigorous shoots to prevent the plant from becoming unbalanced and lopsided.

Remedial pruning

These plants can be cut back quite severely—often back to the main framework of branches—to promote new growth or to overcome wind damage.

Remove all of the smaller (sublateral) branches and cut the framework branches back to within 18 inches of the main stem.

WHICH TOOLS

Pruning saw
Long-handled pruners (loppers)
Hand pruners
Thick gloves

WHEN TO PRUNE MOST SPECIES

	early	mid	late
Spring	/////////////		
Summer			
Fall			
Winter			/////////

Forsythia
Forsythia

A welcome harbinger of spring, the flowers of this popular and easy-to-grow shrub are borne on usually bare stems.

Even people with little interest in gardening can name this plant, familiar in gardens everywhere. In early to midspring, the shrub is usually covered with spikes or arching branches of small golden- or lemon-yellow flowers, which are carried along the younger shoots.

It's a resilient and hardy deciduous shrub. The dark-green leaves, broadly oval in shape, are carried in opposite pairs on light-brown stems, which change to a rough-textured, dull gray as they get to be 3 years old or older. The plant forms a dense, bushy thicket of long, arching branches and often becomes bare at the base, especially if left unpruned.

An adaptable, sometimes ungainly plant, it will grow in a wide range of soils, getting to 10 feet high and across and developing into an erect or broadly dome-shaped bush. The flowers, borne singly or in clusters along the shoots, appear before the leaves emerge. The natural habit of this plant means that it needs regular annual pruning if it's to flower to its full potential.

Formative pruning

Young plants should be pruned to encourage a bushy shape, with strong shoots emerging from soil level.

After planting, cut out any weak or damaged growth. Lightly tip back the remaining shoots to about two-thirds of their length to encourage new shoots from the base of the plant as it becomes established.

Routine pruning

If they are to flower well, forsythias need regular annual pruning to remove the old wood that would gradually develop and to encourage production of new flower-bearing shoots.

Immediately after flowering, cut back all old flower-bearing stems at least halfway along their length to just above a healthy bud or to a well-placed new sideshoot. The old flower-bearing shoots of golden bell (*Forsythia suspensa*)

WHY PRUNE?

To restrict the plant's height and to encourage it to develop an open habit of growth.

PRUNING TIPS

• *Start pruning as soon as possible after flowering to avoid losing next year's flowers.*

• *Remove older shoots with a saw because long-handled pruners (loppers) will easily crush the stems.*

PLANTS PRUNED THIS WAY

Forsythia x intermedia: *in late spring or early summer*
Forsythia ovata: *in late spring or early summer*
Forsythia suspensa: *in late spring or early summer*
Deutzia gracilis *and cvs.*: *in late spring or early summer*
Deutzia scabra *and cvs.*: *in late spring or early summer*

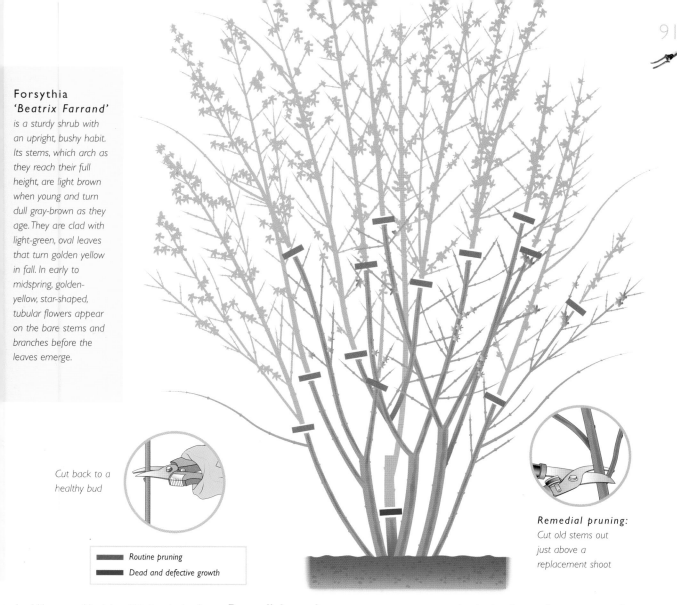

Forsythia 'Beatrix Farrand' is a sturdy shrub with an upright, bushy habit. Its stems, which arch as they reach their full height, are light brown when young and turn dull gray-brown as they age. They are clad with light-green, oval leaves that turn golden yellow in fall. In early to midspring, golden-yellow, star-shaped, tubular flowers appear on the bare stems and branches before the leaves emerge.

Cut back to a healthy bud

Routine pruning
Dead and defective growth

Remedial pruning: Cut old stems out just above a replacement shoot

should be pruned back to within two buds of their base. Do this in late spring or early summer to give the maximum period of growth to produce a good display of flowers the following year.

On mature shrubs, try to remove about one-quarter to one-fifth of the old stems each year to allow in light and make room for new shoots to develop.

Remedial pruning

Forsythia shrubs will naturally become dense and overcrowded as they age, and the thicket of thin, weak, straggly stems will produce few flowers and make the plant susceptible to pests and diseases, especially if the pruning has been neglected. This can be overcome by hard pruning, which must be done in stages over 2 or 3 years rather than by simply cutting the plant down completely.

Leaving just three or four strong stems, in late winter or early spring cut all other shoots back to within 2 to 3 inches of ground level to encourage new replacement shoots to develop.

The following year, completely remove any thin or weak shoots. Prune out the three or four remaining old stems, cutting close to ground level.

WHICH TOOLS

Hand pruners

Pruning saw

WHEN TO PRUNE MOST SPECIES

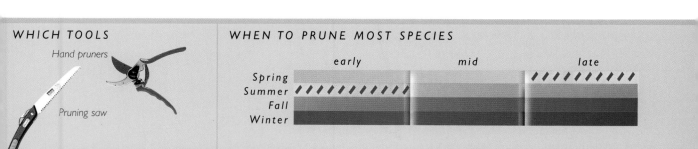

Fremontodendron
Flannel bush

An outstanding wall shrub for a warm, sunny position, the fremontodendron will produce large, saucer-shaped, bright-yellow flowers from late spring until midfall.

Fremontodendron *'California Glory'* is a shrub with a loose, open habit. The stems are golden brown, fading to dull gray-brown as they age. The young stems and the deeply lobed, dark-green leaves are covered with a fine, felty substance that gradually disappears as the plants get older. Large, saucer-shaped, bright-yellow flowers are produced from late spring until midfall. Each bloom contains a cluster of bright-golden stamens and anthers in its center.

Reaching 15 feet high and 12 feet across, fremontodendrons are clad in deeply lobed, dark-green leaves, which, like the young stems, are covered with a fine, feltlike substance (which can be irritating to the skin). As the leaves and shoots age, the felt gradually disappears. The flowers are golden yellow, saucer shaped, and up to 4 inches across, with a cluster of bright-golden stamens and anthers in the center of each bloom. The young stems are rich golden brown but age to dull gray-brown, and the bark often splits and cracks into fissures near the base of the plant.

Fremontodendrons seem to thrive in poor, dry soils with a neutral to alkaline pH. They must have shelter from cold winds and are often damaged by late spring frosts, especially when grown against an east-facing wall. They will always need some support because they have fairly brittle root systems and are often wall-trained.

Formative pruning

Prune young plants to encourage them to grow bushy and well-structured, with a central main stem and plenty of branches originating from it.

Remove the top 4 to 6 inches of the main stem to encourage branching along its length.

In spring, cut any weak, leggy shoots back to two or three buds. Remove the end one-third of any long, straggly shoots.

WHY PRUNE?

To maintain a bushy habit and a framework of strong branches.

PRUNING TIPS

• *Wear gloves and a face mask, because the stems and young leaves are covered with irritating hairs.*

PLANTS PRUNED THIS WAY

Fremontodendron californicum *and cvs.: in midsummer, after the first flush of flowers*
Fremontodendron mexicanum *and cvs.: in midsummer, after the first flush of flowers*

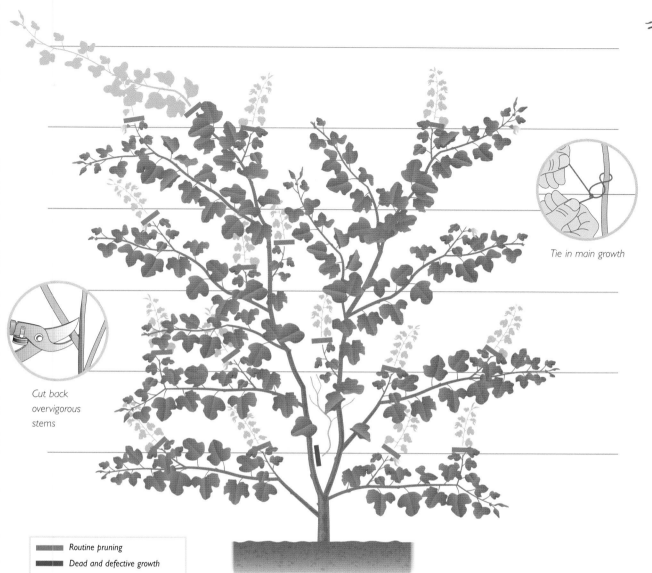

Tie in main growth

Cut back
overvigorous
stems

Routine pruning
Dead and defective growth

Routine pruning

Fremontodendron will grow well for many years with little or no pruning, but shortening the previous season's growth by about one-quarter in summer, immediately after the first flush of flowers, will produce a bushy, free-flowering plant. This is also a good way to keep the plant from getting too bare and leggy.

In summer, cut the flower-bearing shoots back to within three to five buds of the old wood to encourage the plant to develop many short, flowering stems.

In summer, shorten by one-third any overly vigorous shoots so that the plant doesn't become unbalanced and lopsided.

Remedial pruning

These plants may become bare at the base, but they do not respond well to severe pruning, and it is better to replace an old plant than to attempt to revive it.

Dig up the old plant and replace it.

WHICH TOOLS

Face mask
Hand pruners
Long-handled pruners (loppers)
Gloves

WHEN TO PRUNE MOST SPECIES

	early	mid	late
Spring			
Summer		/////////	
Fall			
Winter			

Fuchsia

Lady's eardrops

Outdoor fuchsias are among the most reliable flowering shrubs you can plant in your garden. They will flower from early summer until the frosts stop them, and as long as they are watered regularly, they will grow in most conditions.

Fuchsia magellanica *is a hardy shrub with slender, arching stems and twiggy branches. These are pale brown when young and become grayish brown with flaking bark as they age. The leaves are lance shaped, pale to midgreen in color, paler on the underside with a lightly toothed margin. Small, pendant flowers with red outer sepals and a purple bloom inside are produced throughout the summer to be followed by small, purple fruits in the fall.*

Fuchsias can grow into large shrubs, up to 6 feet high and 10 feet across, forming dense thickets of thin, spindly branches and side branches. The leaves are broadly oval in shape, with finely toothed margins, and they are arranged in opposite pairs along slender stems, which are red when young, turning light brown before changing to a dull gray-brown as they age. The small, bell-like flowers are made up of an outer case of four brightly colored sepals and an inner cluster of petals (which are usually a different color than the sepals). There are many interesting color combinations. In fall, the flowers may be followed by edible, black-purple, oval fruits up to 1 inch long.

Fuchsias prefer moist, well-drained soil and a position in full sun or partial shade; they do especially well in coastal gardens.

The popular fuchsias developed from *Fuchsia triphylla* are not hardy, but *F. magellanica* and cultivars such as 'Ricartonii' and forms such as 'Mrs. Popple' can tolerate frost and should be pruned in early spring, once growth has started.

WHY PRUNE?

To encourage the development of healthy new shoots and regular flowers.

PRUNING TIPS

• Prune after the last spring frost.

PLANTS PRUNED THIS WAY

Fuchsia magellanica: *in early spring, once growth has started*
Fuchsia 'Mrs. Popple': *in early spring, once growth has started*
Fuchsia 'Ricartonii': *in early spring, once growth has started*

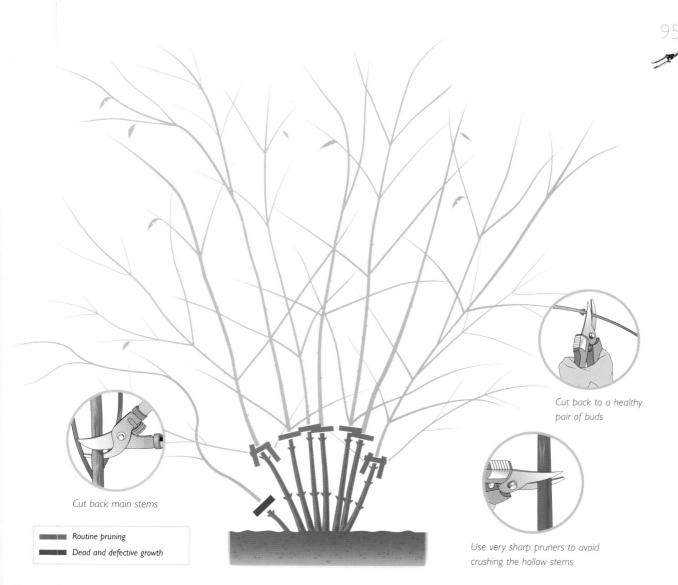

Cut back to a healthy
pair of buds

Cut back main stems

| | Routine pruning |
| | Dead and defective growth |

Use very sharp pruners to avoid
crushing the hollow stems

Formative pruning

Prune young plants to encourage them to
grow bushy, with plenty of strong, vigorous
shoots emerging from soil level.

After planting, remove any weak or
damaged growth. Cut the remaining shoots
back to about one-third of their length to
encourage the development of new shoots
from the base of the plant.

Routine pruning

Regular pruning will encourage the
development of strong, young, flower-bearing
stems or lateral branches, but wait until the
new growth has started so that you notice any
frost-damaged shoots.

Cut all the main stems back to about 12
inches above ground level. Prune back all lateral
shoots to a strong pair of buds close to the
main stem.

Remedial pruning

If fuchsias are left unpruned for a number of
years, they produce many weak, short, thin
stems and much smaller flowers. They also
become bare at the base of the stems.

In spring, cut all the stems back to within 2
to 3 inches of ground level, and in summer
remove up to about one-third of the weakest
and thinnest shoots to prevent overcrowding.

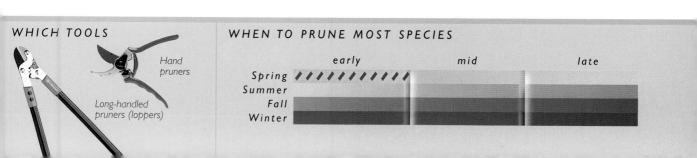

WHICH TOOLS

Hand
pruners

Long-handled
pruners (loppers)

WHEN TO PRUNE MOST SPECIES

	early	mid	late
Spring	/////////////		
Summer			
Fall			
Winter			

Hedera
Common ivy, climbing ivy

Its numerous cultivars make ivy one of the most useful of all climbers, whether you are covering horizontal or vertical surfaces.

Hedera colchica *'Dentata Variegata'* *is a vigorous, evergreen, self-supporting climber grown for its distinctive leaves. It may take time to establish before growing well. The young shoots are purplish brown, turning gray-green as they mature. It has large, deep gray-green, glossy leaves with creamy-white margins that vary in width from leaf to leaf. In fall, small clusters of yellow-green flowers are produced, followed by round, black berries.*

Ivies are tough, evergreen, woody-stemmed climbers that cling to supports with aerial roots, so they're ideal for covering unsightly objects. They can also grow over the ground or up and across a wall or fence to provide additional color, interest, and shelter for wildlife. In the garden, they are adaptable and tolerant, although they will do best in slightly alkaline, moist but well-drained soil. In the forest, they can outcompete natives and become an invasive problem. Once established, however, they will grow well in drier conditions. The foliage of many plants can be quite variable, with the juvenile shoots carrying typical three- to five-lobed leaves, while the adult leaves on the flower-bearing stems are broadly oval with no lobes. These adult stems do not produce aerial roots for support and climbing, which is why plants often become top-heavy and fall away from their supporting structure as they age.

Ivies are equally at home climbing or spreading across the ground as weed-suppressing groundcover, and they are ideal for deep shade, where few other plants will survive. In shade, the leaves eventually become broader and thinner, and variegated forms will revert to deep green. The tough, glossy green leaves, usually paler on the underside, grow on pinkish-green stems, which turn green or purple-brown as they mature.

The numerous variegated cultivars are the most popular garden plants, and gold- and purple-leaved forms are also readily available. Several foliage forms have been developed, including leaves with narrow lobes, finely cut leaves, and even crinkled leaves. Clusters of greenish-yellow flowers appear in fall and are followed by black or yellow-orange fruits.

WHY PRUNE?

To control plant growth and to encourage even coverage of the allotted area.

PRUNING TIPS

• *Before pruning, spray the plants with a garden hose to wash away the dust.*

PLANTS PRUNED THIS WAY

Hedera canariensis *and cvs.: in early spring and throughout the season as needed*
Hedera colchica *and cvs.: in early spring and throughout the season as needed*
Hedera helix *and cvs.: in early spring and throughout the season as needed*
Parthenocissus quinquefolia *and cvs.: in fall or early winter, when stems are visible*
Parthenocissus tricuspidata *and cvs.: in fall or early winter, when stems are visible*

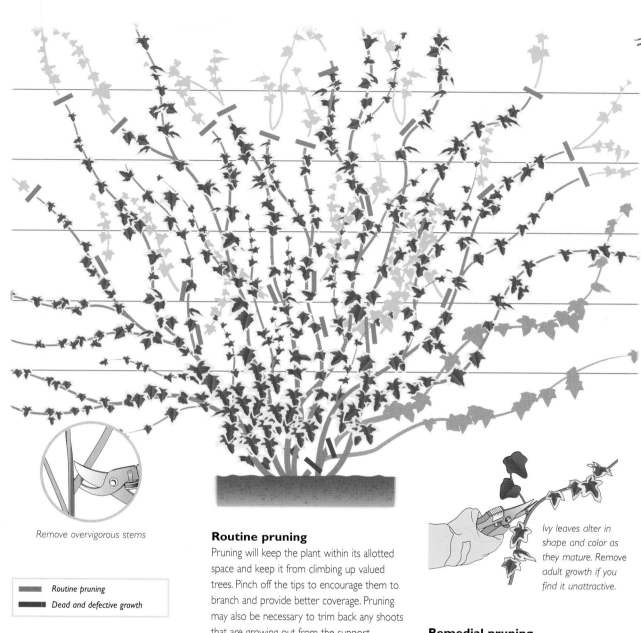

Remove overvigorous stems

Routine pruning
Dead and defective growth

Formative pruning

Try to develop a multistemmed plant, with strong shoots emerging close to ground level.

In the first spring after planting, cut the shoots back by removing about one-third of their length.

Routine pruning

Pruning will keep the plant within its allotted space and keep it from climbing up valued trees. Pinch off the tips to encourage them to branch and provide better coverage. Pruning may also be necessary to trim back any shoots that are growing out from the support.

In spring, before new growth starts, prune all shoots that are growing beyond their allotted space, cutting back to 2 feet inside the area to allow the shoots to branch.

Cut all vigorous, outward-facing growth back to its point of origin.

Ivy leaves alter in shape and color as they mature. Remove adult growth if you find it unattractive.

Remedial pruning

Renovate plants that are totally overgrown and out of control, especially when they become bare at the base, with severe pruning.

In spring, cut all the shoots back to within 2 feet of ground level. Train in the new shoots as they emerge.

WHICH TOOLS

Hand pruners

Pruning saw

Long-handled pruners (loppers)

WHEN TO PRUNE MOST SPECIES

	early	mid	late
Spring			
Summer			
Fall			
Winter			

Hibiscus
Rose mallow, tree hollyhock

Hibiscus are grown for their large, attractive, colorful blooms, which are produced on the new growth in late summer and early fall.

All types of hibiscus must have some shelter in cold-winter climates because none can be described as fully hardy, and even the hardiest members of the genus, *Hibiscus syriacus* and its cultivars, need a sheltered spot. Other forms, including *H. rosa-sinensis*—which is also known as Chinese hibiscus, Hawaiian hibiscus, and rose of China—will do well in mild, reliably frost-free gardens, but they should be treated as indoor plants or annual, potted plants in colder areas. Outdoors, plants should be grown in a south-facing, sheltered position. All hibiscus prefer to grow in full sun, and they need a light, well-drained, slightly alkaline soil if they are to do well. Newer cultivars are long flowering and produce few seeds, making them better landscape choices.

The plants have an erect to bushy habit, with slightly hairy stems carrying oval to diamond-shaped leaves that are shallowly lobed and have deeply toothed margins. The leaves are dark green, but they may turn pale green or even yellow in soil that contains too much lime. The brightly colored, trumpetlike flowers range in color from bright crimson through shades of pink, yellow, and blue, to white. Some petals have a darker base, making each bloom look as if it has an eye. In warmer climates, plants often grow to 10 to 15 feet high and 6 to 10 feet across, but in cooler areas they can be slow growing, often putting on only a small amount of extension growth each year.

Hibiscus syriacus 'Woodbridge' *is a hardy shrub with upright branches that turn pale-gray and arch as they age. The leaves are dark green with three lobes and a deeply toothed margin, turning pale yellow before dropping in fall. From midsummer, large pink flowers with a darker "eye" in the center and shaped like an open trumpet are produced, each with a large column of stigma and stamens protruding from the center.*

WHY PRUNE?

To keep the plant healthy and flowering regularly.

PRUNING TIPS

• *Prune as the plant starts to grow in spring so that any dead or dying shoots are easily seen.*

PLANTS PRUNED THIS WAY

Hibiscus rosa-sinensis *and* cvs.: *in late winter or early spring, as new growth begins*

Hibiscus syriacus *and* cvs.: *in late winter or early spring, as new growth begins*

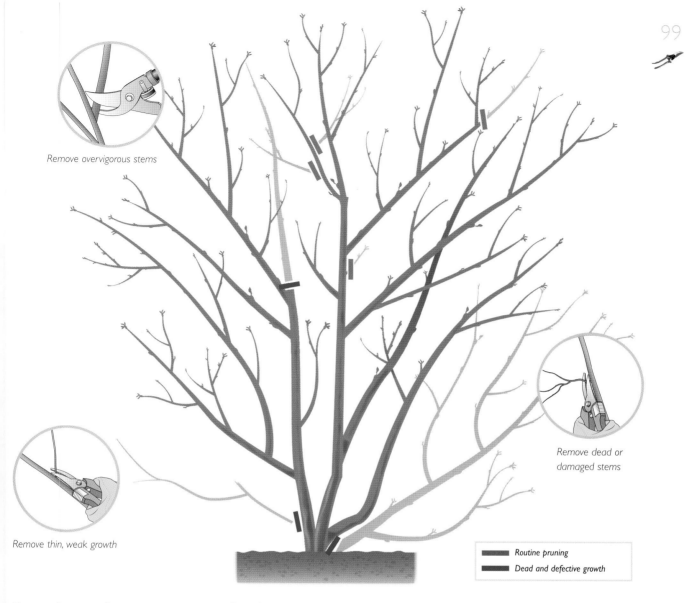

Remove overvigorous stems

Remove thin, weak growth

Remove dead or damaged stems

| | Routine pruning |
| | Dead and defective growth |

Formative pruning

Prune young plants to encourage them to develop a bushy habit, with strong shoots emerging from just above ground level.

After planting, cut out any weak or damaged growth. Cut the remaining shoots back to about half their length to encourage new shoots to develop from the base of the plant.

Routine pruning

These plants need little regular pruning, although you need to remove weak or dead growth and to cut back any very vigorous shoots, which may cause the plant to become lopsided.

Pinch off the tips of any thin, weak shoots by cutting them back to half their length. Remove any dead or dying shoots, cutting back cleanly to healthy growth.

Remedial pruning

It may be necessary to rebalance a one-sided plant, to reduce overall plant size to prevent damage to brittle root systems, and to remove any dead shoots to prevent fungal attacks.

Completely remove older branches. Cut the remaining branches back by two-thirds of their original length.

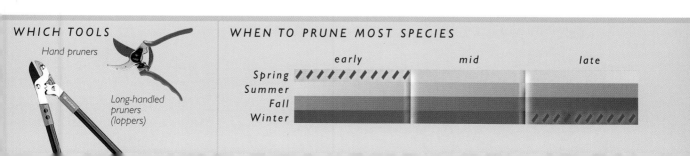

WHICH TOOLS

Hand pruners

Long-handled pruners (loppers)

WHEN TO PRUNE MOST SPECIES

	early	mid	late
Spring	/////////////		
Summer			
Fall			
Winter			/////////////

Hydrangea
Hydrangea, common hydrangea

The massed flowers of hydrangeas are familiar sights in all but the very coldest of gardens, bringing delicate shades from summer to early winter.

Hydrangea macrophylla 'Teller Rosa' *is a large, spreading shrub with light-brown stems that turn gray with age. The shrub is covered with large, deep-green, oval-shaped leaves that narrow to a sharp point and have a deeply toothed margin. The flower heads appear in midsummer and are made up of tiny, cream or pink inner flowers and larger, outer flowers with deep-red bracts. The dead flowers persist for many months.*

Hydrangeas are good indicator plants for telling the gardener what the soil is like: A predominance of pink flowers indicates alkaline conditions, while blue flowers signify acidic soil. White blooms rarely respond to the lime content in the soil by changing color either way. It is hardly worth going to the trouble of amending your soil to try to make the flowers of pink forms turn blue and vice versa; it's just not easy to change the pH in your soil over the long haul.

Naturally woodland plants, hydrangeas must have reliably moist but well-drained soil to which plenty of well-rotted organic matter has been added. Apply an annual mulch of well-rotted compost to keep the root run cool and moist. They also need the protection of dappled shade.

Mature plants can grow from 3 feet tall to 10 feet or more, depending on the species. Some form a dense thicket of green stems, which turn brown with age, and the oldest stems have frayed, shedding bark. The broadly oval leaves are bright midgreen and slightly paler on the underside; each ends in a sharp point at the tip. All the foliage has coarsely toothed margins.

The flowers are minute, and the main color is provided by four brightly colored bracts, which surround all or some of the flowers. *Hydrangea arborescens* and *H. paniculata* flower on new growth. The flowers of *H. macrophylla* are mainly borne on the previous season's wood.

Prune *H. arborescens* and *H. paniculata* and their cultivars in spring, just as the growth starts. *H. quercifolia* (oakleaf hydrangea) is grown primarily for its oak leaf-shaped foliage and excellent fall color. It's best when grown in a protected area; if grown in an exposed site, it can experience some winter dieback. Prune in early spring to remove dead wood. Cut back to below the point of injury and remove old wood to the base.

H. macrophylla and *H. serrata* can be pruned in late summer after flowering. If spring pruning, remove only dead wood, as the majority of its flower buds form on shoots that develop after the plant blooms. Fall or spring pruning can sacrifice bloom. *H. macrophylla* 'Quadricolor' (a lacecap form) is grown for its attractive leaves, which are variegated pale and dark green, cream-white, and gold, rather than for its flowers.

WHY PRUNE?

To improve flower size and quality and to encourage the plant to develop an open, balanced shape.

PRUNING TIPS

• *Use sharp tools so that you do not accidentally split the stems.*

PLANTS PRUNED THIS WAY

Hydrangea arborescens *and cvs.: in spring, as new growth starts*
Hydrangea paniculata *and cvs.: in spring, as new growth starts*
Hydrangea quercifolia *and cvs.: in spring, as new growth starts*
Hydrangea macrophylla *and cvs.: in late summer, after flowering*
Hydrangea serrata *and cvs.: in late summer, after flowering*

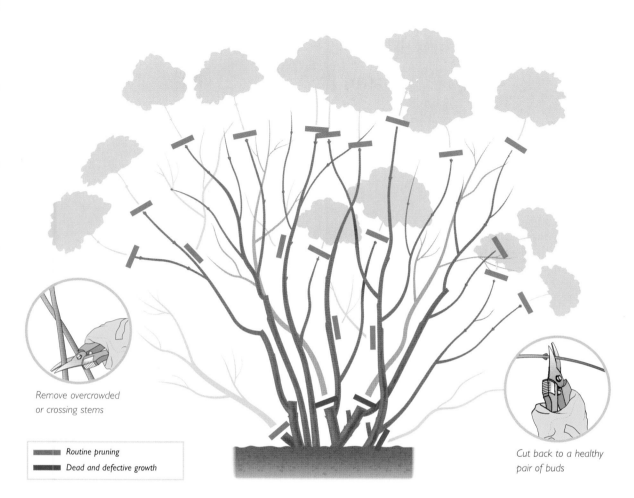

Remove overcrowded
or crossing stems

■■■ *Routine pruning*
■■■ *Dead and defective growth*

Cut back to a healthy
pair of buds

Formative pruning

Prune young plants to encourage them to develop a bushy habit, with strong shoots emerging from just at or above ground level.

After planting, cut out any weak or damaged growth. Lightly pinch off the remaining shoots to about two-thirds of their length so new shoots can emerge from the base of the plant.

Routine pruning

Hydrangeas need regular pruning if they are to flower well. It's important to remove the old wood, which would otherwise gradually accumulate.

In spring, prune species that bloom on new growth by shortening each shoot by about one-third, cutting back to a pair of strong, healthy buds so that there is a good display of flowers later in the year.

Cut thin, spindly shoots back to ground level. Remove any shoots that are crossing and rubbing.

Remedial pruning

Hydrangeas tend to become woody and overcrowded as they age, with lots of thin, weak, straggly stems producing fewer and fewer flowers, especially if pruning has been neglected. This can be overcome with hard pruning, although the following season's flowers may be lost.

In late winter or early spring, cut the old, strong shoots back to within 4 to 6 inches of ground level. Cut out any thin, weak growth so new shoots can develop.

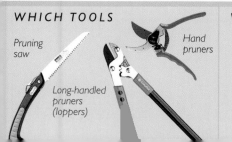

WHICH TOOLS

Pruning saw

Hand pruners

Long-handled pruners (loppers)

WHEN TO PRUNE MOST SPECIES

	early	mid	late
Spring	/////////		
Summer			
Fall			
Winter			

Hydrangea
Climbing hydrangea

Ideal plants for brightening a shady wall, climbing hydrangeas bear wonderful clusters of blooms from summer into late fall.

Hydrangea anomala subsp. petiolaris is a vigorous, deciduous climber with green stems. With age, the stems turn light brown and eventually dark grayish brown and the bark flakes. The leaves are oval to heart shaped with a serrated margin and pointed tip. They are glossy green on the upper surface and slightly paler on the underside, often turning yellow in the fall. In summer, clusters of white flowers are produced on the shoot tips; the dead flower heads often stay on the plant all winter.

Most gardeners are familiar with the shrubby hydrangeas (see pages 100 and 101), but the genus also includes some striking, woody climbers: the deciduous *Hydrangea anomala* subsp. *petiolaris* and the evergreen *H. serratifolia* and *H. seemannii*.

These vigorous, climbing plants are useful for growing in shade or semishade or for growing up into trees. They are true climbers, supporting themselves with clinging aerial roots that attach themselves to any suitable support.

They prefer moderately fertile, well-drained soil with plenty of added organic matter, although once established they seem to grow well in quite dry conditions. Late spring frosts may damage young growth, and cold winds in winter and spring may damage the evergreen plants. They are often slow to become established, but plants climb vigorously once they are attached to a suitable support. Established plants flower abundantly, although most of the flowers are produced on the top one-third of the stems.

The aerial roots are arranged along the stems, which are green when young but turn light brown and eventually dark brown as they age and the bark flakes. The glossy green leaves are oval to heart shaped, slightly paler on the underside, with serrated margins and pointed tips. The foliage of some cultivars turns golden

yellow before falling in autumn. In summer, the flowers are carried on the tips of shoots. They form clusters of white blooms—greenish white on plants grown in shade—up to 10 inches across, and the dead flower heads often last well into the winter. Once established, these climbers can grow up to 45 feet high.

Formative pruning

Young plants need little pruning because they will naturally develop a bushy habit, with strong shoots emerging from just above ground level.

In the first spring after planting, cut out any weak or damaged growth. Train the new growth against the support structure.

WHY PRUNE?

To control the plant and to encourage the production of flowers.

PRUNING TIPS

• After remedial pruning, it may be 2 or 3 years before the plants start to flower again.

PLANTS PRUNED THIS WAY

Akebia quinata: *in late spring, after flowering*
Hydrangea seemannii: *in late summer, after flowering*
Hydrangea serratifolia: *in late summer, after flowering*
Stauntonia hexaphylla: *in late spring, after flowering*

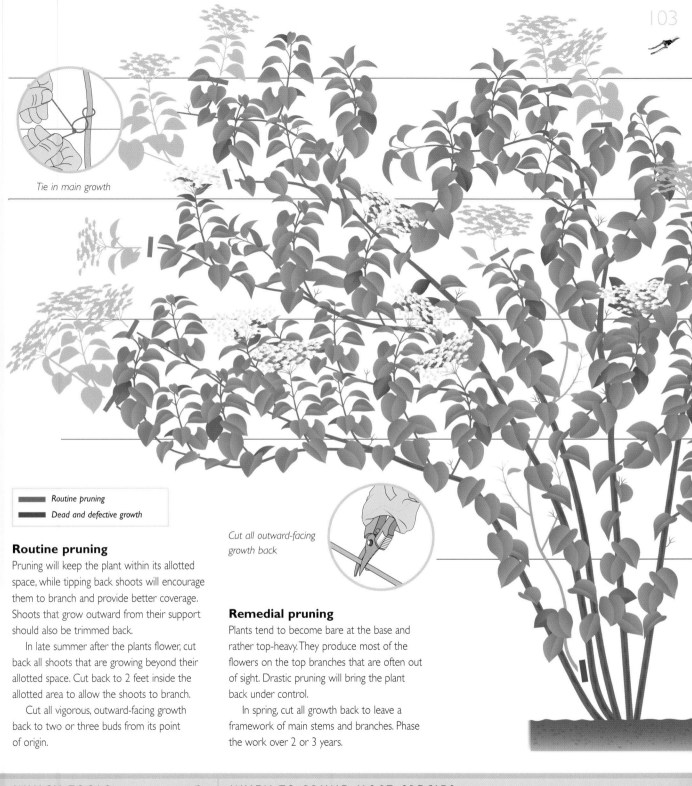

Tie in main growth

Cut all outward-facing
growth back

▬▬ Routine pruning
▬▬ Dead and defective growth

Routine pruning

Pruning will keep the plant within its allotted
space, while tipping back shoots will encourage
them to branch and provide better coverage.
Shoots that grow outward from their support
should also be trimmed back.

In late summer after the plants flower, cut
back all shoots that are growing beyond their
allotted space. Cut back to 2 feet inside the
allotted area to allow the shoots to branch.

Cut all vigorous, outward-facing growth
back to two or three buds from its point
of origin.

Remedial pruning

Plants tend to become bare at the base and
rather top-heavy. They produce most of the
flowers on the top branches that are often out
of sight. Drastic pruning will bring the plant
back under control.

In spring, cut all growth back to leave a
framework of main stems and branches. Phase
the work over 2 or 3 years.

WHICH TOOLS

Hand pruners

Long-handled
pruners
(loppers)

WHEN TO PRUNE MOST SPECIES

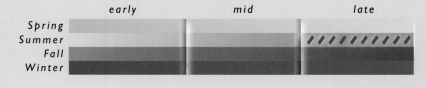

	early	mid	late
Spring			
Summer			/////////
Fall			
Winter			

Ilex
Holly

One plant that everyone knows is holly, even if only because of its association with Christmas.

Although there are a few deciduous hollies in cultivation, these tough, resilient plants are best known as evergreen trees and shrubs, grown for their attractive, glossy leaves and brightly colored berries. The green-leaved forms are excellent choices for city gardens, because they can cope with both dense and partial shade and atmospheric pollution. Although the forms with variegated leaves can tolerate the same conditions, they lose their bright leaf colors when grown in shade. Hollies are tolerant plants, growing well in most conditions. They will do their best, however, in fertile, humus-rich, moist but well-drained soil, and in the right conditions they are long lived. Some hybrids, such as *I.* x *meserveae*, make good hedging plants.

Hollies are usually thought of as having spiny leaves, but some forms have only one spine at the tip of the leaf. Others have so many spines that they are described as spine toothed. One cultivar, *Ilex aquifolium* 'Ferox', known as the hedgehog holly, even has spines over the upper surface of each leaf.

The tough, evergreen leaves have a glossy surface and can be green, green-blue, or variegated in combinations of gold and green, silver and green, or purple. The small, usually cream-white flowers are produced in spring or early summer and are followed by black, red, orange, yellow, or white berries in fall. The berries are borne on female plants only, and both male and female plants must be present if berries are to be produced.

Formative pruning

Hollies usually have a main stem or central leader with a series of laterals or side branches, and pruning keeps the main shoot growing strongly while encouraging the laterals to become bushy.

After planting, trim back any broken or damaged growth and remove the end 2 inches of growth from the sideshoots to encourage them to branch.

If striving to maintain a pyramidal shape, remove any strong shoots that compete with the central leader.

WHY PRUNE?

To maintain an open, balanced, well-shaped plant.

PRUNING TIPS

• *Do not prune in fall because the new growth may be damaged by frosts.*

PLANTS PRUNED THIS WAY

Ilex aquifolium *and cvs.:* *in mid- to late summer*
Ilex crenata *and cvs.:* *in late winter or early spring*
Ilex glabra *and cvs.:* *in late winter or early spring*
Ilex opaca *and cvs.:* *in mid- to late summer*
Ilex x altaclarensis *and cvs.:* *in mid- to late summer*

Long-handled pruners (loppers)

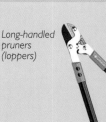

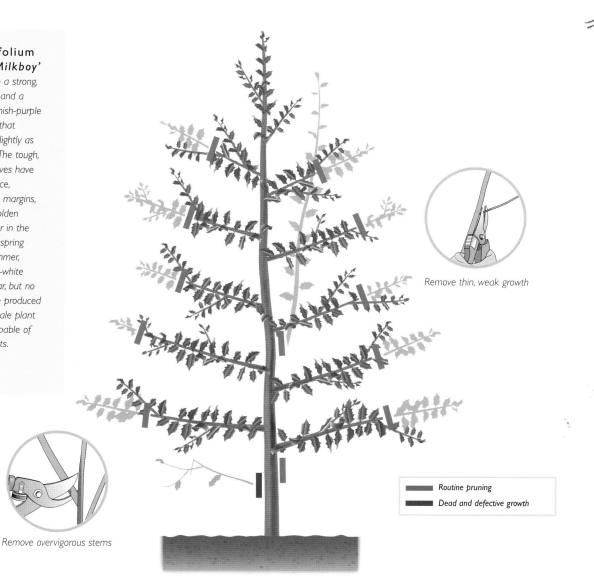

**Ilex aquifolium
'Golden Milkboy'**
*is a holly with a strong,
upright habit and a
mass of greenish-purple
young stems that
often droop slightly as
they mature. The tough,
evergreen leaves have
a glossy surface,
spine-toothed margins,
and a vivid golden
splash of color in the
center. In the spring
and early summer,
small, creamy-white
flowers appear, but no
berries will be produced
as this is a male plant
and is not capable of
producing fruits.*

Remove thin, weak growth

Remove overvigorous stems

	Routine pruning
	Dead and defective growth

Routine pruning

Hollies grown in a tree form do not require regular pruning to keep growing well, but you can pinch off the tips when the plant is young to keep it in a desired shape. Vigorous shoots should be cut back to balance the growth and shape of the plant.

In late summer, remove the tips of shoots, cutting off 2 to 4 inches of growth to encourage branching. Remove any competing leaders.

Prune vigorous stems by at least half their length, cutting back to just above a healthy bud or to a well-placed sideshoot. Remove any thin, weak growth from the center of the plant.

Remedial pruning

As they age, hollies make less extension growth at the tip of each shoot, and they increase in overall size very slowly. At the same time, they often become bare and straggly at the base.

Holly trees (*I. aquifolium* and *I. opaca*) are slow growing and generally do not require renovation.

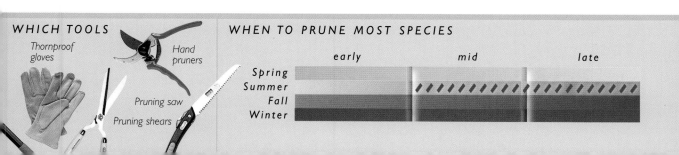

WHICH TOOLS

Thornproof gloves

Hand pruners

Pruning saw

Pruning shears

WHEN TO PRUNE MOST SPECIES

	early	mid	late
Spring			
Summer			
Fall			
Winter			

Jasminum
Jasmine, jessamine

These scrambling climbers are grown for their attractive and often fragrant blooms. They make ideal screens to camouflage or hide items and parts of the garden that you'd prefer to keep out of sight.

Jasminum nudiflorum *is a hardy shrub with lax, green stems that turn brown with age. It is often grown as a wall shrub or climber. The small, dark-green leaves are each divided into three equal lobes and carried in opposite pairs along the stems. The deep-golden flowers are tubular, opening out to a five-petaled, starlike shape during the winter and early spring.*

The genus contains both evergreen and deciduous shrubs and climbers. Most climbing jasmines have mid- to dark-green leaves, but there are gold- and silver-variegated forms of *Jasminum officinale*. The leaves are made up of three to seven oval leaflets arranged along a green central stalk and positioned along the midgreen stems in opposite pairs. The small, tubular flowers open at the mouth to form five- or six-segmented, star-shaped blooms, usually in shades of golden yellow or white, with the white blooms often tinged pink when in bud. Flowers are usually formed in small clusters in the leaf joints, although the flowers of *J. nudiflorum* are often borne singly. These plants grow best in a fertile, well-drained soil in full sun or partial shade, but need protection from cold winds. Plants with variegated leaves will revert to solid green if they're grown in shade.

Climbing jasmines should be pruned after flowering, which will vary according to species.

WHY PRUNE?

To maintain balanced growth and to encourage flowering.

PRUNING TIPS

• *Prune jasmine after flowering so that you don't remove blooming shoots.*

PLANTS PRUNED THIS WAY

Jasminum nudiflorum: *in spring, after flowering*
Jasminum officinale: *in winter, after flowering*
Jasminum polyanthum: *in summer, after flowering*

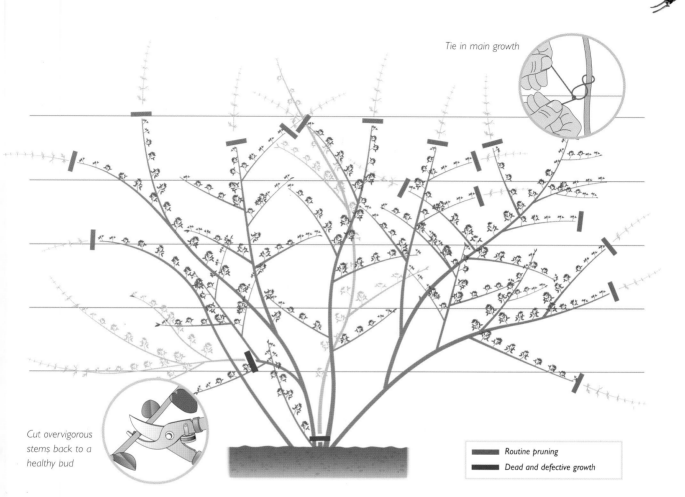

Tie in main growth

Cut overvigorous stems back to a healthy bud

▬	Routine pruning
▬	Dead and defective growth

Formative pruning

Prune young plants to encourage them to grow bushy, with a number of strong, vigorous shoots emerging from close to soil level.

In the first spring after planting, cut out any weak or damaged growth, and cut all strong, healthy stems back to about two-thirds of their original length. Train the new shoots into the support structure as they develop.

Routine pruning

Try to produce a framework of strong, healthy shoots and encourage the formation of flower-bearing spurs. Also, prune mature plants to keep them within their allotted space.

Cut the lateral flower-bearing shoots back to two or three pairs of strong buds; these will bear the current season's flowers. Remove any weak or straggly growths.

To encourage branching, cut back to a strong bud any vigorous shoots that are growing out of their allotted space.

Remedial pruning

Jasmines often become leggy and bare at the base, but they will respond well to severe pruning.

In late winter or early spring, use hand pruners or long-handled pruners (loppers) to cut all the stems back to within 2 feet of ground level. This will encourage the development of new shoots.

Six to eight weeks after cutting down the plant, remove all the weak, thin shoots and start to train the new replacement shoots into position on the support structure.

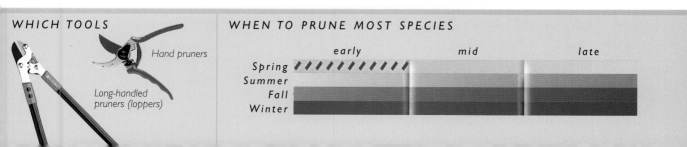

WHICH TOOLS

Hand pruners

Long-handled pruners (loppers)

WHEN TO PRUNE MOST SPECIES

	early	mid	late
Spring	/////////		
Summer			
Fall			
Winter			

Lagerstroemia
Pride of India, crape myrtle

These shrubs and trees are suitable only for reliably warm gardens with hot summers, but in the right conditions they flower profusely and for long periods. As well as brightly colored flowers, they have decorative foliage and attractive peeling bark.

Lagerstroemia indica *is a small tree with an upright habit. Its attractive, gray-brown bark turns red-brown as it ages before peeling away from the stems and branches. The leaves are broadly oblong and bronze-green at first, turning dark green as they expand. They are arranged in opposite pairs along the branches. The flowers vary greatly in color and can be white, pink, or shades of red and purple.*

The species of large shrubs or small trees in the genus can vary in size from 25 feet high and across to 6 feet high and across. They have mid- to dark-green leaves arranged in opposite pairs along young green stems, which often turn a light gray-brown, and as the bark ages it turns red-brown before it begins to peel away from the trunk and branches. The flowers appear mainly in summer and fall (*Lagerstroemia speciosa* starts to flower in spring). Colors range from white through shades of pink, red, and purple. The common name crape myrtle derives from the crinkled edges of the petals, which resemble crepe paper. The broadly oval to oblong leaves on the deciduous forms often turn bright orange-red before dropping in fall.

Lagerstroemias prefer moderately fertile, well-drained soil. They need a position in full sun and must be protected from cold winds and late spring frosts.

Although there are about 50 species, the most widely grown are *L. fauriei*, *L. indica* and its cultivars, and *L. speciosa* (giant crape myrtle).

WHY PRUNE?
To encourage balanced growth and regular flowering.

PRUNING TIPS
• *Prune so that plenty of light can get into the center of the plant.*

PLANTS PRUNED THIS WAY
Lagerstroemia fauriei: *in early spring*
Lagerstroemia indica: *in early spring*
Lagerstroemia speciosa: *in early spring*

Remove crossing stems

Cut stems back to
two or three buds

■ Routine pruning
■ Dead and defective growth

Formative pruning

When they are grown as shrubs, young plants should be pruned so they grow bushy and well-structured, with a central main stem and plenty of branches originating from it. This could be converted into a standard with a single stem later on if wished.

Remove the top 4 to 6 inches of the main stem to encourage branching along its length.

In early spring, cut any weak, leggy shoots back to two or three buds. Remove the end one-third of any long, straggly shoots.

Routine pruning

Once a framework of branches has been established, annual pruning will remove about one-half of the smaller (sublateral) branches to encourage new flower-bearing shoots.

In early spring, cut shoots back to within two or three buds of the lateral stems, which form the plant's main framework of branches. Remove any branches that cross through the middle of the plant.

Remedial pruning

These plants can be cut back quite severely—even back to the main framework of branches—to promote new growth or to overcome frost damage.

Remove all the small branches and cut the framework branches back to within four or five buds of the main stem.

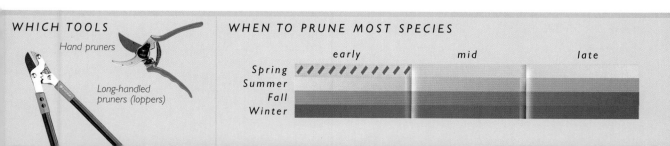

WHICH TOOLS

Hand pruners

Long-handled
pruners (loppers)

WHEN TO PRUNE MOST SPECIES

	early	mid	late
Spring	////////		
Summer			
Fall			
Winter			

Lavandula
Lavender

The wonderful scent and beautiful colors of both flowers and foliage have made lavender one of the best known and best loved of all garden plants.

Lavandula angustifolia 'Hidcote' *is a compact, evergreen shrub with erect silvery-green stems that turn silvery brown as they mature. The aromatic, silvery-gray leaves are narrow and straplike with a covering of silvery down. In midsummer, short, dense clusters of fragrant, dark-purple flowers are produced above the leaves.*

Lavenders are fully hardy to half-hardy evergreen plants, and their strongly aromatic leaves and distinctive flowers make them instantly recognizable, even by people who have little interest in gardening. They prefer fertile, well-drained, alkaline soil and can withstand long periods of hot, dry weather. Lavenders should always be planted in full sun. In winter, especially if they are grown in a heavy, waterlogged, or poorly drained soil, their roots are susceptible to rot. Compared with most other shrubs, they are not long lived; they can be too old to save after 7 or 8 years. As they age, they develop into open, rather spreading plants with old, bare wood.

Lavenders are compact and bushy shrubs with small, narrow, gray to gray-green leaves held on thin, square, gray-green stems. Young leaves and stems are covered with gray, downy felt to protect them from hot, dry conditions. The flowers, which are held in erect spikes at the ends of long, slender stems, come in many shades of blue as well as white and pink. *Lavandula dentata* and *L. stoechas* have a tuft of bracts directly above the flower—the bracts are usually colored similarly to the flowers beneath. All parts of the plant are aromatic.

WHY PRUNE?

To promote flowering and to create a compact, bushy plant.

PRUNING TIPS

• Trim the dead flowers off L. stoechas after flowering but leave the main pruning until spring.

PLANTS PRUNED THIS WAY

Lavandula angustifolia and cvs.: *after flowering*
Lavandula x intermedia and cvs.: *after flowering*
Lavandula stoechas and cvs.: *in spring*
Hebe pinguifolia and cvs.: *after flowering*
Hebe speciosa and cvs.: *in spring*

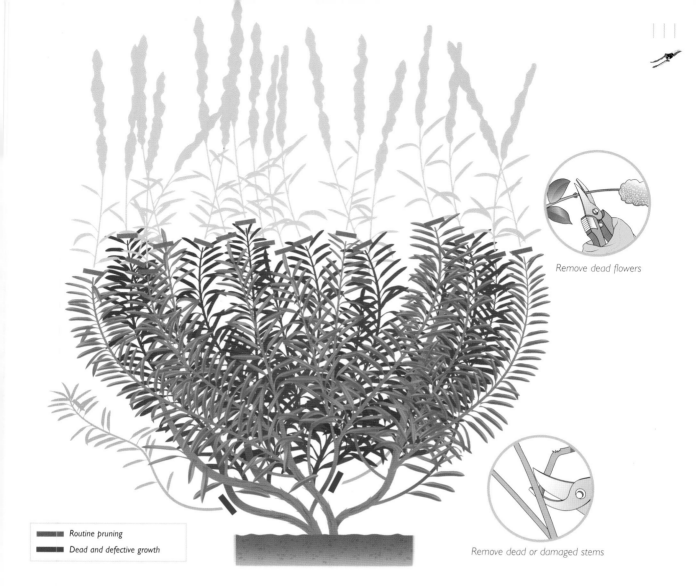

Remove dead flowers

Remove dead or damaged stems

■ Routine pruning
■ Dead and defective growth

Formative pruning

Prune young plants to encourage them to develop a bushy habit, with strong shoots emerging from the base of the plant.

After planting, cut out any weak or damaged growth. Cut the remaining shoots back to about half of their length to encourage new shoots to form at the base of the plant.

Routine pruning

Pruning is necessary not only to remove spent flowers and keep the plants compact and bushy, but also to encourage production of plenty of new shoots to prevent bareness at the base. Remove any broken, damaged, or winter-killed shoots and trim back tall stems in spring.

Prune after flowering by removing the dead flowerheads with about 2 to 3 inches of leafy growth.

Remedial pruning

These short-lived shrubs often become bare and leggy at the base. They do not respond to severe pruning, and the old wood does not produce new shoots.

Remove and replace old, straggly plants.

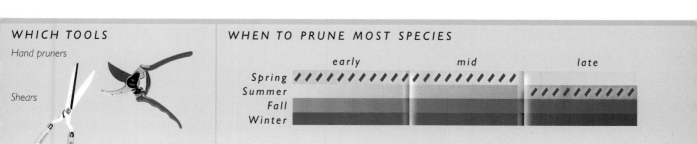

WHICH TOOLS

Hand pruners

Shears

WHEN TO PRUNE MOST SPECIES

	early	mid	late
Spring			
Summer			
Fall			
Winter			

Lonicera
Climbing honeysuckle

There is nothing to compare with the scent of honeysuckle on a warm summer evening. If there is one fragrant plant that should be grown close to open windows, this is it.

These woody climbers support themselves by twining their stems around other plants and structures so they can climb and spread. They often form a huge, tangled mess of leaves, stems, and flowers. They prefer moist, well-drained soil but will grow in almost any soil and soon fall victim to fungal diseases when they lack water. If possible, keep the roots shaded. Because they are pollinated mainly by moths and butterflies, they tend to be at their most fragrant in the afternoon and evening.

The plants are vigorous climbers, eventually reaching up to 15 feet high and often spreading to over 18 feet—they must be allowed plenty of room, or they will quickly swamp other plants. The leaves are oval, straplike, or almost circular in shape, midgreen with a slightly hairy underside, and arranged on the green-pink stems in opposite pairs. The twining stems, which turn woody and gray-brown with age, bear clusters of long, tubular flowers on the tips of each sideshoot and on the stems. The fragrant flowers, which range in color from white, cream, and pale yellow to shades of pink, deep red, and orange, are followed by red berries in fall.

Lonicera periclymenum **'Serotina'** *is a vigorous climber with twining stems that turn from pinkish green to pale brown and eventually gray. The younger shoots carry broadly oval, midgreen leaves that are arranged in opposite pairs at irregular intervals. Clusters of tubular flowers, pink in bud and opening to white, are produced from midsummer onward. The flowers are highly fragrant, particularly in the evening.*

Formative pruning

Prune young plants to encourage them to develop a bushy habit, with strong shoots emerging from the base of the plant.

After planting, cut out any weak or damaged growth. Cut the remaining shoots back to about one-third of their length to encourage development of new shoots from the base of the plant as it becomes established.

Select the strongest shoots and tie them to the support until they start to twine of their own accord.

Routine pruning

Try to produce a framework of strong, healthy shoots and to encourage formation of flower-producing spurs. Mature plants need to be pruned to stay contained within their allotted area.

In late summer after flowering, cut back all shoots that are growing beyond their allotted space. Cut back to 2 feet inside the allotted area to allow the shoots to branch. Thin out congested growth. Cut all lateral shoots back to within two or three buds of the main stems— these will bear next season's flowers.

WHY PRUNE?

To control the plant and to encourage production of flower-bearing shoots.

PRUNING TIPS

• *Use sharp pruners, because the stems are easily crushed.*

PLANTS PRUNED THIS WAY

Lonicera caprifolium *and cvs.: in late summer, after flowering*
Lonicera etrusca *and cvs.: in late summer, after flowering*
Lonicera henryi *and cvs.: in late summer, after flowering*
Lonicera japonica *and cvs.: in spring, after flowering*
Lonicera periclymenum *and cvs.: in late summer, after flowering*
Lonicera sempervirens *(native honeysuckle): in late summer, after flowering*

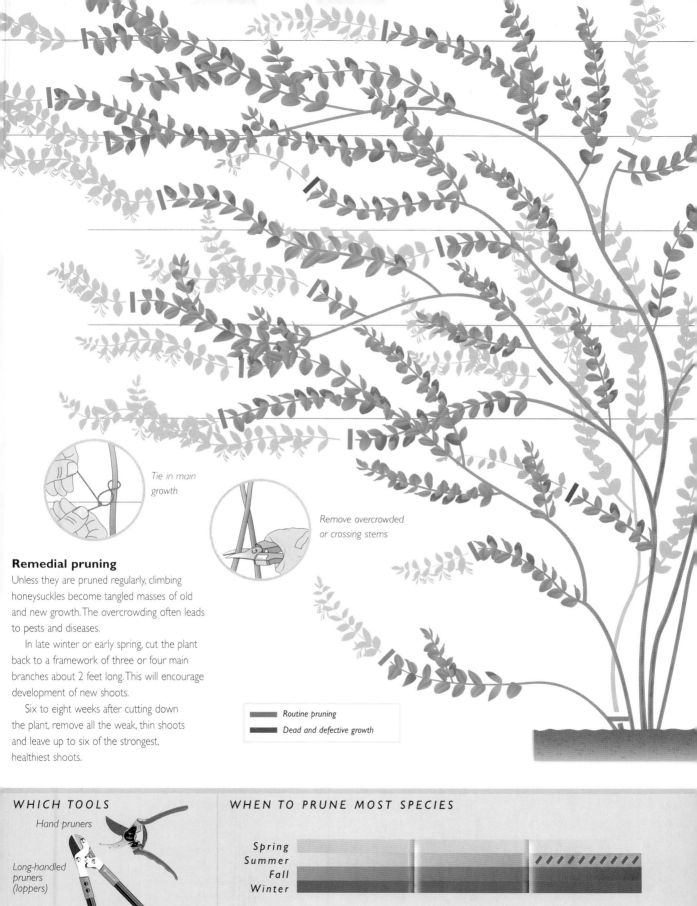

Tie in main growth

Remove overcrowded or crossing stems

Remedial pruning

Unless they are pruned regularly, climbing honeysuckles become tangled masses of old and new growth. The overcrowding often leads to pests and diseases.

In late winter or early spring, cut the plant back to a framework of three or four main branches about 2 feet long. This will encourage development of new shoots.

Six to eight weeks after cutting down the plant, remove all the weak, thin shoots and leave up to six of the strongest, healthiest shoots.

▬	Routine pruning
▬	Dead and defective growth

WHICH TOOLS

Hand pruners

Long-handled pruners (loppers)

WHEN TO PRUNE MOST SPECIES

Spring			
Summer			///////////
Fall			
Winter			

Lonicera
Shrubby honeysuckle, twinberry

Shrubby forms of honeysuckle are invaluable hedging plants, and freestanding specimens make good focal points, especially when they are topiarized.

The genus contains a large number of easy-to-grow deciduous and evergreen shrubs, which often carry strongly fragrant flowers on stems formed the previous year. Evergreen species, such as *Lonicera nitida*, sometimes known as box-leaved honeysuckle, and their cultivars grow well as low hedges, while the spreading *L. pileata* is often used for groundcover.

These plants prefer moist, well-drained soil but will grow in almost any conditions. If possible, plant in full sun or partial shade. Once established, the shrubs often develop a suckering habit; the suckers can be dug up in the winter and transplanted to other areas.

Loniceras can grow quite large, with some plants reaching 10 feet high and 12 feet across when they mature. Most have a dense, bushy habit with masses of thin, twiggy growth. The leaves are arranged along the stems in opposite pairs and are a bright, glossy mid- to deep green. They are oblong to oval in shape, often turning yellow before dropping in fall. The fragrant flowers are tubular and arranged in pairs or clusters along the stems. Colors range from creamy whites through pinks and reds, followed in the fall by bright-red or black berries. Some species, *L. maackii* and *L. tartarica* in

Lonicera nitida 'Baggesen's Gold' is an evergreen, shrubby honeysuckle with an arching habit forming a mass of dense, twiggy shoots and golden-yellow foliage. The leaves are small, round to oval in shape, and arranged in opposite rows along the branches and stems. Bright sunlight may bleach the leaves. In spring, small, creamy-white flowers are produced on the stems, followed later by bluish-purple berries.

particular, have become invasive in some parts of the country.

Pruning timing is dictated by the time of flowering—you should prune immediately after flowering unless you want a display of the brightly colored berries. Prune the deciduous *L. tartarica* and its cultivars in midsummer.

Formative pruning

Prune young plants to encourage them to develop a bushy habit, with strong shoots emerging from close to ground level.

After planting, cut out any weak or damaged growth. Lightly pinch off the remaining shoots to about two-thirds of their length so that new shoots grow from the base of the plant.

WHY PRUNE?

To restrict height and to encourage the plant to develop a more open, balanced habit.

PRUNING TIPS

• *Use a pruning saw to remove older stems, which might be crushed by long-handled pruners (loppers).*

PLANTS PRUNED THIS WAY

Deutzia gracilis *and cvs.: in late spring or early summer*
Forsythia x intermedia *and cvs.: in late spring or early summer*
Lonicera tartarica *and cvs.: in midsummer*
Lonicera fragrantissima: *in late spring or early summer*
Lonicera x purpusii *and cvs.: in late spring or early summer*
Lonicera standishii: *in late spring or early summer*

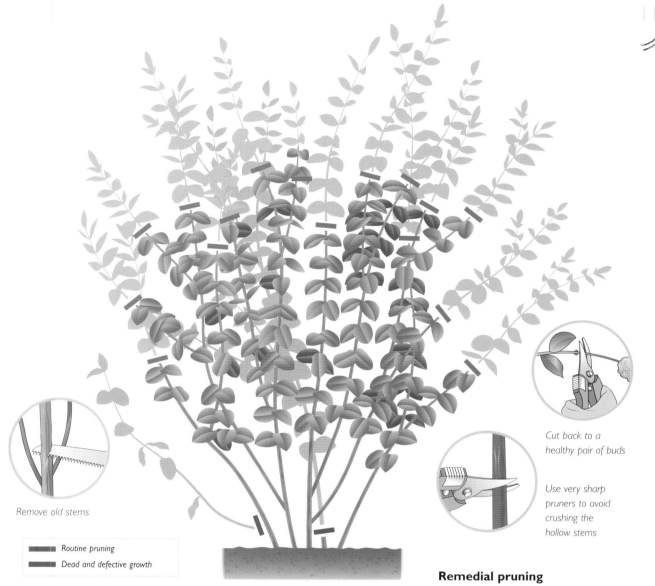

Remove old stems

| | Routine pruning |
| | Dead and defective growth |

Cut back to a healthy pair of buds

Use very sharp pruners to avoid crushing the hollow stems

Routine pruning

Shrubby honeysuckles should be pruned regularly if they are to flower well. It's important to remove the old wood, which would gradually accumulate, and to encourage production of new flower-bearing shoots.

Immediately after flowering, cut the old flower-bearing stems back to a strong pair of buds or down to lower, younger shoots. Pruning in early summer gives the plant the maximum period of growth for a good display of flowers the following year.

Cut old flower-bearing stems back by at least half, cutting to just above a healthy bud or to a well-placed new sideshoot. Remove about one-quarter of the old stems each year to allow new shoots to develop.

Remedial pruning

Old shrubs, especially if they have not been pruned regularly, will naturally become overcrowded as they age and develop into a thicket of thin, weak, straggly stems that produce few flowers. This can be remedied with hard pruning.

In late winter or early spring, cut the shoots back to a framework of four or five shoots within 18 to 24 inches of ground level to encourage new growth.

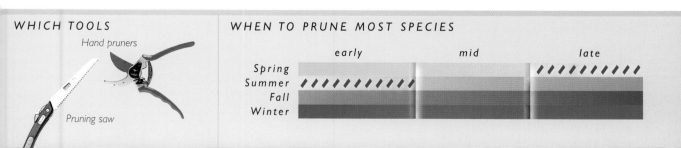

WHICH TOOLS

Hand pruners

Pruning saw

WHEN TO PRUNE MOST SPECIES

	early	mid	late
Spring			/////////
Summer	/////////		
Fall			
Winter			

Magnolia
Magnolia

Magnolia flowers are among the most beautiful of all blooms, and a tree laden with the spectacular flowers is an unforgettable sight.

Magnolia x soulangeana *is a large, vigorous, deciduous shrub or small tree with a spreading habit. From mid- to late spring, large goblet shaped flowers with pale, rose-pink petals marked with a deeper pink appear on the bare branches. The oval-shaped, glossy green leaves emerge from gray, down-covered buds after the flowers have appeared.*

Many gardeners think that magnolias are difficult to grow, but if you get the correct type for the conditions in your garden, it will usually do well. There are both deciduous and evergreen species, and most prefer well-drained, acidic to neutral soil with plenty of organic matter incorporated into it. However, some species, such as *Magnolia kobus* and *M. stellata* (star magnolia), can grow in moist, alkaline soils, and the evergreen *M. grandiflora* (Southern magnolia) will grow in dry, alkaline conditions.

Magnolias can range in size from shrubs of 10 feet high and 12 feet across to trees 30 feet high and 18 feet across. The leaves are mostly oval to oblong. They are midgreen in color (some with a felty covering on the underside) and are carried on stout stems, which are green when young, changing to a light gray-brown as they age. Flowers have from six to more than 30 tepals (star magnolia cultivars have many-tepaled flowers) and come in an range of colors: white, yellow, green, pinks, purples, and reds, many with a white and darker-color combination. They will grow in full sun or partial shade.

WHY PRUNE?

To maintain a balanced shape and to encourage flowering.

PRUNING TIPS

• *Always prune when plants are in full leaf so that the cuts don't bleed excessively.*

PLANTS PRUNED THIS WAY

Magnolia grandiflora *and other evergreen species: in spring*
Magnolia liliiflora: *in midsummer, while in leaf*
Magnolia x soulangeana *and cvs.: in midsummer, while in leaf*
Magnolia stellata *and cvs.: in midsummer, while in leaf*

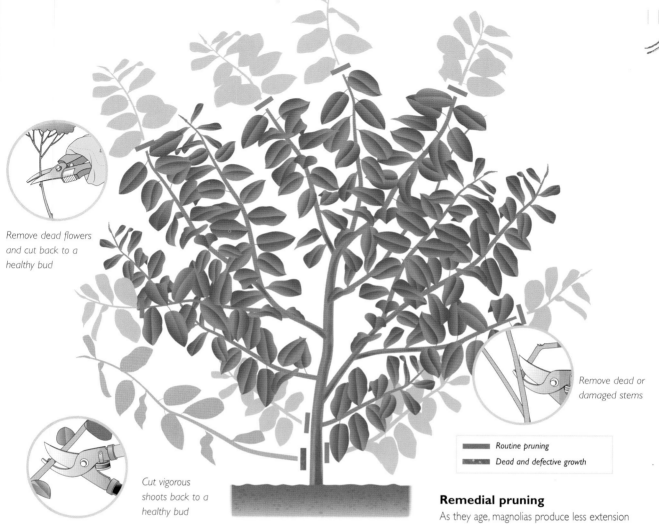

Remove dead flowers and cut back to a healthy bud

Cut vigorous shoots back to a healthy bud

Remove dead or damaged stems

Routine pruning
Dead and defective growth

Formative pruning

Young plants require only light pruning to encourage the development of multistemmed plants that are evenly balanced with strong shoots.

In spring, remove any weak, damaged, or broken shoots. Cut out any shoots growing across the center of the bush.

Tip any long, vigorous shoots by removing the end one-third of each shoot.

Routine pruning

Magnolias do not require regular pruning to keep growing well, but vigorous shoots can be cut back to balance the growth and shape of the plant.

Cut vigorous stems back at least halfway along their length to just above a healthy bud or to a well-placed sideshoot. Cut back any shoots or branches that have been damaged by wind.

Immediately after flowering, deadhead by cutting back the old flower-bearing spikes to a strong, healthy bud or down to a lower, strongly growing shoot.

Remedial pruning

As they age, magnolias produce less extension growth at the tip of each shoot and only slowly increase in overall size. Because the wood is brittle, they are often damaged by strong winds, and remedial pruning should be carried out in stages over 3 or 4 years.

Multistemmed plants can be revived by cutting between one-quarter and one-third of the old stems back to 2 to 3 feet above soil level.

The following year, repeat the process, and thin out any overcrowded new shoots to allow the stronger stems to grow.

Repeat this process over several years until all the old wood has been replaced.

WHICH TOOLS

Hand pruners

Pruning saw

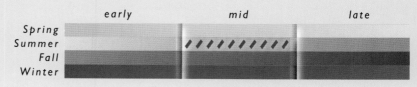

WHEN TO PRUNE MOST SPECIES

	early	mid	late
Spring			
Summer		/////////	
Fall			
Winter			

Mahonia
Mahonia

There can be few sights more heartening in winter than the golden-yellow flowers of mahonia. As if this was not enough, the flowers carry their heady lily-of-the-valley fragrance on the winter breezes.

By selecting different forms of mahonia, you can have a plant in flower from early winter until mid- to late spring.

This is a tough, hardy shrub, with leathery green leaves arranged in circular whorls around the stem. The leaves are armed with sharp spines on their tips, so they resemble holly leaves—and they feel just as painful. It's a beautiful plant, but it does grow upward, often up to 12 feet high, producing few sideshoots and always carrying its flowers in the growing point of the previous year's growth. This natural habit makes the plant hard to appreciate because the flowers are out of reach and difficult to get to. Moreover, when the plant is allowed to grow too tall, the branches splay outward, totally spoiling its appearance and growth pattern.

All the widely grown and popular species and cultivars of mahonia, including Oregon grape *(Mahonia aquifolium)*, M. fortunei, M. repens, and the hybrid *M. x media* are pruned as described here.

Mahonia x media 'Charity' *forms an erect shrub with midgreen stems. As they age, the stems become grayish brown with deeply fissured bark. The tough, leathery leaves are made up of numerous broadly oval, deep-green leaflets with sharply toothed margins. During the winter, dense spikes of small, fragrant, golden-yellow flowers are produced on the tips of the new shoots, followed by numerous grapelike berries later in the season.*

Formative pruning

Try to encourage the development of a multistemmed plant with strong shoots forming close to ground level.

In the first spring after planting, cut back the woody stems to the lowest whorl or cluster of leaves, preferably to 6 to 8 inches above ground level.

Routine pruning

Although no regular pruning is required, its goal would be to form a multibranched plant and to prevent it from becoming too tall, straggly, and unmanageable.

In spring, after the flowers have faded, cut back stems to the desired height. This will allow the maximum period of growth to produce a good display of flowers the following year, but

WHY PRUNE?

To restrict the plant's height and to encourage it to develop a bushy habit of growth.

PRUNING TIPS

• *Start pruning before the new shoots form to avoid losing next year's flowers.*
• *Use bypass pruners, because anvil-type pruners will easily crush the stems.*
• *Wear thick leather gloves to protect yourself from the spiny leaves.*

PLANTS PRUNED THIS WAY

Mahonia aquifolium *and cvs.: in spring, after flowering*
Mahonia fortunei *and cvs.: in spring, after flowering*
Mahonia repens *and cvs.: in spring, after flowering*
Mahonia x media *and cvs.: in spring, after flowering*
Nandina domestica *and cvs.: in midsummer, after flowering*

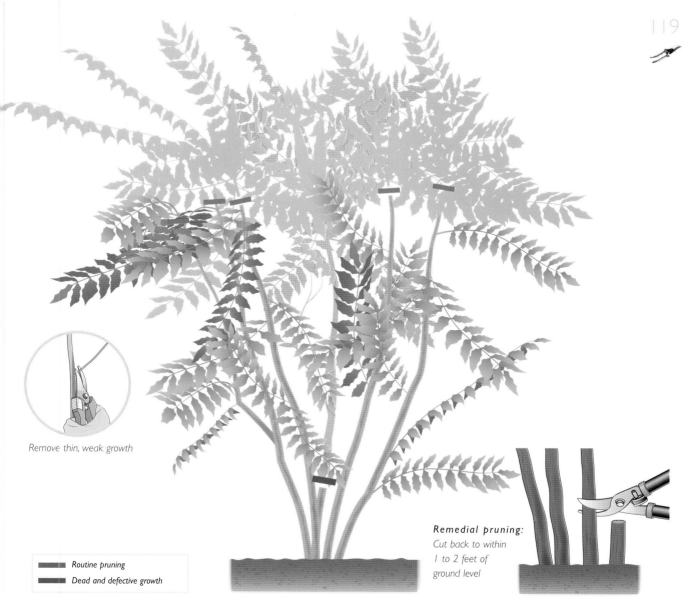

Remove thin, weak growth

Routine pruning
Dead and defective growth

Remedial pruning:
Cut back to within
1 to 2 feet of
ground level

it will also sacrifice the current year's berries.

Cut the stems at a point just above a whorl of leaves to encourage the dormant buds to produce between three and five new stems from this point.

Cut out any thin, straggling growths because they rarely produce good flowers and often harbor pests and diseases.

Remedial pruning

As it ages—especially if it has been neglected for a number of years—mahonia tends to shed its lower leaves, often leaving the base of each stem bare and leggy and exposing old bark, which is marked with deep cracks and fissures. Plants will, however, usually respond to hard pruning.

Cut the plant back to a framework of strong shoots within 1 to 2 feet above ground level in late spring. Pruning too early in the year leaves the new shoots at risk from spring frosts.

Prune any thin or weak shoots back to stronger stems or to ground level.

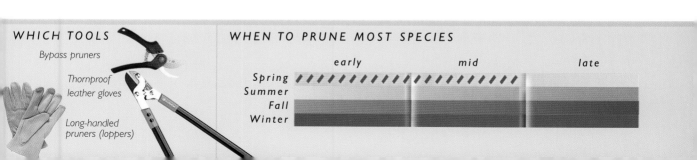

WHICH TOOLS

Bypass pruners

Thornproof
leather gloves

Long-handled
pruners (loppers)

WHEN TO PRUNE MOST SPECIES

	early	mid	late
Spring			
Summer			
Fall			
Winter			

Malus
Crab apple

These ornamental relatives of the fruiting apple (Malus domestica) are among the most widely grown of spring-flowering trees. The glorious display of blossom is often accompanied by attractive young foliage in shades of lime green, bronze, or red-purple.

Malus *'Profusion'* forms a medium-size tree with a spreading habit. Its dense, tangled branches turn deep brown with age. The bronze-green leaves are broadly oval with a serrated margin. They are purple tinted when young, turning orange and crimson before dropping in fall. In late spring, clusters of purple-pink flowers are produced and are followed by copious amounts of small, cherrylike, reddish-purple fruits.

Although flowering crab apples used to be regarded as too large for most modern gardens, the practice of propagating them onto dwarfing rootstocks means that there are forms suitable for almost any size of garden. It is possible to find small, shrubby forms no more than 12 feet high to large, majestic trees up to 40 feet tall. There are also some with a lax, weeping habit. The mid- to dark-green leaves are broadly oval, with serrated margins, and are often bronze tinted when young, turning orange and crimson before dropping in fall. The main flowering period is late spring. Single flowers have only five petals, but double and semidouble blooms with large numbers of petals have been hybridized. The blooms are white or creamy-white, or in shades of pink, crimson, and red. Many crab apples also produce masses of small fruits, exhibiting almost as many shape variations as the flowers and in shades of yellow, orange-yellow, red, and red-purple. They grow in a wide range of conditions but prefer moist, fertile, well-drained soil and a position in full sun.

Formative pruning

Crab apples are usually trained as standard trees with a main, single stem, but the branch structure or head (crown) of the tree can be developed after the plant has started to grow in your garden. Prune young plants to encourage the development of a well-balanced head with a central stem and laterals coming from it.

After planting, cut out any damaged growth. Cut the remaining shoots back to about half of their length, leaving the main stem in the head slightly longer than those around it.

Cut back any small, lateral shoots to 3 to 4 inches to encourage the development of new shoots.

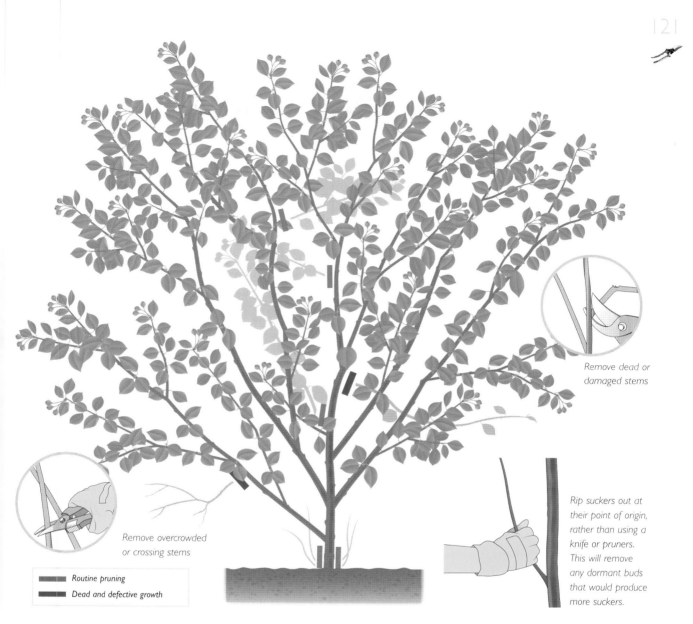

Remove dead or
damaged stems

Remove overcrowded
or crossing stems

Rip suckers out at
their point of origin,
rather than using a
knife or pruners.
This will remove
any dormant buds
that would produce
more suckers.

| | Routine pruning |
| | Dead and defective growth |

Routine pruning

Once the branch structure has developed—
which will take about 5 years—little routine
pruning is needed, although you should
remove any damaged growth. Any pruning is
best done in summer as soon as possible after
flowering, when it will not encourage

excessively vigorous growth and will minimize
the chances of fungal attack.

Cut back any shoots that are rubbing
or split.

Remove any competing or overcrowded
branches. Remove suckers originating below
the graft.

Remedial pruning

Crab apples often become thick and congested
with age, with thin, weak, straggly branches.
They then produce fewer flowers, especially if
pruning has been neglected. This can be
overcome by removing weak or diseased
growth, opening up the tree in the center for
good air circulation.

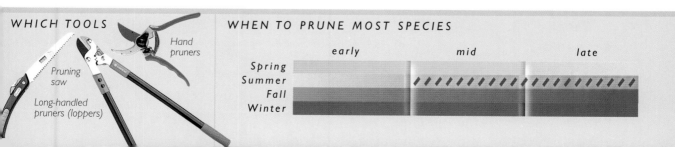

WHICH TOOLS

Hand
pruners

Pruning
saw

Long-handled
pruners (loppers)

WHEN TO PRUNE MOST SPECIES

	early	mid	late
Spring			
Summer			
Fall			
Winter			

Osmanthus
Sweet olive, devil wood

These compact, easy-to-grow shrubs or small trees produce small but wonderfully fragrant flowers, which are followed by attractive berries.

Osmanthus fragrans *forms a vigorous, dense, upright shrub with a framework of pale-brown, slender branches that become grayish green with age. The glossy, dark-green leaves are oval to oblong in shape and thick and leathery in texture. In fall and intermittently through spring and summer, small, white, fragrant flowers are produced in clusters along the stems. These are often followed by small, blue-black, olivelike fruits that last well into the following season.*

Osmanthus are perfect plants for city gardens, because the evergreen leaves can cope with dense or partial shade and with atmospheric pollution—the leaves may be covered in dirt and grime, but it washes off as soon as it rains. They prefer well-drained, fertile soil but must have shelter from cold winds in winter and spring. All can be grown as freestanding shrubs, and *Osmanthus delavayi* makes an excellent wall shrub. Others, including *O. x burkwoodii* and *O. heterophyllus*, make excellent hedges and can also be grown as topiary specimens. All the species produce fragrant flowers.

When they are mature, most of these plants will be large, dense shrubs or small trees up to 15 feet high and often spreading to 12 feet across. They have glossy, dark-green, oval to oblong leaves arranged along thin, woody, pale-brown stems. *O. heterophyllus* has hollylike leaves with deeply notched margins, and of its cultivars 'Aureomarginatus' has gold-edged green leaves and 'Purpureus' has young leaves and shoots that are blackish purple, turning green with age. Small, white, tubular, fragrant flowers are produced in clusters along the stems in spring or fall, and these are often followed by small, blue-black, olivelike fruits, which last well into the winter.

WHY PRUNE?

To encourage flowers and to encourage the plant to develop a bushy, well-balanced habit.

PRUNING TIPS

• *Osmanthus species can be sheared in summer where they are used as hedge plants or topiaries, but this removes many of the following year's flower buds.*

PLANTS PRUNED THIS WAY

Osmanthus armatus *and cvs. (bloom in late summer or fall): in early spring*
Osmanthus delavayi *and cvs.: in late spring, after flowering*
Osmanthus fragrans: *in early spring*
Osmanthus heterophyllus *and cvs. (bloom in late summer or fall): in early spring*
Osmanthus x burkwoodii *and cvs.: in late spring, after flowering*

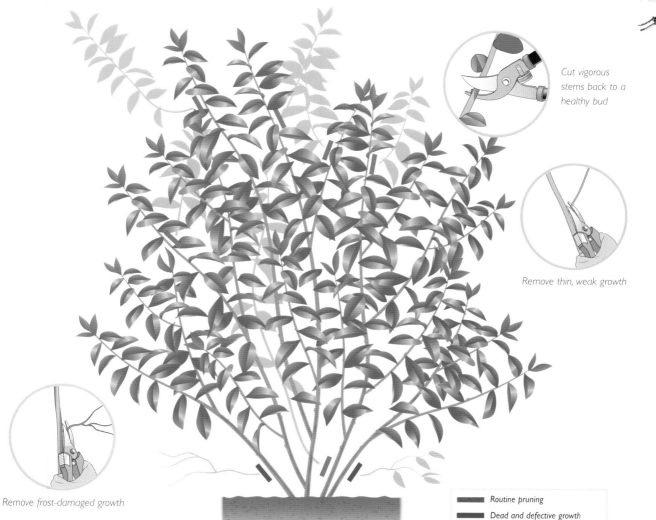

Cut vigorous stems back to a healthy bud

Remove thin, weak growth

Remove frost-damaged growth

Routine pruning

Dead and defective growth

Formative pruning

Light pruning will encourage development of a multistemmed shrub, with strong shoots forming an evenly balanced plant.

In spring, remove any damaged or broken shoots. Cut back any shoots growing across the center of the bush. Prune the remaining shoots by removing about one-third of each shoot.

Cut back vigorous shoots by about half to keep the growth even and balanced.

Routine pruning

These plants do not require regular pruning to keep growing well, but vigorous shoots should be cut back to balance the growth and shape of the plant.

Cut vigorous stems back by at least half their length to just above a healthy bud or to a well-placed sideshoot. Remove any thin, weak growth from the center of the plant.

Remove any new growth that has been damaged by late frosts.

Remedial pruning

As they age, these shrubs produce less extension growth at the tip of each shoot and increase in overall size only slowly. At the same time, they often become bare and straggly at the base, and sometimes the branches splay out, leaving an open center.

Cut back all stems to 18 to 24 inches above ground level in late spring. In summer, remove any thin, overcrowded shoots to allow the stronger stems to grow.

WHICH TOOLS

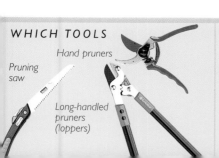

Pruning saw

Hand pruners

Long-handled pruners (loppers)

WHEN TO PRUNE MOST SPECIES

	early	mid	late
Spring			/////////
Summer			
Fall			
Winter			

Passiflora
Granadilla, passionflower

The spectacular flowers alone make these plants worth growing, but they have the added advantage of producing edible yellow fruits in late summer and fall.

Passiflora caerulea *is an evergreen or semievergreen climber with thin, square stems, often trailing for many feet and supported by tough, coiling stem tendrils that will grip to any form of support. The midgreen leaves are deeply divided and palmlike in structure; they are arranged at regular intervals along the stem. Large, attractive flowers are produced from sideshoots during mid- to late summer, often followed by egg-shaped fruits.*

These deciduous to semievergreen climbing plants bear stunning flowers. Few people can walk past a passionflower in full bloom without stopping to marvel at the intricate detail.

The plants support themselves by wrapping the tips of their tendrils around any object they can reach. The tendrils then tighten to draw the stem of the plant as close as possible to the supporting object, which can be a trellis or tree. They prefer well-drained, fertile soil, with the topgrowth in full sun or partial shade. *Passiflora caerulea* can be grown outdoors in areas that are not subject to harsh, penetrating frosts, but other species and cultivars should be grown in a sunroom or glasshouse except in reliably frost-free areas. Provide shelter from cold winds in winter and spring, because they are susceptible to frost damage and may be killed down to ground level in harsh winters.

Passionflowers are fast-growing plants, achieving heights of 30 feet or more once they are established, although the thin, pale-green, angular stems often seem too frail to sustain so much growth. The rich green leaves are divided into three to six oblong lobes, so they look like the fingers of a green hand. From summer to fall, large bowl-shaped flowers open flat to reveal the floral parts in the center

(the outer colored "petals" are actually modified leaves). Flower colors range from white through shades of red and blue to deep purple, and are often followed in fall by oval green fruits, which turn yellow or orange as they ripen.

Prune *P. caerulea* and its cultivars in spring, after the last frosts. Prune other forms after flowering.

Formative pruning

Prune young plants to encourage them to develop a bushy habit, with strong shoots emerging from the base of the plant or to climb a supporting structure.

After planting, cut out any weak or damaged growth. Cut the remaining shoots back to about one-third of their length to encourage new shoots to grow from the base of the plant.

Select the strongest four or five shoots and tie them to the trellis or wires until they form tendrils and start to take hold of the support.

WHY PRUNE?

To control the plant and to encourage flowers.

PRUNING TIPS

• *Avoid hard pruning, which may reduce flowering for the next year or two.*

PLANTS PRUNED THIS WAY

Lonicera etrusca: *in spring*
Lonicera japonica: *in spring*
Lonicera periclymenum: *in late summer, after flowering*
Passiflora caerulea: *in spring*

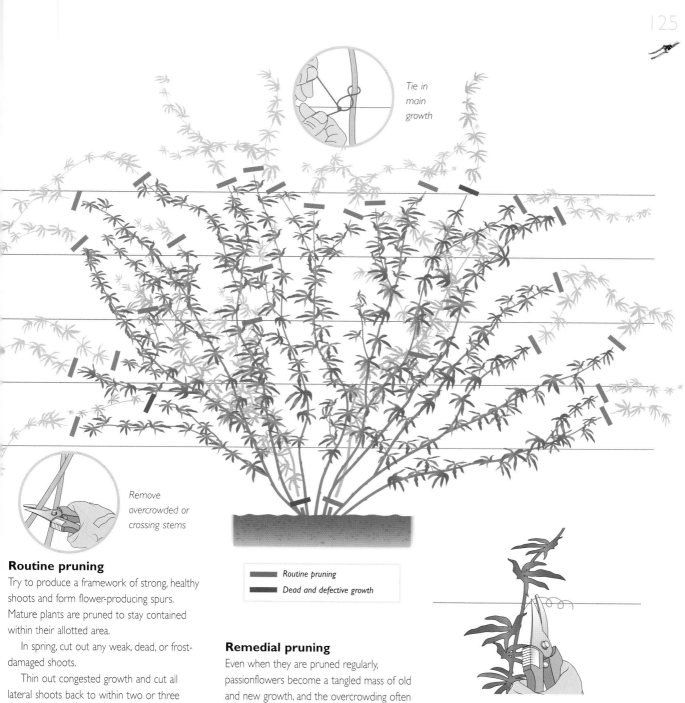

Tie in main growth

Remove overcrowded or crossing stems

Routine pruning
Dead and defective growth

Routine pruning

Try to produce a framework of strong, healthy shoots and form flower-producing spurs. Mature plants are pruned to stay contained within their allotted area.

In spring, cut out any weak, dead, or frost-damaged shoots.

Thin out congested growth and cut all lateral shoots back to within two or three buds of the main stems—these will bear the new season's flowers.

Remedial pruning

Even when they are pruned regularly, passionflowers become a tangled mass of old and new growth, and the overcrowding often leads to pests and diseases.

Remove old, straggly plants and replace them with a new specimen.

Remove tendrils before pruning stems to ease removal of the stems from the support

WHICH TOOLS

Hand pruners

Long-handled pruners (loppers)

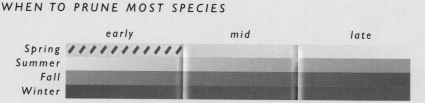

WHEN TO PRUNE MOST SPECIES

	early	mid	late
Spring	/////////		
Summer			
Fall			
Winter			

Philadelphus
Mock orange

If there is one shrub you should get when you start gardening, it is a mock orange. In early to midsummer, it will be covered with cascades of small, fragrant flowers, carried along the arching branches.

Philadelphus 'Lemoinei' is an upright, deciduous shrub with arching branches. These are light brown when young and turn grayish brown with age. The midgreen leaves are broadly oval in shape with a toothed margin, turning bright yellow before dropping in fall. The extremely fragrant, white, cup-shaped flowers have a single row of petals and are carried in clusters along the stems from early to midsummer.

This resilient, hardy shrub has broadly oval, midgreen, deciduous leaves, which are carried in opposite pairs on light-brown stems, that become a roughly textured, dull gray as they age. Plants can vary greatly in size, and there is something for every garden. Some forms develop into large shrubs, 10 feet high and 12 feet across, while *Philadelphus* 'Manteau d'Hermine' reaches 3 to 4 feet high. There are some outstanding forms with decorative foliage: *P. coronarius* 'Aureus' has golden-yellow leaves, which turn paler in full sun, and the leaves of *P. coronarius* 'Variegatus' have broad, white margins. The flowers, which may be single, semidouble, or double, are carried singly or in clusters along the stem. These plants prefer a moderately fertile, well-drained soil in full sun or partial shade.

Formative pruning
Prune young plants to encourage them to develop into bushy shrubs with strong shoots emerging from soil level.

After planting, cut out any damaged growth. Cut the remaining shoots back to about half of their length to encourage new shoots to develop from the base of the plant.

WHY PRUNE?
To encourage the plant to develop new flower-bearing shoots.

PRUNING TIPS
• Use bypass hand pruners, because the stems are easily crushed by anvil-type hand pruners.

PLANTS PRUNED THIS WAY
Philadelphus coronarius *and cvs.: in late summer, after flowering*
Philadelphus 'Manteau d'Hermine' *and all other named cvs: in late summer, after flowering*
Kerria japonica *and cvs.: in late spring, after flowering*

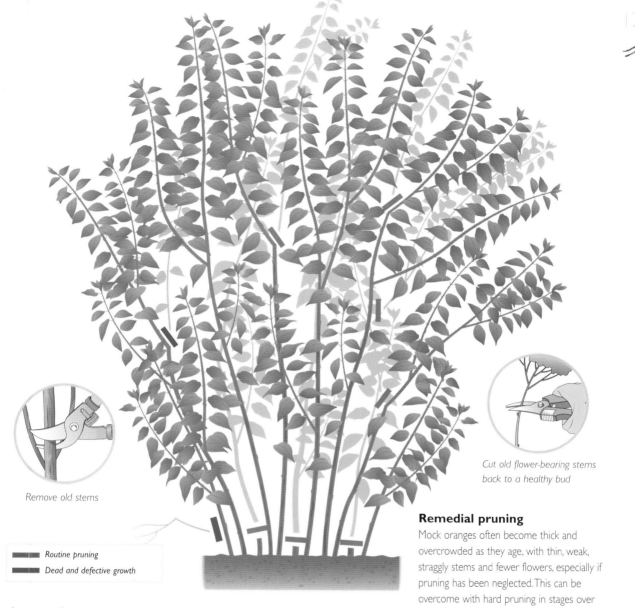

Remove old stems

Cut old flower-bearing stems
back to a healthy bud

▬▬▬	Routine pruning
▬▬▬	Dead and defective growth

Routine pruning

If they are to flower well, mock oranges need regular annual pruning to remove the old wood that would gradually accumulate, and to encourage the production of new flower-bearing shoots. Try to remove about one-quarter of the old stems each year to allow in light and make room for new shoots to develop.

Cut back the old wood as close to the ground as possible in late summer to allow maximum period of growth to produce a good display of flowers the following year.

Shape the plant by cutting old flower-bearing stems back to just above a healthy bud or to a well-placed new sideshoot.

Remedial pruning

Mock oranges often become thick and overcrowded as they age, with thin, weak, straggly stems and fewer flowers, especially if pruning has been neglected. This can be overcome with hard pruning in stages over several years.

Select three or four strong stems and cut them back to about half of their length. Cut the remaining shoots back to within 2 to 3 inches of ground level to encourage new shoots to develop to replace the old ones.

The following year, completely remove any thin or weak shoots. Cut out the three or four remaining old stems close to ground level

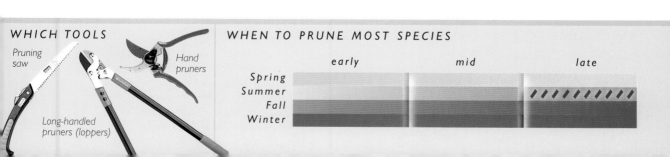

WHICH TOOLS

Pruning saw

Hand pruners

Long-handled pruners (loppers)

WHEN TO PRUNE MOST SPECIES

	early	mid	late
Spring			
Summer			
Fall			
Winter			

Photinia
Photinia, Chinese hawthorn

Brilliant foliage color, pretty flowers, and colorful berries make photinias among the best value in hardy garden shrubs.

Photinia x fraseri 'Red Robin' is a large shrub with an erect habit. It has stiff, upright branches that often splay out, spoiling the shape as the plant ages. It has large, oval-shaped, evergreen leaves that are bright red when young and mature to a glossy, dark green. They have a leathery texture and a slightly crinkled margin. In late spring, small, white flowers are produced in large, flat clusters. This cultivar is grown for its bright red new growth.

Many of these large shrubs originated in China and Japan. Several modern cultivars are now available, providing more intense foliage color or larger berries. There are both deciduous and evergreen species, and all make excellent freestanding shrubs, especially in larger gardens. Some species (for example, *Photinia x fraseri* or *P*. 'Birmingham') are also used for hedges. They prefer well-drained, fertile soil and should be grown in full sun or partial shade, although they must have shelter from cold winds in winter and spring because the brightly colored new shoots are susceptible to frost damage. The deciduous types must have acidic or neutral soil and need partial shade to thrive.

Photinias make large shrubs, growing from 9 to 30 feet high. The larger plants spread to 18 feet across, making them appear more like a small plantation than an individual shrub. On evergreen plants, the large leaves are often brightly colored in shades of red and purple when they are young; they turn a glossy dark-green as they age and unfold. The mature leaves have a leathery texture with a slightly crinkled margin. *P. davidiana* 'Palette' has green-, cream-, and white-variegated leaves as well as young red shoots. The leaves of deciduous plants, such as *P. beauverdiana*, turn vivid shades of bronze-red before they drop in fall.

In spring or summer, photinias produce small, white flowers in large, flat clusters that are followed by orange or red fruits.

Prune the upright, evergreen *P. davidiana* in early spring and the spreading evergreen *P. serratifolia* after flowering and in early spring.

Formative pruning

Pruning encourages a multistemmed plant, with strong shoots emerging close to ground level.

In the spring after planting, prune the shoots lightly, removing about one-third of each shoot to form stocky, bushy plants.

Cut back vigorous shoots by half to keep growth even and balanced.

WHY PRUNE?
To maintain a balanced shape and to encourage new shoots.

PRUNING TIPS
• *Remove dead flowerheads to encourage decorative branching shoot tips.*

PLANTS PRUNED THIS WAY
Photonia davidiana: *in early spring*
Photonia x fraseri: *after flowering and in early spring*
Photonia serratifolia: *after flowering and in early spring*
Pieris floribunda: *in spring, after flowering*
Pieris formosa *and cvs.*: *in spring, after flowering*
Pieris japonica *and cvs.*: *in spring, after flowering*

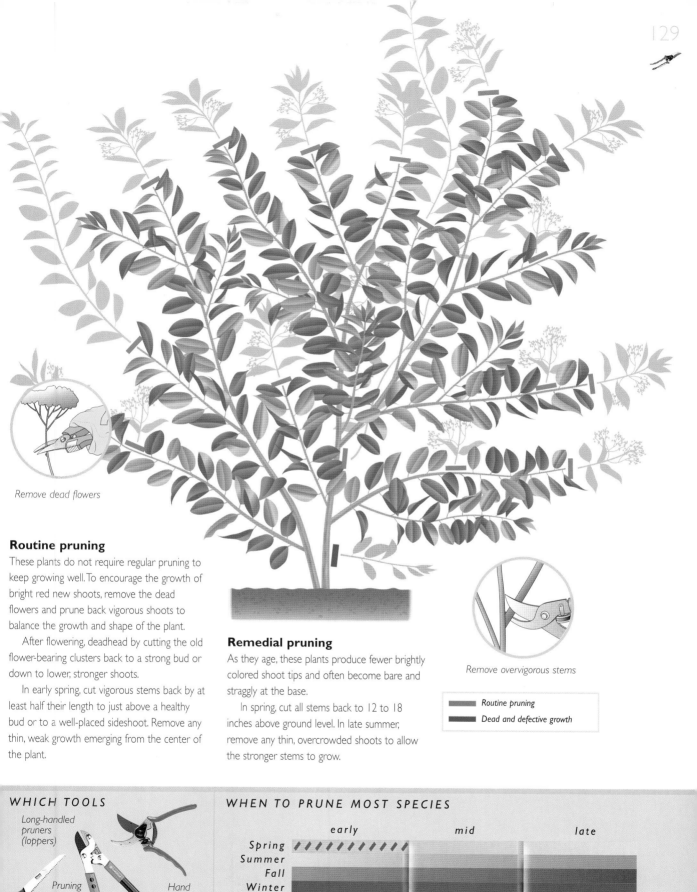

Remove dead flowers

Remove overvigorous stems

	Routine pruning
	Dead and defective growth

Routine pruning

These plants do not require regular pruning to keep growing well. To encourage the growth of bright red new shoots, remove the dead flowers and prune back vigorous shoots to balance the growth and shape of the plant.

After flowering, deadhead by cutting the old flower-bearing clusters back to a strong bud or down to lower, stronger shoots.

In early spring, cut vigorous stems back by at least half their length to just above a healthy bud or to a well-placed sideshoot. Remove any thin, weak growth emerging from the center of the plant.

Remedial pruning

As they age, these plants produce fewer brightly colored shoot tips and often become bare and straggly at the base.

In spring, cut all stems back to 12 to 18 inches above ground level. In late summer, remove any thin, overcrowded shoots to allow the stronger stems to grow.

WHICH TOOLS

Long-handled pruners (loppers)

Pruning saw

Hand pruners

WHEN TO PRUNE MOST SPECIES

	early	mid	late
Spring			
Summer			
Fall			
Winter			

Potentilla fruticosa
Cinquefoil, shrubby cinquefoil

These tolerant, easy-to-grow shrubs are covered with colorful flowers, and it's possible to choose forms that will provide flowers from summer through late fall.

Potentilla fruticosa forms a compact, bushy shrub with a low, spreading, moundlike habit. The silvery-green stems turn light brown and eventually gray and woody with flaking bark as they age. The dark-green, slightly hairy leaves are divided into five to seven leaflets. Small, yellow, saucer-shaped flowers are held in small clusters of three to five blooms from late spring until the fall.

Potentilla fruticosa and its many named cultivars are ideal starter shrubs for the new gardener, and they have a long flowering period, providing plenty of color. Even better, they grow well in sandy or poor to moderately fertile soils as long as they are well drained. In fact, they actually flower better in poor soil, but they must be in bright sunshine. Potentillas are also trouble free, not susceptible to pests or disease, although roots in heavy clay or waterlogged soils may rot.

Potentillas are compact, bushy shrubs with a low, spreading habit, reaching up to 3 feet high and to about 5 feet across, creating a moundlike profile. Most have silver-green leaves, equally divided into five to seven narrow segments. The leaves are arranged along thin, silver-green stems, which turn light brown as they age, later becoming quite woody with flaking bark. From late spring until midfall, small, saucer-shaped flowers are held in small clusters of three to five blooms. The colors range from white and yellow through shades of pink and orange to red.

WHY PRUNE?

To promote flowering and to create a compact, bushy plant.

PRUNING TIPS

• *Use shears to trim the plants after flowering.*

PLANTS PRUNED THIS WAY

Cistus *spp. and cvs.: in midspring*
Hebe albicans: *in spring and after flowering*
Hebe rakaiensis: *in spring and after flowering*
Potentilla fruticosa *and cvs.: in midspring*

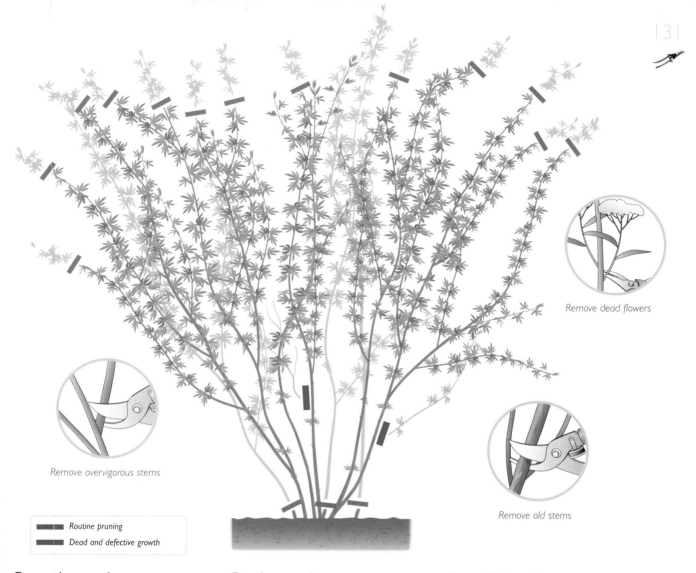

Remove dead flowers

Remove overvigorous stems

Remove old stems

Routine pruning

Dead and defective growth

Formative pruning

Prune young plants to encourage a bushy habit, with strong shoots emerging from the base of the plant.

After planting, cut out any weak or damaged growth. Cut the remaining shoots back to about half their length to promote new shoots at the base of the plant.

Routine pruning

It's important to remove the spent flowers and to keep the plants compact and bushy. Pruning should encourage plants to produce lots of new shoots so that they do not become bare at the base.

In midspring, trim back any long, vigorous shoots. Cut about one-third of the oldest stems back to ground level and cut out any congested growth.

After flowering, prune the dead flowerheads along with 2 to 3 inches of leafy growth.

Remedial pruning

Potentillas become woody and overcrowded as they age, with lots of thin, weak, straggly stems producing fewer and smaller flowers. This can be overcome with hard pruning, but the flowers will be lost for the following season.

In late winter or early spring, cut the old, strong shoots back to within 4 to 6 inches of ground level, and cut out any thin, weak growth to develop new shoots.

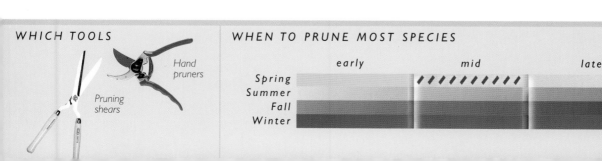

WHICH TOOLS

Hand pruners

Pruning shears

WHEN TO PRUNE MOST SPECIES

	early	mid	late
Spring			
Summer			
Fall			
Winter			

Prunus (deciduous species)

Flowering cherry, ornamental cherry

Flowering cherries provide glorious displays of blossoms, often on bare stems in early to midspring and often leaving a dense carpet of fallen petals at the base of the plant when flowering is finally over.

Although flowering cherries will always be associated with Japan and Japanese gardening, they are distributed over a wide area of the world. They vary greatly in size and shape, and you can choose from small, shrubby plants no more than 5 feet high to large, majestic trees that will grow to 120 feet tall. Some forms are grown for their attractive peeling bark. The mid- to dark-green leaves are broadly oval with serrated margins and are often bronze tinted when young, turning orange and crimson before dropping in fall. Most flower for a short period in spring. The single flowers have only five petals, but double and semidouble blooms have large numbers of petals. They are available in white and creamy white, and in almost every shade of pink you can imagine. The cultivars developed from *Prunus subhirtella* flower intermittently through fall and again in spring. Flowering cherries grow in a wide range of conditions but prefer moist, fertile, well-drained soil and a position in full sun.

Prunus incisa 'Praecox' is a large shrub or small tree with an upright habit when young but becomes openly spreading as it matures. The leaves are broadly oval, with a very finely toothed margin. They are tinted reddish orange when young but turn midgreen as they age. The small flowers are white, flushed with pink, and appear in the spring before the leaves emerge.

Formative pruning

Prune young plants to encourage them to grow bushy and well structured, with a main central stem and plenty of well-spaced branches originating from it.

Remove the top 4 to 6 inches of the main stem to encourage branching along its length.

In summer, cut out any weak, leggy shoots. Remove the end one-third of any long, straggly shoots.

WHY PRUNE?

To maintain a balanced framework of branches.

PRUNING TIPS

• *Prune after flowering, to reduce the risk of fungal diseases.*

PLANTS PRUNED THIS WAY

Prunus subhirtella *and cvs.: in late spring, after flowering (if necessary)*

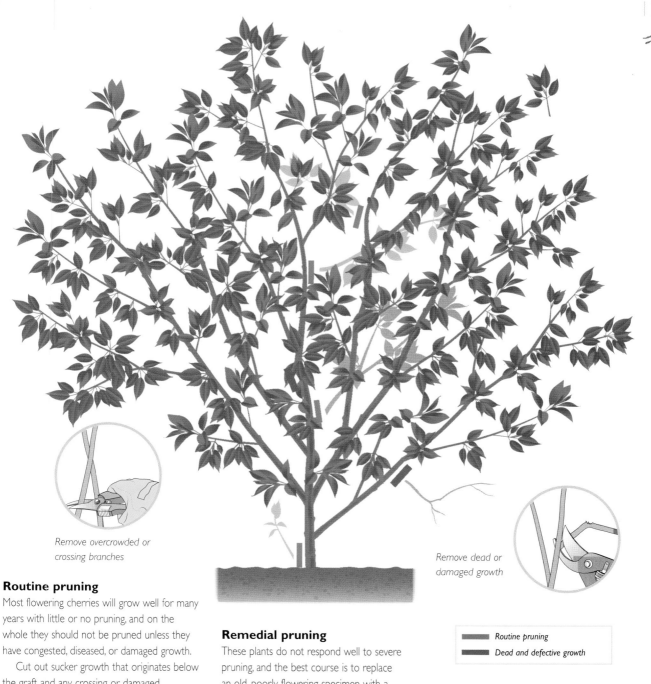

Remove overcrowded or
crossing branches

Remove dead or
damaged growth

| | Routine pruning |
| | Dead and defective growth |

Routine pruning

Most flowering cherries will grow well for many years with little or no pruning, and on the whole they should not be pruned unless they have congested, diseased, or damaged growth.

Cut out sucker growth that originates below the graft and any crossing or damaged branches by pruning them back to their point of origin.

Remedial pruning

These plants do not respond well to severe pruning, and the best course is to replace an old, poorly flowering specimen with a new plant.

Remove and dispose of old, misshapen plants.

WHICH TOOLS

Hand pruners

Pruning saw

WHEN TO PRUNE MOST SPECIES

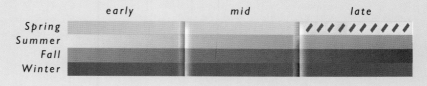

	early	mid	late
Spring			
Summer			
Fall			
Winter			

Prunus (evergreen species)

Cherry laurel, Portugal laurel

The evergreen forms of Prunus are not usually grown for their flowers but often to help give a garden a framework. They are some of the best evergreen plants for use as hedges, as freestanding shrubs, or as groundcover.

These plants form dense, bushy shrubs; some species become treelike with age. *Prunus lusitanica* can reach 50 feet or more in its native land. *P. laurocerasus* 'Otto Luyken', a dwarf cultivar, grows to only 3 feet. They all have glossy, dark-green, leathery leaves, often paler on the underside and usually with smooth margins, although *P. ilicifolia* (holly-leaved cherry) has sharply toothed leaves. There are cultivars of both *P. laurocerasus* (cherry laurel) and *P. lusitanica* (Portugal laurel) with silver-variegated foliage. The fragrant, white flowers are produced in erect spikes on the tips of shoots and branches from spring to summer, and they are followed by red-black, cherrylike fruits in fall. They grow in a wide range of conditions but prefer moist, fertile, well-drained soil and a position in full sun or partial shade. The leaves may become yellow if they are grown in chalky soils. When they are young, plants need protection from cold, drying winds.

Prunus lusitanica ssp. azorica *forms a small tree with a compact, rounded habit. The sturdy branches are covered in grayish-brown bark that turns almost black with age. The glossy, leathery leaves are tinged bronze when young and turn dark green as they age. Fragrant, white flowers are produced as erect spikes on the tips of shoots and branches from early to midsummer, followed by red-black, cherrylike fruits in fall.*

WHY PRUNE?

To keep a well-balanced and rounded shape and to prevent plants from becoming bare and straggly at the base.

PRUNING TIPS

• Keep pruning to a minimum by choosing a cultivar that will grow to the desired size.

PLANTS PRUNED THIS WAY

Prunus ilicifolia *and cvs.: in late winter, after the berries have gone*
Prunus laurocerasus *and cvs.: in late winter, after the berries have gone*
Prunus lusitanica *and cvs.: in late spring or early summer*

Cut back to a healthy bud

Remove overvigorous stems

Routine pruning

Dead and defective growth

Formative pruning

Prune young plants to encourage them to grow bushy, with strong shoots emerging from within 12 inches of soil level.

After planting, cut out any weak or damaged growth. Cut the remaining shoots back by about one-third to encourage development of new shoots from the base of the plant as it becomes established.

Routine pruning

Pruning is done in the late winter after the brightly colored berries are gone and after the risk of severe frost has passed or after flowering. Try to maintain a well-balanced shape and encourage healthy, glossy foliage.

Cut back any excessively vigorous shoots to help the plant retain its natural shape. On variegated plants, remove any all-green shoots.

Prune back to a strong bud all the old flower- and fruit-bearing spikes from the previous year.

Remedial pruning

These shrubs often produce long, bare shoots with only a few leaves on the ends. They also often become bare at the base, revealing dull-green stems.

Cut down the oldest stems to within 6 to 8 inches of soil level. Cut down to ground level any thin, weak shoots.

WHICH TOOLS

Long-handled pruners (loppers)

Hand pruners

WHEN TO PRUNE MOST SPECIES

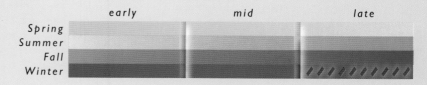

	early	mid	late
Spring			
Summer			
Fall			
Winter			

Pyracantha
Firethorn

This is one of the best plants you can choose to train against a wall or other flat surface. Once established, it will produce a regular display of brightly colored berries, which often last well into the following spring.

Pyracanthas make excellent freestanding shrubs and superb hedges, but they are best known as wall shrubs. They have small, oval to almost straplike leaves arranged along green stems, which ripen to red-brown before turning almost black as they age. All have thorny stems that persist for many years. Pyracanthas produce large, flat heads of hawthornlike flowers in spring, and these are followed by yellow, orange, or red berries in fall and winter. When grown against a wall, they will often reach 15 feet high and 25 feet across, but plants grown as freestanding shrubs or as hedges usually reach only two-thirds of this height. All forms prefer free-draining but moisture-retentive soil and a position in full sun or partial shade.

Pyracanthas grown as freestanding shrubs need no regular pruning, although overlong stems can be cut back before flowering for the best berry production. Plants trained as a hedge need trimming at least three times each year.

Pyracantha 'Orange Charmer' *is a vigorous, bushy shrub with arching, spine-covered branches. The oval, glossy, deep-green leaves are arranged in clusters close to the spines. In early summer, clusters of creamy-white flowers appear, followed by berries that turn bright orange as they ripen in fall.*

WHY PRUNE?

To produce healthy growth and to keep the plant in its allotted space.

PRUNING TIPS

• Avoid severe pruning, which can lead to fireblight disease (symptoms include the death of new shoots and scorched-looking flowers and leaves).
• Wear strong gloves, because the stems are armed with sharp spines.

PLANTS PRUNED THIS WAY

Pyracantha coccinea: *in late spring, after flowering, and late summer*
Pyracantha gibbsii: *in late spring, after flowering, and late summer*
Pyracantha koidzumii: *in late spring, after flowering, and late summer*
Colletia hystrix: *in midspring*
Colletia paradoxa: *in midspring*

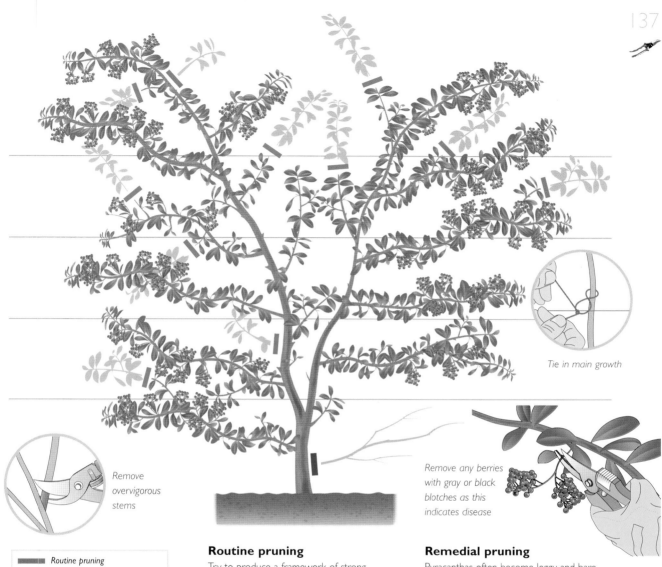

Tie in main growth

Remove overvigorous stems

Remove any berries with gray or black blotches as this indicates disease

	Routine pruning
	Dead and defective growth

Formative pruning

Prune young plants to encourage them to grow bushy, with strong shoots emerging from just above soil level that can be trained onto a supporting structure.

In the first spring after planting, cut out any weak or damaged growth. Prune the tips of the main shoots by removing the end one-third of each shoot.

Routine pruning

Try to produce a framework of strong, healthy shoots and encourage more shoots. Prune mature plants to keep them within their allotted space. Late-summer pruning will show off the bright berries.

To keep the plant tight against the wall, cut back outward-growing shoots to about 4 inches in spring. Remove all old fruit-bearing trusses.

In late summer, cut overly vigorous shoots back to two or three buds if they are not required to tie in as part of the framework.

Remedial pruning

Pyracanthas often become leggy and bare at the base, but they will respond well to severe pruning.

In late winter or early spring, use long-handled pruners (loppers) or a saw to cut all the stems back to within 12 inches of ground level. This will encourage development of new shoots.

Six to eight weeks after cutting down the plant, remove all the weak, thin shoots and start to train the new replacement shoots into position on the support structure.

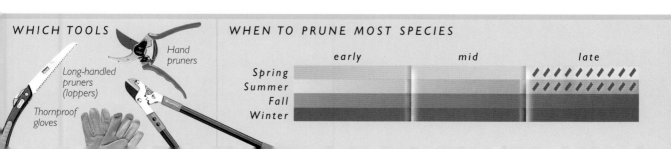

WHICH TOOLS

Hand pruners

Long-handled pruners (loppers)

Thornproof gloves

WHEN TO PRUNE MOST SPECIES

	early	mid	late
Spring			/////////
Summer			/////////
Fall			
Winter			

Rhododendron

Rhododendron, azalea

These lovely plants range from small specimens, which can be grown in containers, to large shrubs suitable for woodland gardens.

Rhododendron 'Cilpinense' *is a compact, semievergreen shrub with a spreading, mound-forming habit and small, oval, glossy, dark-green leaves held on stocky, light-brown branches. In early spring, deep-pink buds open to produce dense clusters of light-pink, bell-shaped flowers with deeper pink markings on the inside and outside of the blooms.*

This is a large genus, containing about 800 species, and over the years many cultivars have been developed. They are tough, mostly hardy plants, and the leathery green leaves often have a feltlike covering on the underside. The leaves, which range from 1 inch up to 8 to 12 inches long, are broadly strap shaped and are arranged in spirals around the stems. Some plants are deciduous, but most are evergreen. All rhododendrons need acidic soil in order to grow well and maintain good leaf color.

There's a wide range of flower sizes, and the individual blooms can be tubular, funnel-like, trumpet shaped, or saucer shaped. The flower colors are even more varied, ranging from white and shades of yellow through pinks and mauves to deep red. The blooms are often produced in multiflowered clusters on the tips of stems and sideshoots, often with many small, brown seed capsules remaining long after the flowers have finished.

The natural habit of these plants can vary from low mounds, spreading over several feet, to small trees almost 40 feet high and 12 to 15 feet across. Many cultivars are grafted, and vigorous shoots—known as suckers—may emerge from the rootstock to form erect new shoots.

Formative pruning

Try to encourage the development of a multistemmed plant with strong shoots forming close to ground level.

In the first spring after planting, prune the shoots lightly to remove the end third of each shoot. This will form stocky, bushy plants. Cut back vigorous shoots by about half to keep the plant's growth even and balanced.

Routine pruning

These plants don't require regular pruning to keep them growing well, but they will do better if dead flowers are removed to prevent the formation of seedheads, which can suppress flowering in subsequent years. Vigorous shoots can be pruned back to keep the growth and shape of the plant balanced.

In midsummer, immediately after flowering, cut off the old flower-bearing spikes (deadheading) to a strong, healthy bud or down to lower, stronger shoots.

WHY PRUNE?

To encourage flower production and to encourage the plant to develop a bushy habit of growth.

PRUNING TIPS

• *Start pruning immediately after flowering to avoid losing next year's flowers.*

PLANTS PRUNED THIS WAY

Azalea (Rhododendron spp. and cvs.) deciduous and evergreen cvs.: *in midsummer, after flowering*

Rhododendron carolinianum and cvs.: *in midsummer, after flowering*

Rhododendron catawbiense and cvs.: *in midsummer, after flowering*

Rhododendron maximum and cvs.: *in midsummer, after flowering*

Cut old flower-bearing stems
back to a healthy bud

Cut vigorous stems back
to a healthy bud

■ Routine pruning

■ Dead and defective growth

Cut off (and burn) any flower buds that
have not opened but that have turned moldy,
as these will only spread fungal disease to other
parts of the plant.

Cut back vigorous stems at least halfway
along their length to just above a healthy bud
or to a well-placed sideshoot. Remove any thin,
weak growths from the center of the plant, and
any deadwood.

Remove any obvious suckers from the base
of the plant by removing them from their
below-ground point of origin.

Remedial pruning

As they age, rhododendrons produce less
extension growth at the tip of each shoot and
increase in overall size slowly. They often
become bare and straggly at the base.

Cut back just the older stems to 12 to 18
inches above soil level in spring. In late summer,
remove any thin or overcrowded shoots to
allow the stronger stems to grow.

Remedial pruning:
Cut back old stems

WHICH TOOLS

Hand pruners

Long-handled
pruners (loppers)

Pruning saw

WHEN TO PRUNE MOST SPECIES

	early	mid	late
Spring		/////////	
Summer			
Fall			
Winter			

Rosa

Large-flowered roses

These popular plants, known for their colorful and often fragrant flowers, are possibly the most widely grown of all hardy plants. There can be few gardens without at least one rosebush in them.

Also known as hybrid tea roses, large-flowered roses were originally created by interbreeding hybrid perpetual roses with the tea roses from China. They produce heads of three or more blooms, usually on shoots that formed earlier in the flowering season. Many of these roses will flower several times during the same year, and the most recently introduced forms are often the more prolific.

The leaves are subdivided into a number of small, broadly oval-shaped leaflets with toothed margins arranged along a central rib that often has small thorns on its underside. The young leaves and shoots range in color from reddish bronze to pale green, often turning deep green as they age. Although most large-flowered roses are grown as multistemmed bushes to provide attractive flowers, the same cultivars can also grow as standards on extended stems about 3 feet above ground level. Almost all roses are grafted or budded onto a rootstock. Suckers originating from this rootstock should be removed as soon as they are noticed.

Formative pruning: First spring

Rosa 'Peace' is possibly the most well-known and best-loved rose of all time. The large, high-centered blooms are creamy golden-yellow in color. Each petal has a deep-pink edge that intensifies to red as the flower ages. The flowers are slightly fragrant. The glossy, deep-green foliage is relatively disease resistant and is carried on stout, reddish-green stems that are clad with large, red thorns.

Formative pruning

Try to encourage the development of a multistemmed plant with strong shoots forming close to ground level to create a balanced framework of branches.

Remove damaged or broken shoots and cut back any shoots growing across the center of the bush.

Prune back strong, healthy shoots to within 3 to 6 inches of ground level, cutting to an outward-facing bud.

Routine pruning

The aim is to produce an open-centered plant with good circulation of air around the branches. This type of rose needs regular annual pruning to remove all old and diseased wood and any weak, thin shoots and to encourage the production of vigorous new stems.

In late winter or early spring, cut back any dead, diseased, or damaged stems as close to the healthy branches as possible. Always try to cut back to an outward-facing bud so that the center of the bush does not become congested.

WHY PRUNE?

To encourage the production of strong, new shoots and flushes of blooms.

PRUNING TIPS

• *Don't prune when a frost is forecast because the pruned stems may split, especially if the sap is flowing.*

PLANTS PRUNED THIS WAY

Rosa 'Fragrant Cloud': *in late winter or early spring*
Rosa 'Piccadilly': *in late winter or early spring*
Rosa 'Ruby Wedding': *in late winter or early spring*
Rosa 'Silver Jubilee': *in late winter or early spring*

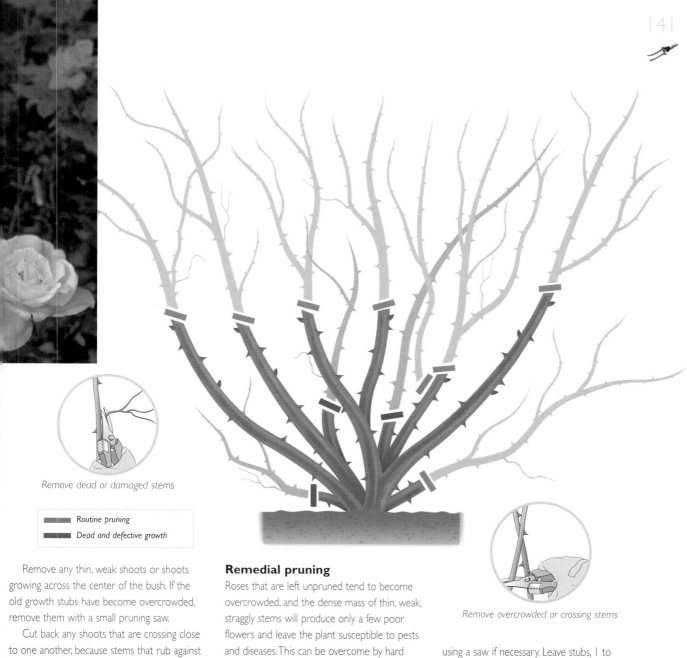

Remove dead or damaged stems

Routine pruning
Dead and defective growth

Remove overcrowded or crossing stems

Remove any thin, weak shoots or shoots growing across the center of the bush. If the old growth stubs have become overcrowded, remove them with a small pruning saw.

Cut back any shoots that are crossing close to one another, because stems that rub against each other will damage the bark and leave the rose open to disease.

Finally, cut back all remaining shoots to about 10 inches above soil level, cutting just above an outward-facing bud. Thinner shoots can be cut back to 6 inches.

Remedial pruning

Roses that are left unpruned tend to become overcrowded, and the dense mass of thin, weak, straggly stems will produce only a few poor flowers and leave the plant susceptible to pests and diseases. This can be overcome by hard pruning, which is better done in stages to minimize the likelihood of suckers emerging from the rootstock.

In winter, cut back half of the old stems as close to the old branch framework as possible,

using a saw if necessary. Leave stubs, 1 to 2 inches long, from which the new shoots will emerge.

In the second year, completely cut out any thin or weak shoots and remove any old branches that still remain.

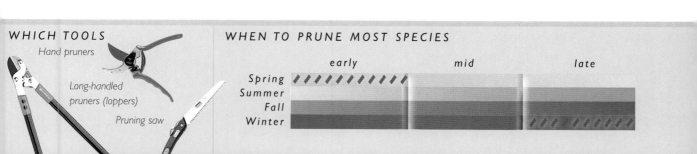

WHICH TOOLS
Hand pruners

Long-handled pruners (loppers)

Pruning saw

WHEN TO PRUNE MOST SPECIES

	early	mid	late
Spring	/////////		
Summer			
Fall			
Winter			/////////

Rosa
Cluster-flowered roses

These popular plants have colorful—often fragrant—flowers and are most commonly grown for a mass display of color rather than for the individual blooms.

Cluster-flowered roses, also known as floribundas, were originally created through intensive breeding of polyantha roses to impart repeat flowering into newer generations of bush roses. They produce clusters of flowers, with anywhere from 3 to 25 individual blooms, though 12 to 15 blooms are most usual. Each flower opens to expose its center. The flowers are borne on the tips of shoots that formed earlier in the year, and most cultivars produce an almost continuous display of flowers, with many of the newer introductions flowering until the fall frosts.

The leaves are subdivided into a number of small, broadly oval-shaped leaflets with toothed margins arranged along a central rib that often has small thorns on its underside. The young leaves and shoots range from reddish bronze to pale green in color, often turning deep green as they age. Although they are often grown as bushes or even sometimes as low hedges, to provide attractive flowers, the same cultivars can also be grown as standards on extended stems about 3 feet above ground level. The majority of roses are grafted or budded onto a rootstock. Suckers originating from the rootstock may be a problem and should be removed as soon as they are noticed.

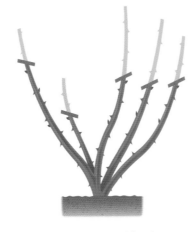

Formative pruning: After planting

Formative pruning

Try to encourage the development of a multistemmed plant with strong shoots forming close to ground level to create a balanced framework of branches.

Remove damaged or broken shoots and cut back any shoots growing across the center of the bush.

Prune back all strong, healthy shoots to within 3 to 6 inches of ground level, cutting to an outward-facing bud.

Rosa 'Iceberg' is a popular floribunda (cluster) rose with an upright habit. It has strong, pale-green stems appearing from dormant buds close to the base of the plant. These turn gray-green as they mature. The pale-green leaves are arranged as seven to nine leaflets along a rib or stalk and, in cold weather, may have a purple tinge along the margins. From early summer until late fall, bunches of double white blooms are produced on the stem and branch tips.

WHY PRUNE?

To encourage the production of strong new shoots and flushes of blooms.

PRUNING TIPS

• Don't prune when a frost is forecast because the pruned stems may split, especially if the sap is flowing.

PLANTS PRUNED THIS WAY

Rosa 'Anne Harkness': *in late winter or early spring, before new growth begins*
Rosa 'Iceberg': *in late winter or early spring, before new growth begins*
Rosa 'Margaret Merril': *in late winter or early spring, before new growth begins*
Rosa 'Queen Elizabeth': *in late winter or early spring, before new growth begins*

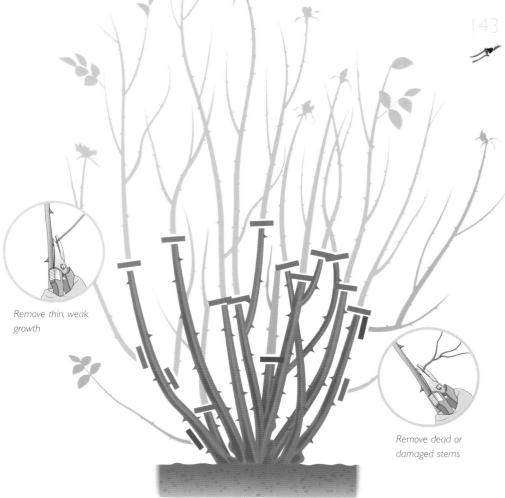

Remove thin, weak growth

Remove dead or damaged stems

Routine pruning

These roses need regular annual pruning to produce an open-centered plant that allows good circulation of air around the branches. The aim is to remove the old and diseased wood and any weak, thin stems and to encourage the production of vigorous new shoots.

In late winter or early spring, cut back any dead, diseased, or damaged stems as close to the healthy branches as possible. Always try to cut back to an outward-facing bud so that the center of the bush does not become congested.

Completely remove any thin, weak shoots or shoots growing across the center of the

bush. If the old stubs of growth have become overcrowded, remove them with a small pruning saw.

Cut back any shoots that are crossing close to one another and those that are rubbing together and causing damage.

Finally, cut back all remaining shoots to about 4 inches above where the previous year's growth started. After about 4 years of this treatment, cut these stems to about 10 inches above soil level. Also remove thinner shoots.

Routine pruning

Dead and defective growth

Remedial pruning

Roses that are left unpruned tend to become overcrowded and the dense mass of thin, weak stems will produce few, poor flowers and leave the plant susceptible to pests and diseases. This can be overcome by hard pruning, which is better done in stages to minimize the likelihood of suckers emerging from the rootstock.

In winter, prune half of the old stems as close to the old branch framework as possible, using a saw if necessary. Leave stubs, 1 to 2 inches long, from which the new shoots will emerge.

In the second year, cut out any weak shoots and any remaining old branches. Cut the strong stems back to 10 inches above soil level.

WHICH TOOLS

Pruning saw

Hand pruners

Thornproof leather gloves

WHEN TO PRUNE MOST SPECIES

	early	mid	late
Spring	///////////		
Summer			
Fall			
Winter			/////////

Rosa
Shrub and species roses

Many of the roses in this group are included in gardens for their colorful—sometimes fragrant—flowers. They can be grown for a mass display of color or as individual plants, and some will also produce attractive fruits, known as hips.

The term shrub rose covers a wide range of plants, from species roses collected from the wild to modern hybrids, which are only distant relatives of the original species but may have similar patterns of growth.

These roses can produce both clusters of several blooms and individual blossoms, some with just a single row of petals opening to expose the center of the flower. Others have flowers with many rows of petals that never fully open. The flowers can form on short, lateral branches originating from shoots or on the tips of shoots. Species roses usually flower only once a year, but the hybrids may be repeat flowering (remontant).

These plants can vary greatly in terms of vigor and habit. Some have an arching, rather lax habit, while others have a stiff, erect pattern of growth. The leaves are subdivided into a number of small, broadly oval-shaped leaflets with toothed margins arranged along a central rib that often has small thorns on its underside. The young leaves and shoots range in color from reddish bronze through to pale green, often turning deep green as they age. Some, including *Rosa glauca*, are grown for their attractive foliage. The majority of shrubs are grafted or budded onto a rootstock and some can be grown from cuttings.

Rosa gallica 'Versicolor' *is an unusual shrub rose with an open, spreading habit and thin, pale green, thorny stems which grow from close to the base of the plant and turn grayish green as they mature. The pale-green leaves are arranged as seven to nine leaflets along a rib or stalk, and have a toothed margin. During the summer, clusters of red-, pale pink-, and white-striped blooms are produced on the stem and branch tips.*

Formative pruning: After planting

Formative pruning

Try to encourage the development of a multistemmed plant with strong shoots forming close to ground level to create a balanced framework of branches.

Remove damaged or broken shoots and cut back any shoots growing across the center of the bush.

Prune back the strong, healthy shoots to within 3 to 6 inches of ground level, cutting to an outward-facing bud.

WHY PRUNE?

To encourage the production of strong new shoots, flushes of blooms, and colorful hips.

PRUNING TIPS

• *Check regularly for suckers, which may look similar to the cultivated roses but emerge from below the graft, and remove them as soon as you can.*

PLANTS PRUNED THIS WAY

Rosa xanthina 'Canary Bird': *in late winter to early spring, before new growth begins*
Rosa glauca: *in late winter to early spring, before new growth begins*
Rosa moyesii: *in late winter to early spring, before new growth begins*
Rosa gallica 'Versicolor': *in late winter to early spring, before new growth begins*
Rosa chinensis 'Viridiflora': *in late winter to early spring, before new growth begins*

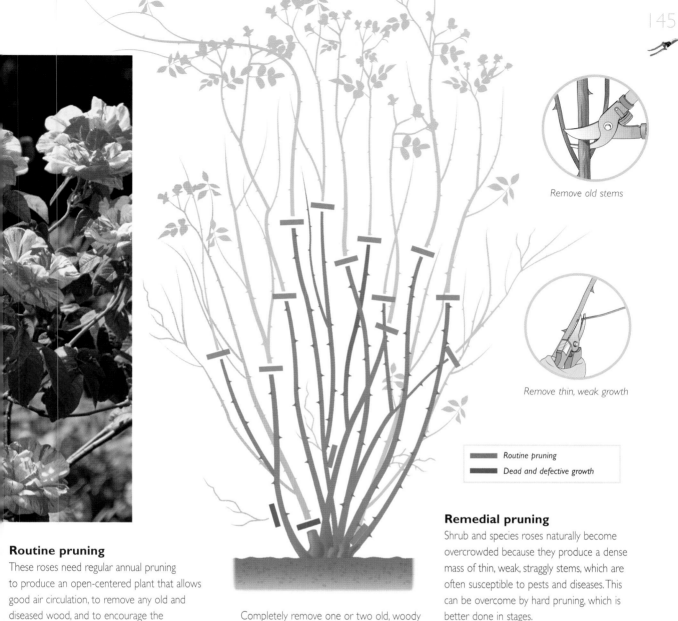

Remove old stems

Remove thin, weak growth

| Routine pruning |
| Dead and defective growth |

Routine pruning

These roses need regular annual pruning to produce an open-centered plant that allows good air circulation, to remove any old and diseased wood, and to encourage the production of vigorous new shoots.

In late winter or early spring, cut back any dead, diseased, or damaged stems as close to the healthy branches as possible. You can prune healthy stems of modern shrub roses by one third to one half. Always try to cut back to an outward-facing bud so that the center of the bush does not become congested.

Completely remove one or two old, woody stems close to the base. Cut out thin, weak shoots or shoots growing across the center of the bush. If the old stubs of growth have become overcrowded, remove them with a small pruning saw.

After flowering, remove the end third of each flowering shoot (unless the plants are being grown for their colorful hips).

Remedial pruning

Shrub and species roses naturally become overcrowded because they produce a dense mass of thin, weak, straggly stems, which are often susceptible to pests and diseases. This can be overcome by hard pruning, which is better done in stages.

In late winter, cut back half the old stems as close to ground level as possible. Reduce the remaining shoots to about half their original length.

In the following summer, completely cut out any thin or weak shoots and remove any old branches, leaving only the strong, healthy growth.

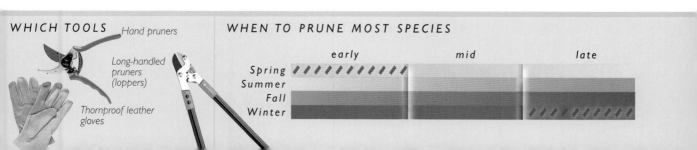

WHICH TOOLS

Hand pruners

Long-handled pruners (loppers)

Thornproof leather gloves

WHEN TO PRUNE MOST SPECIES

	early	mid	late
Spring	/////////		
Summer			
Fall			
Winter			/////////

Rosa
Climbers

In high summer, a wall or pergola covered with a climbing rose in full bloom is an unforgettable sight, with the beautiful flowers nestling among the vivid green leaves.

Climbing roses are mostly either hybrids or climbing sports—that is, naturally occurring climbing versions of large-flowered or cluster-flowered roses. All forms, however, will need to be supported and tied into place, because they are not true climbing plants.

The roses in this category can produce both clusters of several blooms or individual flowers, some opening to expose the center of the flower, others never fully opening. The flowers can form on short, lateral branches originating from shoots or on the tips of shoots that formed earlier in the year, and produce these roses often in an almost continuous display of flowers in a season year, with the new cultivars flowering until the fall frosts.

These plants have only about half the vigor of rambling roses, and their stems tend to be much less flexible. They are included in gardens for their colorful, sometimes fragrant flowers, and they can be grown for a mass display of color or for their individual blooms. The leaves are subdivided into a number of small, broadly oval-shaped leaflets with toothed margins arranged along a central rib, which often has small thorns on its

underside. The young leaves and shoots range in color from reddish bronze to pale green, often turning deep green as they age. Most climbers are grafted or budded onto a rootstock, and any suckers that arise from below the graft should be removed as soon as they are noticed.

Rosa gentiliana *is a very vigorous climbing rose with bronzed-green stems coated in both broad, hooked thorns and numerous bristlelike thorns. The large, glossy leaves are made up of many small leaflets, copper colored when young and turning light green as they age. The semidouble, creamy-white flowers are produced in dense, cascading clusters and are followed by small, orange hips in the fall.*

Formative pruning

Try to encourage the development of a multistemmed plant with strong shoots forming close to ground level and to create a balanced framework of branches.

Remove damaged or broken shoots. Cut back any shoots that are growing across the center of the plant.

As they develop, prune back the tips of strong, healthy shoots when they reach 30 to 36 inches high by removing the last 4 inches of each shoot to encourage branching.

Formative pruning: After planting

WHY PRUNE?	PRUNING TIPS	PLANTS PRUNED THIS WAY
To encourage the production of strong, new shoots and flushes of blooms.	• *Tie as many shoots as possible into a horizontal position.*	Rosa *'Altissimo':* in fall Rosa *'Handel':* in fall Rosa *'New Dawn':* in fall Rosa *'Zepherine Drouhin':* in fall

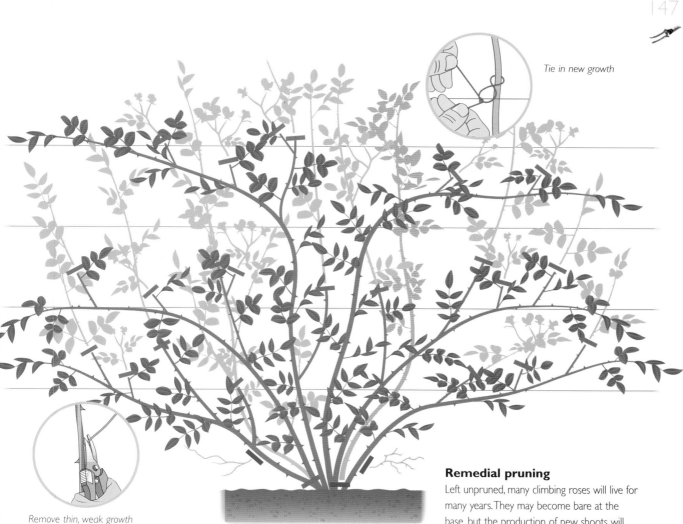

Tie in new growth

Remove thin, weak growth

Routine pruning	
Dead and defective growth	

Routine pruning

Regular pruning should remove old, dead, and diseased wood and any weak, thin shoots and encourage vigorous new shoots. This will create short, flower-bearing spurs, which can be encouraged by training shoots horizontally.

In fall, cut back any dead, diseased, or damaged stems as close to ground level as possible. Each year, try to remove about one-third of the oldest flower-bearing stems to make room for the new shoots.

After flowering has finished, cut back any flower-bearing lateral shoots by two-thirds of their total length.

Cut back any shoots that are crossing close to one another and tie in the remaining shoots, especially any new, young shoots, to the support.

Remedial pruning

Left unpruned, many climbing roses will live for many years. They may become bare at the base, but the production of new shoots will gradually stop, and smaller, poorer flowers will result as the plant slowly declines. This can be overcome by hard pruning, which is better done in stages to minimize the chance of suckers emerging from the rootstock.

In winter, cut back all the old stems to about two-thirds of their original length to a healthy bud or shoot. Prune the lateral shoots to one-third of their original length. This pruning should encourage new shoots to grow.

In the second year, completely cut out any thin or weak shoots. At the same time, remove any old branches that have died.

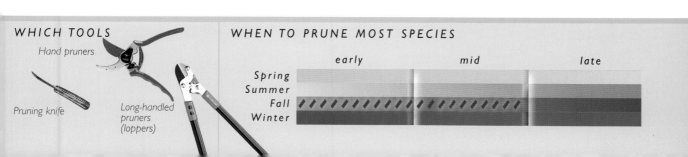

WHICH TOOLS

Hand pruners

Pruning knife

Long-handled pruners (loppers)

WHEN TO PRUNE MOST SPECIES

	early	mid	late
Spring			
Summer			
Fall			
Winter			

Rosa
Ramblers

A rambling rose that has been allowed to climb through a tree or trained over a sturdy arch or pergola is a spectacular summer sight.

Rambling roses are either species or hybrids that are often closely related to *Rosa wichuraiana*. They may be grown as wall shrubs, or trained to climb up pergolas or trellises, or allowed to scramble up into trees. They produce clusters of blooms, with each cluster containing from 3 to 21 individual flowers. The flowers are formed on short, lateral branches originating from shoots that formed in the previous year. Ramblers often produce only one large flush of flowers in summer, although occasionally a few secondary flowers may appear later.

These plants tend to be vigorous, often forming long, lax stems several feet long. They are included in gardens for their colorful and sometimes fragrant flowers and are most commonly grown for a mass display of color.

The leaves are subdivided into a number of small, oval-shaped leaflets with toothed margins arranged along a central rib. The young leaves and shoots are often pale green in color, turning a slightly deeper green as they age.

Some ramblers can be grown as standard roses on extended stems 3 to 5 feet above ground level. Ramblers may be grafted onto a rootstock or grown on their own roots.

Rosa 'Albertine' is a vigorous, climbing rose with long, arching, heavily thorned stems. The glossy, midgreen leaves are arranged as seven to nine leaflets along a rib or stalk with prominent thorns on the underside of the rib. During the summer, clusters of double, pale to salmon pink blooms are produced on short branches originating from the main stems.

Formative pruning

Try to encourage the development of a multistemmed plant with strong shoots forming close to ground level and to create a balanced framework of branches.

Remove any damaged or broken shoots. Cut back any shoots growing across the center of the plant.

Prune back the strong, healthy shoots to within 12 to 16 inches of ground level, cutting to an outward-facing bud.

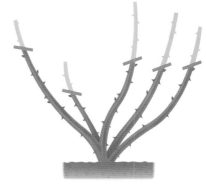

Formative pruning: *After planting*

WHY PRUNE?

To encourage the production of strong new shoots and flushes of blooms.

PRUNING TIPS

• Tie in any new growths immediately after pruning so that they are not damaged by strong winds.

PLANTS PRUNED THIS WAY

Rosa 'Albertine': *after flowering or in early fall*
Rosa 'Emily Gray': *after flowering or in early fall*
Rosa 'New Dawn': *after flowering or in early fall*
Rosa 'Rambling Rector': *after flowering or in early fall*
Rosa 'Wedding Day': *after flowering or in early fall*

Long-handled pruners (loppers)

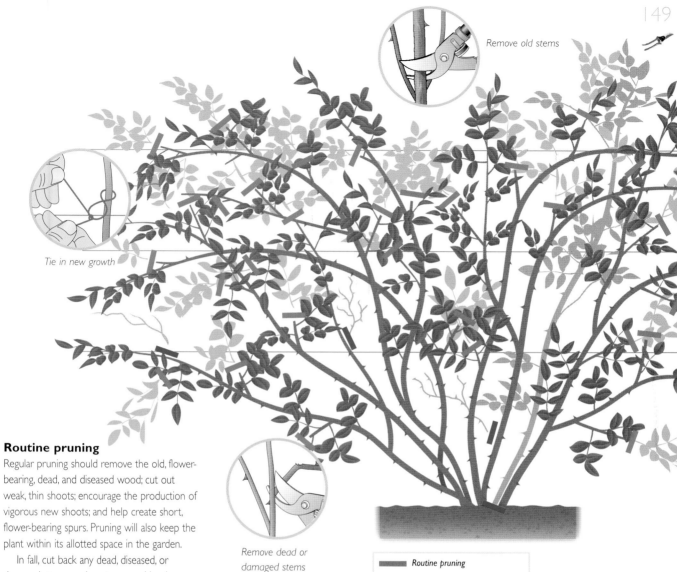

Remove old stems

Tie in new growth

Remove dead or damaged stems

| | Routine pruning |
| | Dead and defective growth |

Routine pruning

Regular pruning should remove the old, flower-bearing, dead, and diseased wood; cut out weak, thin shoots; encourage the production of vigorous new shoots; and help create short, flower-bearing spurs. Pruning will also keep the plant within its allotted space in the garden.

In fall, cut back any dead, diseased, or damaged stems as close to ground level as possible. Each year, try to remove about one-third of the oldest flower-bearing stems to make room for the new shoots.

Cut back any shoots that are crossing close to one another and those that are rubbing together and causing damage. Tie in the remaining shoots securely to the support.

After flowering has finished, cut back any flower-bearing lateral shoots to a point about 4 inches from the base of the shoots.

Remedial pruning

Old, neglected ramblers tend to become a dense, tangled mass of thin, weak, straggly stems, leaving the plant susceptible to pests and diseases as well as producing only a few poor flowers. This can be overcome by hard pruning, which can be done in stages. Alternatively, the whole plant can be cut down to ground level in late summer.

In winter, cut back all old stems to about 18 inches above ground level. This should encourage new shoots to grow.

In early summer, cut out any dead and diseased shoots, and remove any thin, weak stems. Tie in the strongest shoots to form the main framework. Prune any lateral shoots to within 4 inches of the main stem or branch.

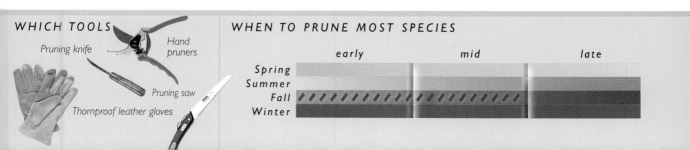

WHICH TOOLS

Pruning knife

Hand pruners

Pruning saw

Thornproof leather gloves

WHEN TO PRUNE MOST SPECIES

	early	mid	late
Spring			
Summer			
Fall			
Winter			

Rosmarinus

Rosemary

Valued in the kitchen for its aromatic leaves, rosemary is equally useful in the garden for its structure and vibrant flower color.

This is where the shrub border and herb garden meet. Rosemary is a hardy evergreen plant in much of the country with strongly aromatic flowers, leaves, and stems, and it is so versatile that it can be a small wall shrub or a low dividing hedge within the garden. Originally from the Mediterranean, it will grow perfectly well in sandy or poor to moderately fertile soils, as long as they are well drained. Plants actually flower much better in poor soil, but they must be placed in bright sunshine. Plants tend to become tall and leggy and sometimes simply collapse because the brittle root system cannot support them. On exposed, windy sites they do far better if they are grown as wall shrubs.

The most commonly grown plant is *Rosmarinus officinalis* or one of its many cultivars. The species forms a dense, bushy shrub about 5 feet high and across with an upright habit. The species and most of the cultivars have thin, straplike, aromatic, leathery leaves, dark-green on the upper side and covered in a white felt on the underside. The cultivar *R. officinalis* 'Aureus' has mottled green and yellow foliage. The small, tubular, aromatic flowers are produced along the stem in small groups of up to three from midspring until early summer and again in fall. Flower colors range from the most common purple-blue to bright blue, pink, and white.

Rosmarinus officinalis *forms a bushy shrub with an erect habit and tangled branches. The plant often opens in the center as it ages, causing the branches to split and snap away. The thin, twiggy branches are densely covered with narrow, dark-green, leathery leaves that are aromatic and slightly felty on the underside. From midspring until early summer and again in the fall, small, pale-blue, tubular flowers are produced along the stem in groups of up to three.*

Formative pruning

On the whole, plants should be allowed to develop naturally. Pruning may be necessary to prevent them from becoming unbalanced.

After planting, remove any weak or damaged growth. Cut back any excessively vigorous shoots.

WHY PRUNE?

To promote balanced growth.

PRUNING TIPS

• To avoid crushing the stems, use a pruning saw for remedial pruning.

PLANTS PRUNED THIS WAY

Rosmarinus officinalis *and cvs.: in late summer, after flowering*
Santolina spp. and cvs.: *in late summer, after flowering*

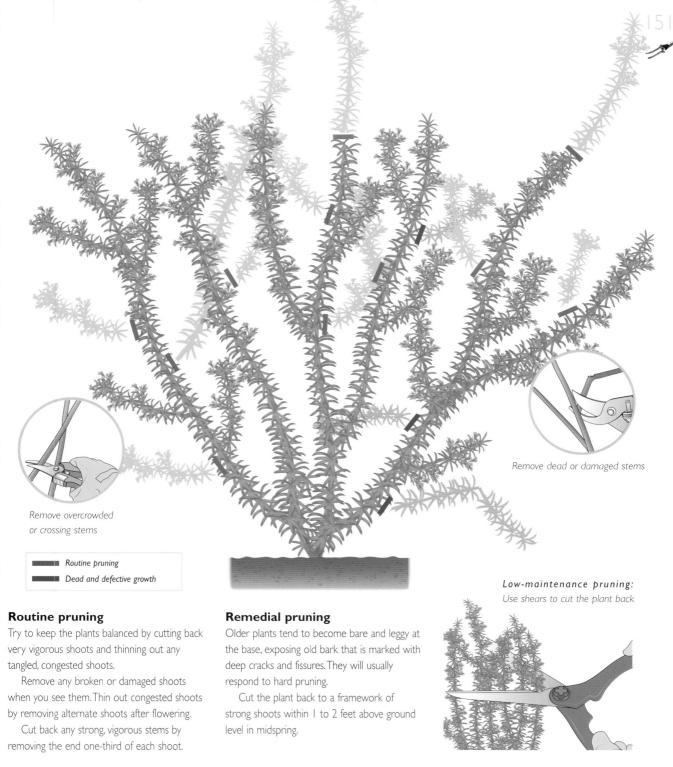

Remove overcrowded
or crossing stems

Remove dead or damaged stems

	Routine pruning
	Dead and defective growth

Low-maintenance pruning:
Use shears to cut the plant back

Routine pruning

Try to keep the plants balanced by cutting back
very vigorous shoots and thinning out any
tangled, congested shoots.

Remove any broken or damaged shoots
when you see them. Thin out congested shoots
by removing alternate shoots after flowering.

Cut back any strong, vigorous stems by
removing the end one-third of each shoot.

Remedial pruning

Older plants tend to become bare and leggy at
the base, exposing old bark that is marked with
deep cracks and fissures. They will usually
respond to hard pruning.

Cut the plant back to a framework of
strong shoots within 1 to 2 feet above ground
level in midspring.

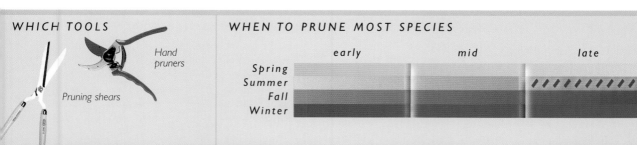

WHICH TOOLS

Hand
pruners

Pruning shears

WHEN TO PRUNE MOST SPECIES

	early	mid	late
Spring			
Summer			
Fall			
Winter			

Salix
Willow

Willows are often grown for their vividly colored stems or for their eye-catching, variegated foliage. Some forms have attractive flowers (catkins), while others are selected for their lax weeping habit or contorted stems and leaves.

The plants in this large genus include a number of trees and shrubs that are often associated with wet or waterlogged soils, although they will quite happily grow in a wider range of conditions and soils than most gardeners realize. Many willows are vigorous, and they must always have plenty of room to grow to their natural shape.

These resilient trees and shrubs exhibit a wide range of leaf shapes from round to oval with a covering of thick, downy material to smooth, long, and spear or strap shaped, arranged in spirals around the stem. The flowers (catkins) also vary in color from pale yellow to a blackish purple, and in size from ½ inch to 7 inches long—all producing copious quantities of pollen. The wood of willows is quite soft, sometimes brittle, which means that breaking and splitting branches can be a problem, as can dieback of apparently healthy shoots. Although most garden shrub willows are grown as multistemmed plants for the attractive colors produced by the new bark, one or two forms are grafted onto a rootstock, and suckers may be a problem.

Formative pruning

Try to encourage the development of a multistemmed plant with strong shoots forming close to ground level.

Plants that are to be coppiced (stooled) are cut back hard—to within about 6 inches—after planting in winter or early spring. This will encourage new shoots to develop from the base of the plant as it becomes established.

Plants that are to be pollarded are left for the first year to grow a single stem about 3 feet high. Then the growing point is removed in winter or early spring to encourage new shoots to develop from the top of this 3-foot high leg as the plant becomes established.

WHY PRUNE?

To restrict the plant's height and to promote the production of new, brightly colored shoots.

PRUNING TIPS

• *Start pruning just as the buds start to grow.*
• *Use bypass pruners because anvil-type pruners will easily crush the stems.*

PLANTS PRUNED THIS WAY

Cornus alba *and cvs.: in midspring*
Cornus sanguinea *and cvs.: in midspring*
Cornus stolonifera*: in midspring*
Salix alba *and cvs.: in early spring; remove deadwood in summer*
Salix daphnoides*: in early spring; remove deadwood in summer*
Salix purpurea *and cvs.: in early spring; remove deadwood in summer*

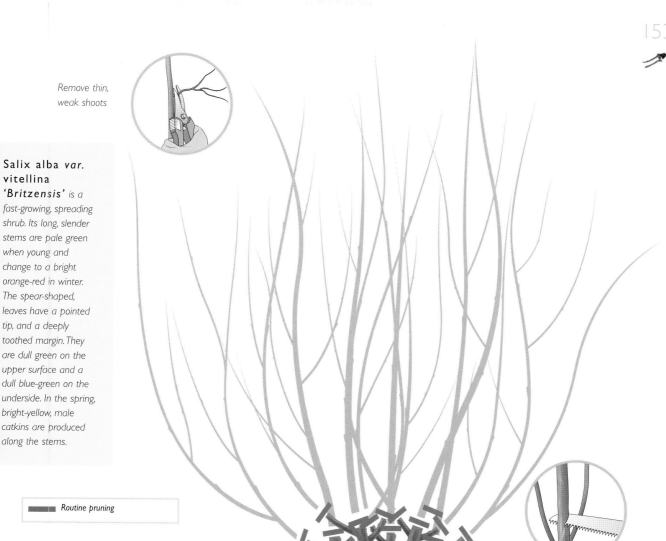

Remove thin, weak shoots

Salix alba *var.* vitellina 'Britzensis' *is a fast-growing, spreading shrub. Its long, slender stems are pale green when young and change to a bright orange-red in winter. The spear-shaped, leaves have a pointed tip, and a deeply toothed margin. They are dull green on the upper surface and a dull blue-green on the underside. In the spring, bright-yellow, male catkins are produced along the stems.*

▬▬ Routine pruning

Remove old stems

Routine pruning

If they are to produce the most attractive winter colors, these plants need regular annual pruning to remove old wood and encourage new shoots. Pruning should cut out any weak or thin shoots.

In spring, cut back the 1-year-old stems as close to the old branch framework as possible. This will leave stubs of growth 1 to 2 inches long, from which the new shoots will emerge.

If the old stubs of growth have become overcrowded, remove them with a small pruning saw.

Remedial pruning

Willows that are left unpruned tend to become thick and overcrowded, with a dense mass of thin, weak, straggly stems that produce poor color and look particularly unattractive. The plant will also be more susceptible to pests and diseases. This can be overcome by hard pruning, which can be done in stages over 2 to 3 years or by cutting down the plant completely.

In winter, cut back all the old stems as close to the old branch framework as possible, using a saw if necessary. Leave stubs 1 to 2 inches long, from which the new shoots will emerge.

In late spring, completely remove any thin or weak shoots. Cut out any branches that are rubbing or crossing over each other.

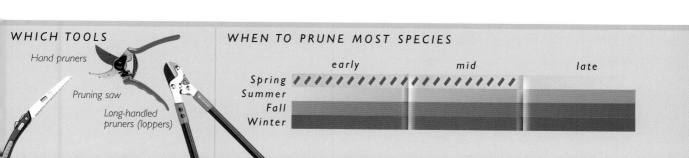

WHICH TOOLS

Hand pruners

Pruning saw

Long-handled pruners (loppers)

WHEN TO PRUNE MOST SPECIES

	early	mid	late
Spring			
Summer			
Fall			
Winter			

Sambucus
Elderberry, elder

*Striking foliage, flowers, and berries make elderberries good-value shrubs
and trees, especially at home in mixed borders and woodland-style gardens.*

Elderberries are among the easiest garden
shrubs you can grow. They will thrive in a
wide range of growing conditions and
soils and will even tolerate a fair amount
of neglect. They are usually grown for
their attractive berries and brightly
colored foliage, which is much larger and
bolder when plants are coppiced. Elders
will grow in partial shade or full sun, but
for the best leaf color they need a
position in dappled shade. The stems are
hollow, and in a wet season some may
bend and topple over as the base of the
stem collapses—these shoots often form
roots where they touch the soil.

These resilient plants can grow up to
10 feet in a single season, and in the right
conditions they often form large clumps
as they establish and spread. The leaves
are made up of five broadly oval segments
arranged in a handlike structure held on
midgreen stems, which turn light brown
and develop a corky texture as they age.
There is a wide range of leaf colors
available, including golden yellow and
purple, and some cultivars have gold and
silver variegation. The cut-leaf form
Sambucus racemosa 'Plumosa Aurea' has
finely cut, gold-colored leaves, which are
bronze when young. From midspring to
early summer, white or pink-tinged
flowers are carried in broad, flat clusters
on the shoot tips, followed by red or
black berries in late summer.

**Sambucus racemosa
*'Plumosa Aurea'*** *is a vigorous,
fast-growing shrub with midgreen stems
that turn light brown with a corky
texture as they age. The finely cut,
golden-yellow leaves are bronze when
young. Each leaf has a deeply toothed
margin and is made up of five broadly
oval segments arranged in a palmlike
structure. In midspring, creamy-yellow
flowers are carried in cone-shaped
clusters on the shoot tips, followed by
red berries in summer.*

Formative pruning

Try to develop a multistemmed plant, with
strong shoots forming close to ground level.

In the winter or early spring after planting,
cut plants back hard—to about 6 inches. At the
same time, remove any thin, weak shoots to
encourage new shoots to grow from the base
of the plant.

WHY PRUNE?

To encourage new, attractive foliage.

PRUNING TIPS

• *Cut close to the buds to prevent
dieback.*

PLANTS PRUNED THIS WAY

Cornus alba *and cvs.: in midspring*
Cornus sanguinea *and cvs.: in midspring*
Salix *spp. and cvs.: in midspring*
Sambucus nigra *and cvs.: in winter*
Sambucus racemosa *and cvs.: in winter*

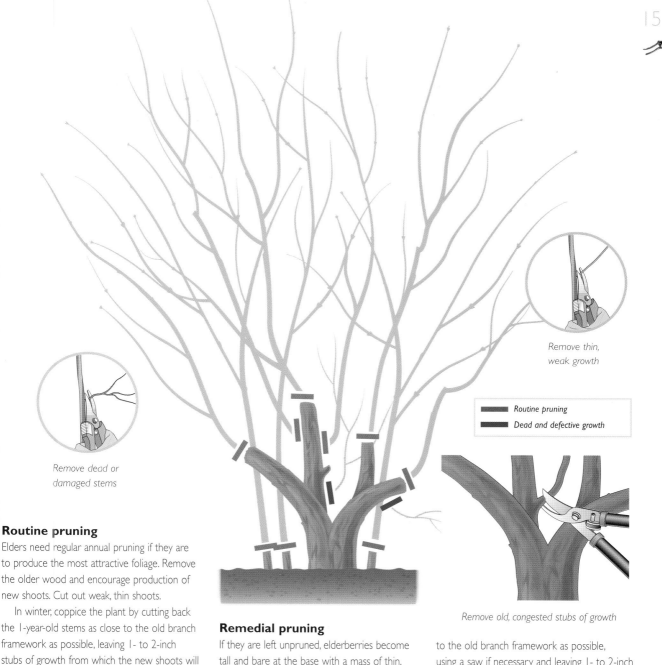

Remove thin, weak growth

Routine pruning	
Dead and defective growth	

Remove dead or damaged stems

Remove old, congested stubs of growth

Routine pruning

Elders need regular annual pruning if they are to produce the most attractive foliage. Remove the older wood and encourage production of new shoots. Cut out weak, thin shoots.

In winter, coppice the plant by cutting back the 1-year-old stems as close to the old branch framework as possible, leaving 1- to 2-inch stubs of growth from which the new shoots will emerge. Alternatively, remove older growth and cut 1-year-old stems by one-third.

If the old stubs of growth become overcrowded, remove them with a small pruning saw.

Remedial pruning

If they are left unpruned, elderberries become tall and bare at the base with a mass of thin, weak, straggly stems that produce poor foliage size and color. This can be overcome with hard pruning, which involves cutting the plant down completely.

In winter, cut back all the old stems as close to the old branch framework as possible, using a saw if necessary and leaving 1- to 2-inch stubs of growth from which the new shoots will emerge.

In late spring, completely remove any thin or weak new shoots.

WHICH TOOLS

Hand pruners

Pruning saw

Long-handled pruners (loppers)

WHEN TO PRUNE MOST SPECIES

	early	mid	late
Spring			
Summer			
Fall			
Winter			

Spiraea 'Arguta'

Bridal wreath, foam of May

This hardy shrub often bears so many flowers that they appear to be a layer of foam coating the leaves, giving the plant one of its common names, foam of May.

This medium-size, hardy, deciduous shrub is one of the easiest plants to grow. It has light-green, broadly oval leaves, which are carried on light-brown stems that turn dark brown and eventually dull gray as they age. In mid- to late spring it can be covered with a display of clusters of small, white flowers, which are carried on the tips of shoots formed in the previous year.

A versatile plant, it will grow in a wide range of soil types, getting to 10 feet high and across and forming a broadly dome-shaped bush. It eventually forms a dense, bushy thicket, especially if left unpruned, and its natural habit of growth means that it needs regular annual pruning if it's to flower to its full potential.

Formative pruning

Young plants should be pruned to encourage a bushy shape with strong shoots emerging from soil level.

After planting, remove any old growth. Cut back the remaining shoots to about half their length to encourage the development of new shoots from the base of the plant as it becomes established.

Spiraea 'Arguta' forms a dense, rounded shrub with a bushy habit and long, arching branches. It is clad with broad, oval-shaped, bright-green leaves with deeply toothed margins. In spring, masses of small, white flowers are produced in short spikes on the tips of the young shoots and side branches of the previous season's growth. In the fall, the leaves will turn pale orange and yellow before falling.

Routine pruning

If it's to flower well, this plant needs regular annual pruning to remove the old wood, which would gradually accumulate, and encourage the production of new flower-bearing shoots.

Cut back the old flower-bearing stems as close to the ground as possible in early summer to allow the maximum period of

---

WHY PRUNE?

To restrict the plant's height and to encourage it to develop a bushy habit.

PRUNING TIPS

• *Start pruning before the new shoots form so that you don't lose next year's flowers.*
• *Use bypass pruners because anvil-type pruners will easily crush the stems.*

PLANTS PRUNED THIS WAY

Dipelta *spp. and cvs.: in midsummer, after flowering*
Forsythia *spp. and cvs.: in mid- to late spring, after flowering*
Kerria japonica *and cvs.: in late spring, after flowering*
Spiraea nipponica: *in early summer, after flowering*
Spiraea japonica: *in very early spring*
Spiraea x vanhouttei: *in late spring, after flowering*
Weigela florida *and cvs.: in midsummer, after flowering*

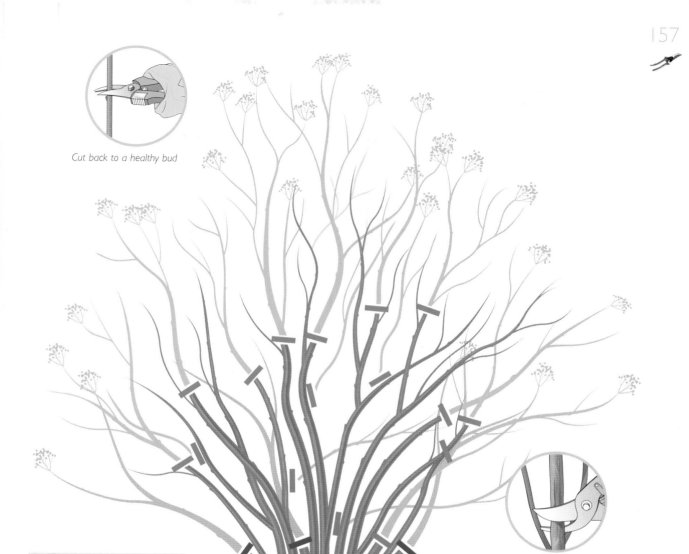

Cut back to a healthy bud

Remove old stems

| | Routine pruning |
| | Dead and defective growth |

growth to produce a good display of flowers the following year.

Prune old flower-bearing stems at least halfway along their length, cutting to just above a healthy bud or to a well-placed new sideshoot.

Try to remove about one-quarter of the old stems each year to allow in light and make room for new shoots to develop.

Remedial pruning

Spiraea 'Arguta' tends to become thick and overcrowded as it ages, especially if the pruning has been neglected, and the resulting thicket of thin, weak, straggly stems will produce few flowers and leave the plant susceptible to pests and diseases. This can be overcome by hard pruning, which must be done in stages rather than by

simply cutting the plant down completely.

Leaving three or four strong stems, in early summer cut the remaining shoots back to within 2 to 3 inches of ground level to encourage new replacement shoots to develop. The following year, completely remove any thin or weak shoots. Cut out the three or four remaining old stems close to ground level.

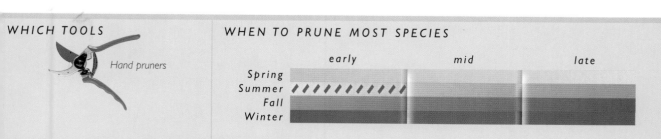

WHICH TOOLS

Hand pruners

WHEN TO PRUNE MOST SPECIES

	early	mid	late
Spring			
Summer			
Fall			
Winter			

Syringa
Lilac

You can always rely on lilac to provide a stunning display of late-spring blooms. They are easy-to-grow shrubs that seem to do particularly well in town gardens.

Most lilacs are cultivars of *Syringa vulgaris*. The small, tubular, often fragrant flowers are carried in large, pyramidal spikes on the tips of young shoots in late spring and early summer. There are forms with flowers in white and shades of pink, red-purple, blue, and blue-pink. The deciduous leaves, which are arranged in opposite pairs on the stems, are broadly oval to heart shaped and usually midgreen in color, sometimes with bronze tints when young and often paler on the underside. Many plants develop an erect habit when young, often becoming open centered and bare at the base as they age. Mature trees may grow to 20 feet high and wide. They prefer a fertile, moist but well-drained, neutral to alkaline soil and a position in full sun or partial shade. They are shallow-rooted plants and always grow better if they are mulched regularly.

Syringa pubescens subsp. microphylla is a large shrub with an erect habit, becoming open and spreading with age. Its many thin, twiggy branches have brownish-gray bark and its leaves are broadly oval to lance shaped. These are glossy dark green in color, paler on the underside, and arranged in opposite pairs on the stems. In early summer, small, lilac, highly fragrant flowers are carried in spikes on the tips of young shoots.

Formative pruning

Prune young plants to encourage them to develop a bushy habit, with strong shoots emerging from just above soil level. These shoots can be trained as a framework onto a supporting structure.

In the first spring after planting, cut out any weak or damaged stems. Prune the tips of the main shoots by removing the end one-third of each.

WHY PRUNE?

To promote flowering and to encourage development of new shoots.

PRUNING TIPS

• *Most lilacs flower on buds formed the previous season. If you choose to remove the fading flowers, take care not to damage the new growth because that produces next year's blooms.*

PLANTS PRUNED THIS WAY

Syringa vulgaris and cvs.: *in midsummer, after flowering*
Syringa x josiflexa: *in midsummer, after flowering*
Syringa x prestoniae: *in midsummer, after flowering*
Syringa x hyacinthiflora: *in midsummer, after flowering*

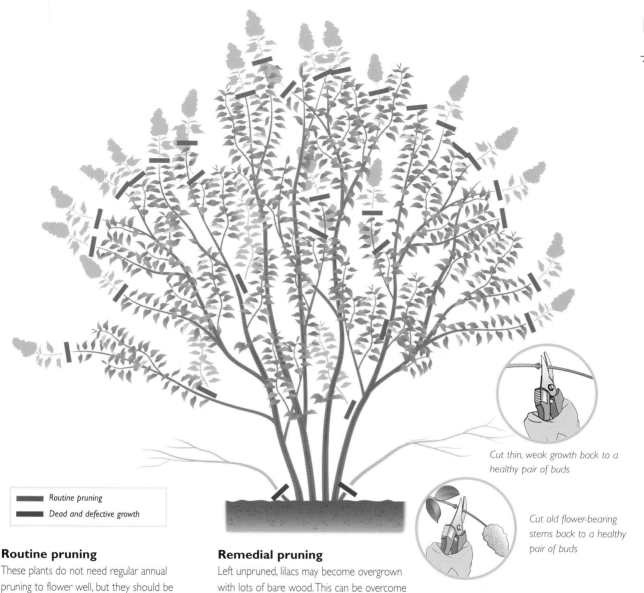

Routine pruning
Dead and defective growth

Cut thin, weak growth back to a healthy pair of buds

Cut old flower-bearing stems back to a healthy pair of buds

Routine pruning

These plants do not need regular annual pruning to flower well, but they should be pruned to avoid long, straggly stems with lots of bare wood and to encourage production of new flower-bearing shoots.

Immediately after flowering, cut the old flower-bearing stems back to a strong pair of buds. This will give the maximum period of growth to produce a good display of flowers the following year.

Cut back any thin, weak, or overcrowded shoots to a strong pair of buds.

Remedial pruning

Left unpruned, lilacs may become overgrown with lots of bare wood. This can be overcome by hard pruning.

In winter, cut half of the old stems back to within 18 inches of soil level. Cut out any thin, weak, or unwanted shoots.

In the second year, completely cut out any thin or weak shoots and remove any old branches that remain from the previous year.

Lilacs are sometimes grafted onto a rootstock. If you know your lilac is grafted, remove any suckers as soon as they are about

12 inches long, or large enough to handle, removing them as close to the main root as possible. Suckers on ungrafted lilacs can be used to rejuvenate the shrub.

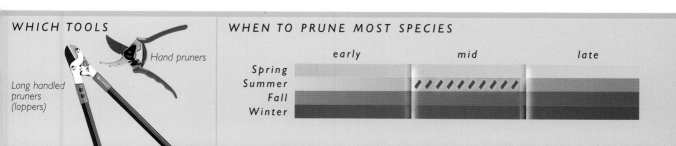

WHICH TOOLS

Hand pruners

Long handled pruners (loppers)

WHEN TO PRUNE MOST SPECIES

	early	mid	late
Spring			
Summer		/////////	
Fall			
Winter			

Taxus

English yew, yew

These hardy, long-lived, evergreen plants are especially valued as freestanding specimen trees, but they are also excellent hedging and screening plants.

Yews are often grown to give a garden year-round structure. Some plants have an upright habit, while some of the prostrate forms make excellent groundcover. They vary in height from 70 feet to as low as about 3 feet, and spread from 30 feet to a little over 6 feet across. It is better to select a cultivar with the desired mature height and width than to annually shear a large shrub. The foliage is composed of small, narrow, straplike leaves, about 1 inch long and usually a glossy, dark green on the upper surface and paler on the underside. There are also some attractive cultivars with golden and variegated leaves, but these are usually less vigorous than the green types. They are resilient plants that will grow in almost any well-drained, fertile soil. They will tolerate dry shade, exposure, and even urban pollution, making them popular in city gardens. They also display a remarkable tolerance to pests and diseases.

Unlike most other conifers, yews will reshoot if you cut back to old wood.

Taxus baccata 'Fastigiata Aurea' is an erect, evergreen shrub with a narrow, columnar habit. Its golden-yellow young shoots turn rich grayish brown on mature parts of the plant. The foliage is made up of small, narrow, straplike leaves with gold markings, often paler in color on the underside. This plant is female and will produce rich red fruits.

Formative pruning

Young plants require only light pruning to develop into multistemmed plants (which yews naturally form anyway), with strong shoots forming an evenly balanced framework.

In late spring, remove any damaged shoots. Cut back any shoots that are growing across the center of the plants. Prune the remaining shoots lightly by removing the end one-third of each shoot. Cut back vigorous shoots by about half to keep the growth even and balanced.

WHY PRUNE?

To promote even, balanced growth and to remove damaged stems.

PRUNING TIPS

• *Don't prune in late fall, because young growths will be damaged by frosts.*

PLANTS PRUNED THIS WAY

Taxus spp. and cvs.: *in mid- to late spring*
Thuja spp. and cvs.: *in mid- to late spring, will not tolerate remedial pruning*
Tsuga spp. and cvs.: *in mid- to late spring, will not tolerate remedial pruning*

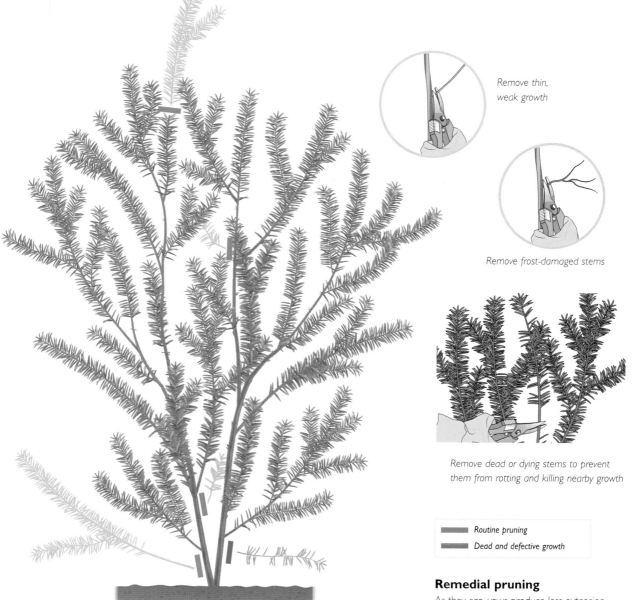

Remove thin, weak growth

Remove frost-damaged stems

Remove dead or dying stems to prevent them from rotting and killing nearby growth

▬▬ Routine pruning
▬▬ Dead and defective growth

Routine pruning

Yews tolerate shearing and are therefore thought of primarily as hedge plants. If possible, though, it is better to remove selected shoots with hand pruners than it is to shear the plants; cut back vigorous shoots to balance the growth and shape of the plant. Cut vigorous stems back at least halfway along their length to just above a healthy bud or to a well-placed sideshoot. Remove any thin, weak growth from the center of the plant.

Remove any new growth that has been damaged by late frosts.

Remedial pruning

As they age, yews produce less extension growth at the tip of each shoot and slowly increase in overall size. At the same time, they may become bare and straggly at the base, or the branches may splay out, leaving an open center.

In late spring, cut all the stems back to 18 to 24 inches above soil level. Cut any side branches back to within 1 inch of the stems. In summer, remove any thin, overcrowded shoots.

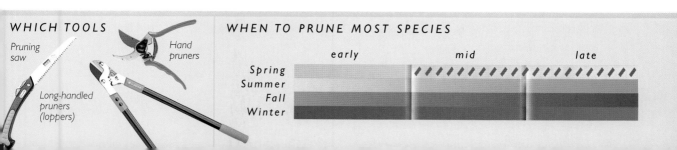

WHICH TOOLS

Pruning saw
Hand pruners
Long-handled pruners (loppers)

WHEN TO PRUNE MOST SPECIES

	early	mid	late
Spring			
Summer			
Fall			
Winter			

Vaccinium
Blueberry

These attractive, deciduous shrubs are close relatives of heathers and pieris and complement them very well with their displays of flowers and fruits. Deciduous forms also produce attractive fall leaf color.

The small, leathery-textured leaves are broadly oval in shape with a slightly toothed margin and usually mid- to dark green in color. They are arranged along reddish-green young stems that turn brownish green with age. These plants have a low, spreading habit; they often grow to less than 3 feet high but spread many feet over the ground, making them much valued as groundcover plants in gardens.

Small, bell- to urn-shaped flowers are produced along the stem or at the end of each shoot in midspring until midsummer. These are colored greenish white, white, or shades of pink or red, and are followed by brightly colored berries in the fall. To grow at all, these plants must have a moist to damp, free-draining, light peaty, or sandy soil with full sun or partial shade. Alternatively they can be grown in containers if the garden soil is unsuitable.

Vaccinium corymbosum *(pictured in fall) is a medium-size shrub with a dense thicket of thin, spindly, reddish-green branches. The small, leathery leaves are midgreen in color and broadly oval in shape, with a slightly toothed margin. They turn vivid reds and oranges in fall. In late spring and early summer, small, white, urn-shaped flowers are produced along the stem, followed by bluish-black berries in the fall.*

WHY PRUNE?

To maintain plant health and vigor and for fruit production.

PRUNING TIPS

• For groundcover plants, use shears for light pruning.

PLANTS PRUNED THIS WAY

Ribes spp *and* **cvs.:** *in late winter*
Vaccinium angustifolium: *in late winter*
Vaccinium corymbosum: *in late winter*

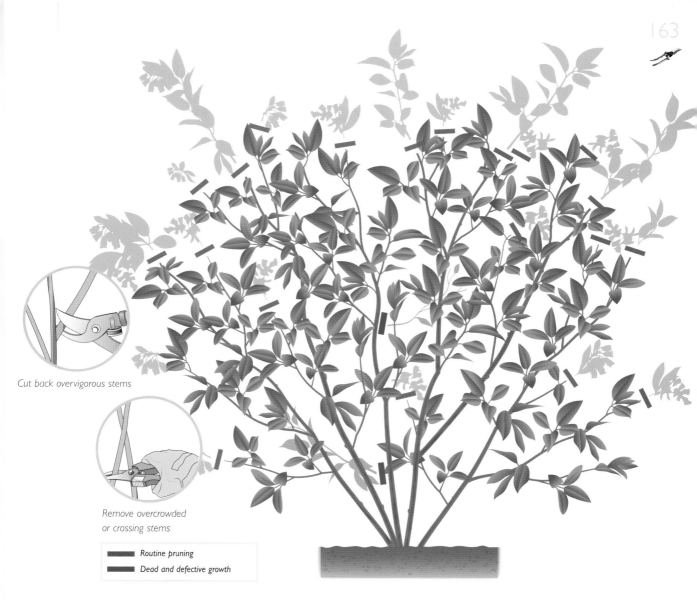

Cut back overvigorous stems

Remove overcrowded
or crossing stems

▬▬	Routine pruning
▬▬	Dead and defective growth

Formative pruning

Prune young plants to encourage them to
develop a bushy habit, with strong shoots
emerging from just above soil level.

After planting, remove any weak or
damaged growth and cut back the remaining
shoots to about half their length to encourage
the growth of new shoots at the base of
the plant.

Routine pruning

Try to produce a compact, bushy framework.
Encourage new shoots to prevent the plant
from becoming bare at the base.

In late winter, trim back any long, vigorous
shoots and remove any congested growth.

Remedial pruning

These shrubs become overcrowded as they age,
with a lot of thin, weak, straggly stems producing
fewer, smaller flowers. This can be overcome by
hard pruning, but the following season's flowers
and fruit will be lost.

In late winter or early spring, cut the old,
strong shoots back to within 4 to 6 inches of
ground level, and cut out any thin, weak growth
to encourage the growth of new shoots.

WHICH TOOLS

Hand pruners

Long-handled
pruners
(loppers)

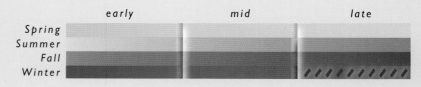

WHEN TO PRUNE MOST SPECIES

	early	mid	late
Spring			
Summer			
Fall			
Winter			//////////

Viburnum (deciduous species)
Viburnum

Viburnums are ideal for small gardens, offering year-round interest from the foliage, flowers, and fruit. They are also easy to grow.

The genus contains both deciduous and evergreen species (see pages 166 and 167). Deciduous forms are grown for their often-fragrant flowers, brightly colored fruits, and the attractive display from the autumn foliage. They prefer to grow in moist, well-drained, fertile soil and will do best in a position in full sun or partial shade. On the whole, viburnums will grow in a wide range of soils. They are versatile and can be grown as freestanding specimens or used to add fragrance and color to a mixed border at a time of year when the number of shrubs in flower is limited.

Deciduous viburnums are fairly diverse, offering a range of growth habits and sizes. Most have oval to round leaves with toothed margins. They are dark-green in color, often slightly bronzed when young, and are arranged in opposite pairs along thin, woody stems. The small, tubular flowers are borne in dense clusters along the often-bare stems in winter and spring or with the foliage in early summer. Colors range from white through a wide range of shades of pink, and most are strongly scented. The flowers are often followed by round fruits, which are usually orange, red, or blue-black.

Viburnum plicatum f. **tomentosum** *'Mariesii' forms a spreading, bushy shrub with tiered layers of branches. The stems have light-brown bark and the deciduous, dark-green leaves are heart shaped with a toothed margin and deeply veined surface. They often turn orange and yellow before dropping in fall. In late spring, broad, flat clusters of saucer-shaped white flowers are produced on the tips of shoots and branches.*

Formative pruning
Plants should be allowed to develop naturally. Pruning may be necessary to prevent them from becoming unbalanced.

After planting, cut out any weak or damaged growth. Cut back any excessively vigorous shoots.

WHY PRUNE?
To promote a well-balanced, open shape and the production of new stems.

PRUNING TIPS
• *Do not deadhead if you want a display of fruits.*

PLANTS PRUNED THIS WAY
Viburnum carlesii: *in late winter*
Viburnum dentatum: *in late winter*
Viburnum dilatatum: *in late winter*
Viburnum farreri: *in late winter*
Viburnum x juddii: *in late winter*
Viburnum opulus: *in late winter*
Viburnum trilobum: *in late winter*

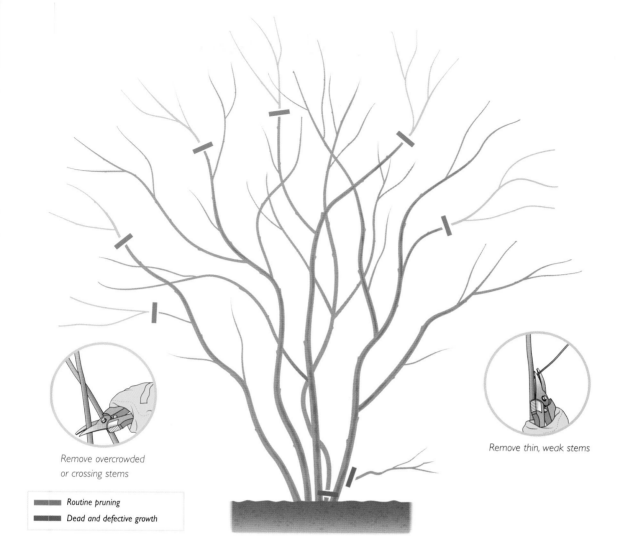

Remove overcrowded
or crossing stems

Remove thin, weak stems

███ Routine pruning
███ Dead and defective growth

Routine pruning

Many viburnums are grown for their berries; it's important to note that if they are deadheaded, the plants will not produce berries. Prune viburnums to control size, or to remove the old wood that would gradually accumulate, and to encourage new flower-bearing shoots.

Viburnums require only light pruning, so remove about one-fifth of the old stems each year to allow light in and to make room for new shoots.

Cut out any thin, weak shoots and any congested, crossing branches to reduce rubbing.

Remedial pruning

If they are left unpruned, viburnums can become overcrowded, with a mass of thin, weak, straggly stems that produce poor stem color and make them susceptible to pests and diseases. This can be overcome by cutting the plant down completely.

In late spring, cut back all old stems close to ground level, using a saw if necessary and leaving 1- to 2-inch stubs of woody stem from which the new shoots will emerge.

In summer, completely remove any thin or weak shoots.

Do not deadhead if berries are desired

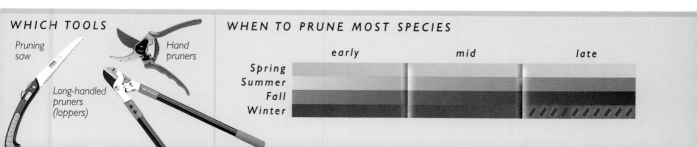

WHICH TOOLS

Pruning saw

Hand pruners

Long-handled pruners (loppers)

WHEN TO PRUNE MOST SPECIES

	early	mid	late
Spring			
Summer			
Fall			
Winter			

Viburnum
(evergreen and semievergreen species)
Viburnum

Evergreen and semievergreen viburnums have glossy green leaves, which provide a handsome background for the fragrant flowers.

Viburnums will grow in a wide range of soils, but they prefer well-drained, fertile soil and full sun or partial shade. The evergreen forms have tough-looking foliage, but they must have shelter from chilling winds in winter and spring because the new shoots are susceptible to frost damage. They are easy to grow and make excellent freestanding specimens. Alternatively, they can add structure and fragrance to a mixed border or grown as wall shrubs. The great diversity of plant type and habit means that there is at least one viburnum to suit your garden.

The evergreen viburnums often have large, leathery leaves, which can be attractive in their own right. In addition to glossy green foliage, purple or even cream- and green-variegated leaves can appear. Many plants have flowers that are stunning for both their color and their fragrance. Colors range from white to shades of deep pink, although it's worth noting that the whites and paler shades often have the most fragrant blooms. Individual flowers are small, but they are usually arranged in large clusters that make them hard to ignore. The flowers are followed by red changing to blue-black fruits.

Viburnum davidii *is a low, spreading, bushy shrub with a dome-shaped habit. The evergreen, dark-green leaves are oval shaped with a toothed margin and deeply veined surface. They have a tough leathery texture. Tiny, tubular, white flowers carried in broad, flat clusters are produced on the tips of shoots and branches in late spring. These are followed by bluish-black berries later in the year.*

Formative pruning

Try to develop a multistemmed plant, with strong shoots forming close to ground level.

In the spring after planting, lightly prune the shoots by removing about one-third of each shoot. This will encourage stocky, bushy plants.

Cut back vigorous shoots by about half their length to keep the plant's growth even and balanced.

WHY PRUNE?

To maintain a well-balanced, open shape and to encourage the production of new stems.

PRUNING TIPS

• *Keep a watch for sucker growth and remove it as soon as possible.*

PLANTS PRUNED THIS WAY

Viburnum betulifolium: *in spring, after flowering*
Viburnum x burkwoodii: *in summer, after flowering*
Viburnum davidii: *in summer, after flowering*
Viburnum rhytidophyllum: *in summer, after flowering*
Viburnum tinus: *in summer, after flowering*

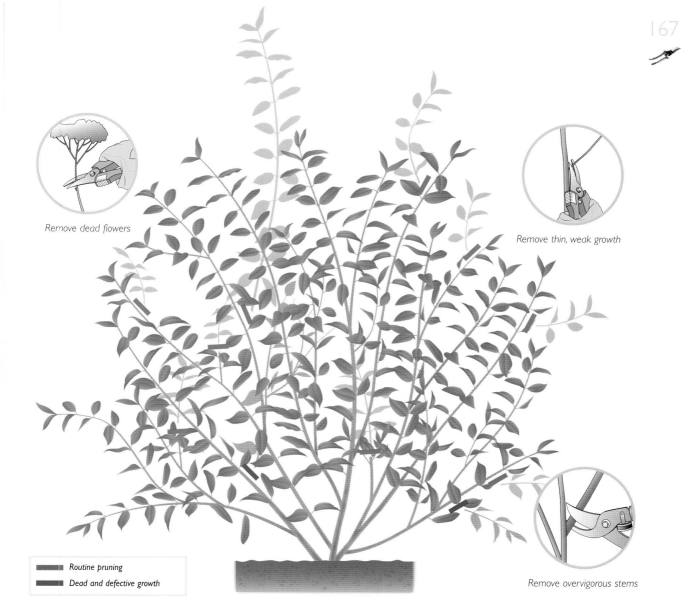

Remove dead flowers

Remove thin, weak growth

Remove overvigorous stems

▬▬▬	*Routine pruning*
▬▬▬	*Dead and defective growth*

Routine pruning

These plants do not require regular pruning to keep growing well, but they will do better if any vigorous shoots are pruned back to balance the growth and shape.

After flowering, the plant can be deadheaded by cutting the old flower-bearing clusters back to a strong bud or down to lower, stronger shoots. Many viburnums are grown for their berries; it's important to note that if they are deadheaded, the plants will not produce berries.

Prune vigorous stems to at least half their length, cutting back to just above a healthy bud or to a well-placed sideshoot. Remove any thin, weak growth emerging from the center of the plant.

Remedial pruning

As they age, these plants become congested and produce fewer flowers. They often become bare and straggly at the base.

In late spring, cut all the main stems back to 1 to 2 feet above ground level. Remove any thin, overcrowded, or crossing shoots.

WHICH TOOLS

Pruning saw

Hand pruners

Long-handled pruners (loppers)

WHEN TO PRUNE MOST SPECIES

	early	mid	late
Spring			
Summer			
Fall			
Winter			

Vitis

Grape vine, vine

This is one of the most rewarding climbers to grow if you want a display of fiery fall colors. Before they drop, the leaves of these vigorous plants turn to brilliant shades of red, crimson, or bright purple.

The best-known members of the genus are the cultivars of *Vitis vinifera* (grape vine), which are grown for fruits that are either eaten or turned into wine. But there are several ornamental vines, grown for their attractive, colorful leaves. These vines are ideal for covering an archway, pergola, wall, or fence, and some forms will even grow up into the tops of large trees. Vines have large, heart-shaped or lobed leaves, which are usually green or purple, with toothed margins. The leaves are held on vigorous stems, which are green when young, maturing to gray-brown and eventually covered in deep

layers of flaking bark as they age. The plants support themselves by means of strong, woody tendrils, which wrap around support structures and enable them to grow to 50 feet high. The small fruits of the cultivar 'Fragola' taste like strawberries.

Ornamental vines prefer well-drained, slightly alkaline soil and will happily grow in full sun or partial shade.

Formative pruning

Prune young plants to encourage them to develop a framework of strong shoots emerging from just above soil level.

In the first winter after planting, remove any weak or damaged growth, cutting back to a strong, healthy bud 18 inches above ground level. As the new shoots develop, select three or four of the strongest ones for training into the supporting structure.

In the second winter, cut the tips of these shoots back by about one-quarter and train them into the support structure. Cut any thin shoots back to one or two buds and remove the weakest shoots altogether.

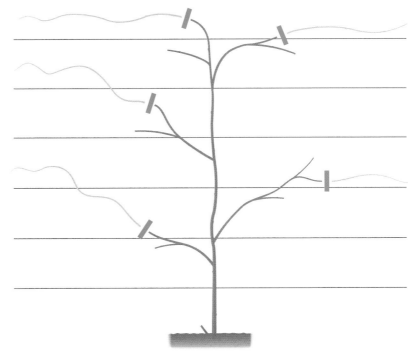

Formative pruning: Second winter

WHY PRUNE?

To produce balanced growth, to control vigor, and for fruit production.

PRUNING TIPS

• Prune in winter or when the plant is in full leaf to minimize the likelihood of excessive bleeding.

PLANTS PRUNED THIS WAY

Vitis amurensis *and cvs.: in late winter, before sap begins to rise*
Vitis coignetiae *and cvs.: in late winter, before sap begins to rise*
Vitis vinifera *and cvs.: in late winter, before sap begins to rise*

Vitis vinifera *is a vigorous climber with slender, woody, light-brown stems. These stems support themselves by means of tendrils that wrap around support structures, enabling them to grow to great lengths. The leaves are large, with three to five lobes, and usually green. They turn vivid oranges and reds before dropping in the fall. Clusters of grapes often follow the small, insignificant flowers.*

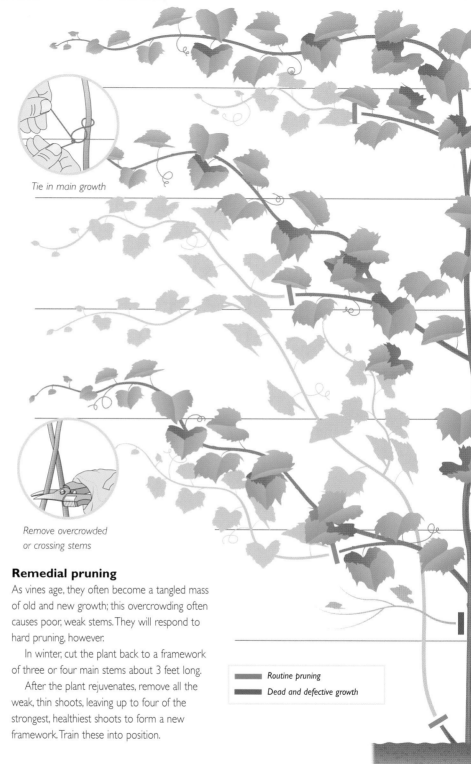

Tie in main growth

Remove overcrowded or crossing stems

▬	Routine pruning
▬	Dead and defective growth

Routine pruning

Try to maintain a framework of strong, healthy shoots and encourage formation of more healthy shoots. Mature plants are also pruned to keep them within their allotted space.

In late winter, shorten the main stems by cutting them back as needed. Tie them into place on the support structure. Cut the sideshoots back to within two or three buds of their point of origin. Remove any shoots that are not needed to prevent overcrowding.

In summer, remove any overcrowded shoots. Cut out any old, bare stems close to ground level to make room for new growth.

Remedial pruning

As vines age, they often become a tangled mass of old and new growth; this overcrowding often causes poor, weak stems. They will respond to hard pruning, however.

In winter, cut the plant back to a framework of three or four main stems about 3 feet long.

After the plant rejuvenates, remove all the weak, thin shoots, leaving up to four of the strongest, healthiest shoots to form a new framework. Train these into position.

WHICH TOOLS

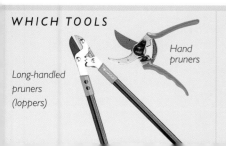

Hand pruners

Long-handled pruners (loppers)

WHEN TO PRUNE MOST SPECIES

	early	mid	late
Spring			
Summer			
Fall			
Winter			

Weigela
Weigela

Weigelas are among the most popular shrubs in the modern garden. They are easy to grow and will perform well over many years with little or no attention. They are often planted close to forsythia, as they flower soon afterward.

Weigelas are deciduous shrubs with an upright to spreading habit, often reaching 6 feet high and 8 feet across when mature. They will grow in any well-drained, fertile soil whether planted in full sun or partial shade, although forms with variegated leaves need full sun to color well. The leaves are broadly oval with toothed margins and are held in opposite pairs on stems that are red when young, changing to green, brown, and eventually gray as they age. The colorful, tubular flowers are borne in late spring and early summer in clusters of up to four blooms on the stems. Colors range from white to green-yellow through shades of pink to dark ruby red. Some cultivars have attractively colored leaves: *Weigela* 'Briant Rubidor' has yellow-green foliage, 'Looymansii Aurea' has golden-yellow leaves, and the popular *W. florida* 'Foliis Purpureis' has bronze-green foliage and outstanding displays of flowers.

Weigela florida *'Briant Rubidor'*
is a deciduous shrub with a lax, spreading habit and slender, pale-brown stems. The bright-yellow leaves are broadly oval shaped with a toothed margin and develop a pale green to yellow edge as they age. They turn orange in fall. The brightly colored, deep-red, tubular flowers are held in clusters of up to four blooms on the stems from late spring until early summer.

WHY PRUNE?

To keep a well-balanced shape and to encourage the plant to develop a bushy habit.

PRUNING TIPS

• *Use bypass hand pruners, because the stems will be easily crushed by anvil-type hand pruners.*

PLANTS PRUNED THIS WAY

Dipelta *spp. and cvs.: in midsummer, after flowering*
Forsythia *spp. and cvs.: in mid- to late spring, after flowering*
Kerria japonica *and cvs.: in late spring, after flowering*
Weigela *ssp. and cvs.: in midsummer, after flowering*

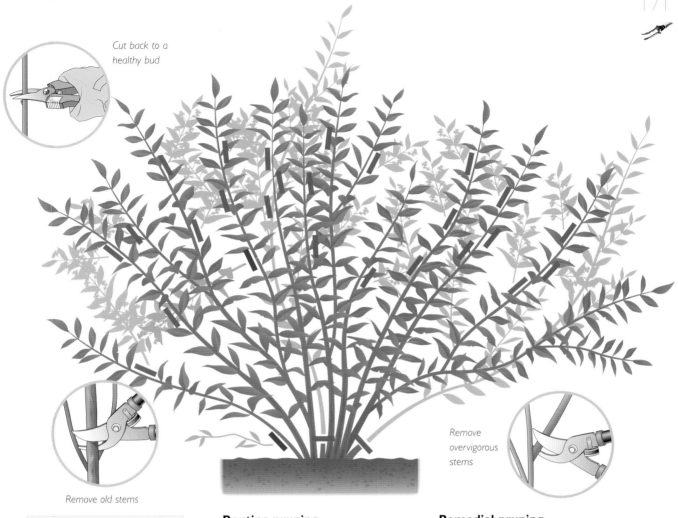

Cut back to a healthy bud

Remove old stems

Remove overvigorous stems

■ Routine pruning
■ Dead and defective growth

Formative pruning

Prune young plants to encourage them to grow bushy, with strong shoots emerging from ground level.

After planting, remove any damaged growth. Cut the remaining shoots back to about half of their length to encourage development of new shoots from the base of the plant as it becomes established.

Routine pruning

If it is to flower well, this plant needs regular annual pruning to remove the old wood that would gradually accumulate, and to encourage production of new flower-bearing shoots.

Cut back old flower-bearing stems at least halfway along their length to just above a healthy bud or to a well-placed new sideshoot. Remove or shorten overvigorous new growth that ruins the shape of the plant.

Aim to remove about one-quarter of the old stems each year to allow in light and make room for new shoots.

Remedial pruning

Weigelas often become thick and congested as they age, with a thicket of thin, weak, straggly stems producing few flowers, especially if the pruning has been neglected. This can be overcome by cutting the plant down completely.

In early spring, cut the old growth back to within 2 to 3 inches of ground level to encourage new shoots to replace the old ones.

In midsummer, completely remove any thin or weak shoots. Prune back the three or four remaining old stems, cutting close to ground level.

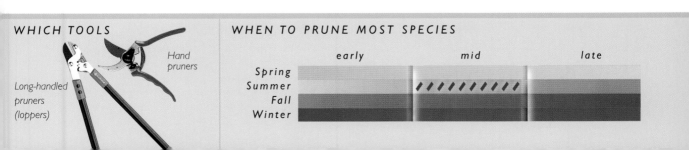

WHICH TOOLS

Hand pruners

Long-handled pruners (loppers)

WHEN TO PRUNE MOST SPECIES

	early	mid	late
Spring			
Summer		/////////	
Fall			
Winter			

Wisteria
Wisteria

Few sights are more impressive than that of a mature wisteria in full flower: The trailing clusters of pealike blooms are one of the highlights of the late spring or summer garden.

But this abundant display does require some attention, and wisteria is best pruned hard twice a year to make sure of the best show of flowers. Its sheer vigor—new shoots can easily grow 12 feet a season—makes it difficult to keep under control, and this is partly to blame for the wariness with which inexperienced gardeners approach the task of pruning wisteria. It really doesn't deserve its reputation as a "difficult" plant to prune, however, as the job is quite straightforward once you grasp a few basic principles.

Wisteria flowers on shoots known as lateral spurs that have developed off main stems the previous year. This is referred to as "flowering on old wood." The aim of pruning is to create the maximum number of well-spaced spurs on a strong and regular framework of branches that will allow the pendulous blooms to hang gracefully without crowding those on the branches below.

All varieties of wisteria flower most profusely in a warm, sunny situation. The plant is at its best grown against a sunny wall, where new shoots are helped to ripen early in the reflected warmth. In this location, the espalier form of training makes the most of the flowers' trailing habit. Fix horizontal support wires to the wall at 15- to 18-inch intervals and at least 2 inches away from the wall for the best effect. Plant the wisteria about 18 inches from the base of the wall and begin training by cutting back the leader immediately after planting. This stimulates the production of sideshoots from which, through successive summer and winter pruning and tying, you will establish a framework of well-spaced, lateral branches studded with flowering spurs to fill the desired area.

Wisteria floribunda *is a vigorous, twining climber with green stems that turn brown and then gray as they mature. The large, midgreen leaves are divided into oval-shaped leaflets, arranged along a central main stalk attached to the stems and branches. In late spring, pealike flowers, bluish pink with white and yellow markings, are produced in dense, hanging clusters. These gradually open down toward the tip and are often followed by grayish-green pods.*

72 inches

36 inches

After planting
Stake and cut back the leader to a healthy bud 3 feet above ground level. Remove all laterals and sideshoots.

First summer pruning
Tie in the vertical leader, then select two strong laterals and tie in at 45 degrees. Prune sideshoots to about 6 inches or three or four buds to begin formation of flowering spurs. Remove any shoots emanating from the base of the plant.

WHY PRUNE?
To create a strong framework for the large, pendulous flowers.

PRUNING TIPS
- *Look at the plant carefully before pruning and decide exactly what it is you want to achieve.*
- *Be brave and decisive. Wisteria is rarely harmed.*

PLANTS PRUNED THIS WAY
Wisteria brachybotrys *and cvs.: in late winter and midsummer, after flowering*
Wisteria floribunda *and cvs.: in late winter and midsummer, after flowering*
Wisteria x formosa *and cvs.: in late winter and midsummer, after flowering*
Wisteria sinensis *and cvs.: in late winter and midsummer, after flowering*

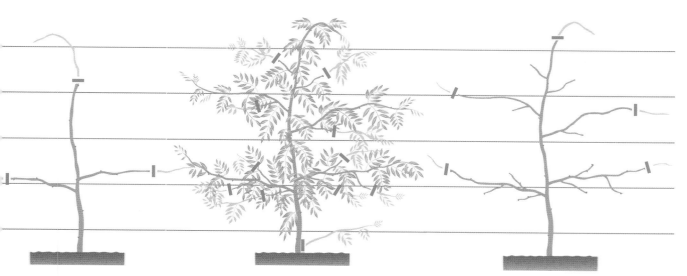

First winter pruning

Cut back leader to about 3 feet above laterals. Pull down laterals previously trained at 45 degrees and tie in horizontally. Cut back by a third of their length.

Second summer pruning

Tie in the leader and horizontal laterals as they grow. Prune sideshoots to three or four buds. Select the next pair of laterals and tie in at a 45-degree angle. Again remove any basal growth.

Second winter pruning

Cut back leader and tie in laterals as in previous winter pruning. Prune back laterals by about a third of their length to ripe wood. Continue this sequence until the available space is covered.

WHICH TOOLS

Hand pruners

Pruning knife

WHEN TO PRUNE MOST SPECIES

	early	mid	late
Spring			
Summer		/////////	
Fall			
Winter			/////////

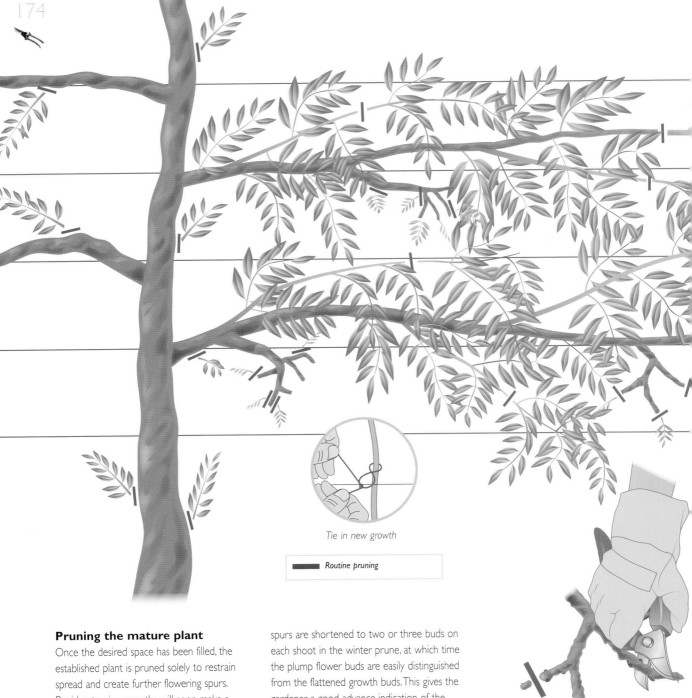

Tie in new growth

▬▬ Routine pruning

Pruning the mature plant

Once the desired space has been filled, the established plant is pruned solely to restrain spread and create further flowering spurs. Rapid extension growths will soon make a tangled mass of whip-like shoots if left uncurtailed, and these must be cut back each summer to form the spurs on which the following year's flowers will appear.

The more frequently these growths are cut back, the more congested the flowering spurs become, and dedicated growers will prune them back to 6 inches every 2 weeks during the summer once flowering has finished. The spurs are shortened to two or three buds on each shoot in the winter prune, at which time the plump flower buds are easily distinguished from the flattened growth buds. This gives the gardener a good advance indication of the following season's flowering potential.

Winter pruning

When the plant is dormant in winter, further shorten the spurs to within 3 to 4 inches of their parent branch, leaving 2 to 3 buds on each spur shoot. Flower buds are plump, dark, and slightly hairy, and are easily distinguished at this stage from the flatter growth buds.

First summer pruning

After all flowering has finished, prune all new shoots back to 6 inches, or four to six leaves, from the main branch. Repeated cutting back of these shoots will result over time in thickly congested spurs producing a profusion of flowers in spring and early summer.

SPECIAL FEATURES

This section includes features on hedging, renovation pruning, and low-maintenance pruning. More specialized pruning techniques such as pollarding, pleaching, and topiary are also discussed. Quick-reference tables show when to prune your plants and a list of plants requiring little or no pruning is provided.

Trees

We plant trees in our gardens to provide the illusion of permanence and the reality of structure. Trees will probably be the longest-lived plants we ever select and grow, and because of this, we tend to assume they can take care of themselves with little or no help or guidance.

In a garden, a tree can serve several purposes, including providing shade and shelter or attractive foliage or flowers and fruits; we may need to manage it to suit these requirements. Trees that produce attractive juvenile foliage or brightly colored young stems in winter need regular pruning so that their most attractive feature is prominent.

Even routine pruning to remove diseased or damaged limbs or branches will help to extend the life of a tree by many years. Selecting the correct time of year to prune certain trees can also help keep them strong and healthy.

Most deciduous trees are pruned in winter during their dormancy, but for some, pruning at this time can be a messy proposition: *Acer* spp. (maple), *Betula* spp. (birch), and *Juglans* spp. (walnut) bleed copious quantities of sap if they are pruned in late winter or early spring. Types of *Prunus* (cherries and their relatives) are also often pruned in summer to avoid the incidence of fungal diseases, especially silver leaf, which are less prevalent in the growing season.

FORMATIVE PRUNING

Formative pruning of ornamental trees often occurs in the nursery before the plants are offered for sale. The young trees you buy have usually been trained to develop a straight stem and well-spaced branches for a structural framework that should last throughout the tree's lifetime.

Some plants are more difficult to train than others, particularly plants with leaves and buds arranged along the stems in opposite pairs—such as *Acer* (maple), *Aesculus* (horse chestnut), and *Fraxinus* (ash)—because they often fork and develop two main stems. The problem will arise in later years when the stems split, causing huge wounds and severe structural damage to the trees, as well as a strong potential for fungal rots.

Prune deciduous shade-producing and flowering trees in the first 3 years to produce a clear stem for the tree and to create an open, well-balanced framework

Producing a single-stemmed tree *After planting, remove the lowest branches. Cut out any top shoots which are competing with the main stem.*

As the tree develops, remove lower branches flush with the main stem and cut the branches immediately above back to about 4 inches.

Repeat the process in subsequent years, removing the lowest branches and reducing the ones immediately above in length, before removing them completely the following year.

As the top or head of the tree develops, trim the branches back to form a balanced structure.

Choose a multistemmed shape for variety in your garden. Many trees and large shrubs look more attractive if grown as a multistemmed plant.

of branches—the crown or the head. It is important to produce a structure that gives each branch plenty of space and light. Also remove competing or rubbing branches.

In late spring or early summer, remove any shoots emerging from the trunk below the branches in the head of the tree because these will compete with the main stem.

Cut back by two-thirds or remove altogether any overcrowded or competing shoots in the head of the tree to prevent branches from crossing and rubbing. Always cut back to an outward-facing bud or shoot so that new shoots do not grow back into the center of the branch network.

Producing a multistemmed tree
Allow the tree to grow for 1 year before cutting the main stem down to about 6 inches above soil level.

Allow three or four strong shoots to grow.

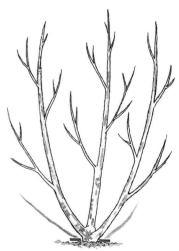

As the new shoots develop and form strong stems, remove any thin, weak shoots which emerge at the base of the plant.

ROUTINE PRUNING

Many established ornamental and shade-producing trees require little routine pruning beyond removing shoots to keep the crown open and tidy and to keep the lower sections of the trunk clear. Severe pruning may, in fact, provoke the tree to produce excessive growth in the form of sappy water (epicormic) shoots. If these are not cut off before they become too large, they will scar the tree trunk when they are eventually removed.

As a tree matures, it may develop an overcrowded head or crown congested with thin, whippy branches in the center. Some branch thinning may be necessary to allow light and air into the center of the tree. Also, as the branches age, some species may tend to droop toward the ground, and some of the lower branches may need to be shortened or removed altogether. Occasionally, a large branch that spoils the balance and shape of the tree may need to be shortened or removed.

In late spring or early summer, cut out any dead, dying, diseased, and damaged wood. This type of growth is much easier to see while the tree is growing rather than in winter when the plant is dormant.

Remove any stem and root suckers. Cut any water shoots off flush with the stem.

Prune out or cut back any crossing or overcrowded branches to an outward-facing bud.

Reduce in length any large branches that spoil the balance of the tree's head (crown).

REMOVING BRANCHES

There may be times when larger branches must be removed from a mature tree. These branches are likely to be heavy, and for safety you should remove them in several sections. Before you begin, make sure that removing one or more branches will not damage the remainder of the tree, which you want to continue to grow after pruning.

There is a procedure that ensures safe removal of large branches by reducing the weight of the branch before you make the final cut. Although it involves extra cutting, the saw will not usually get caught in the pruning cut and the branch will not

Routine pruning For most single-stemmed trees, remove any shoots emerging on the main stem and cut out any shoots growing across the head of the tree.

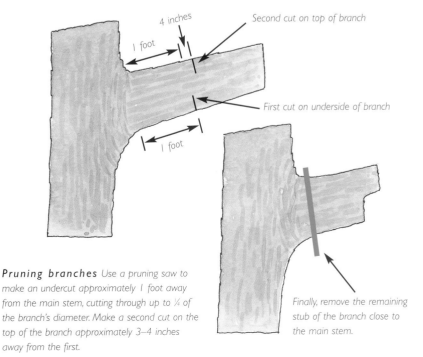

4 inches
1 foot
Second cut on top of branch
First cut on underside of branch
1 foot

Pruning branches Use a pruning saw to make an undercut approximately 1 foot away from the main stem, cutting through up to ¼ of the branch's diameter. Make a second cut on the top of the branch approximately 3–4 inches away from the first.

Finally, remove the remaining stub of the branch close to the main stem.

Most mature trees require little pruning. Simply remove any untidy shoots and keep the base of the trunk clear.

the trunk. Cut up to a quarter of the way through the branch.

Make the second cut on the top of the branch and 4 inches further along the branch (away from the trunk).

Remove the remaining stub close to the trunk.

REMEDIAL PRUNING

Trees may outgrow their allotted space, be damaged by weather, or become unsafe with age, and it is sometimes necessary to remove a tree altogether and plant a new one. Replacement may be the only option, especially if safety is a concern. Contact a qualified arborist (tree surgeon) for advice and guidance.

Remedial pruning is worth doing on trees that are not too old or unsafe. On mature trees extensive remedial pruning is best carried out over several years; remember that in the year following severe pruning, healthy trees may produce large amounts of sappy new growth, which will need to be thinned out to prevent congestion. This type of pruning may also provoke production of sucker growths and water shoots. These will also have to be removed to direct the vigor of the tree into areas that need to be developed, such as the branch framework.

In winter, start by cutting out or reducing the length of any branches that are crossing or rubbing. Thin out any congested growths to balance the tree's branch framework.

In the second year after starting the remedial pruning, thin out any excessive new growth to prevent congestion. Identify the branches needed to form the framework for the head of the tree.

Remove any suckers and water shoots as they emerge.

Post-pruning Remove any strong, new shoots which emerge close to the old pruning point.

tear away when partly cut, injuring the trunk as it falls to the ground.

Rather than immediately cutting the branch off close to the trunk, make an undercut on the underside of the branch at a convenient distance along the branch away from the trunk. Make a second cut on the top of the branch and further out along the branch from the first cut but parallel to it. As this second cut reaches the point where it overlaps the first cut, the branch will snap along the grain and should fall clear. This technique is called a "jump cut". Finally, remove the remaining stump of the branch close to the branch's shoulder—the swollen area at the base of the branch where it joins the trunk. Cutting at this point allows the most rapid healing of the wound caused by branch removal.

Use a suitable saw and start by making an undercut about 12 inches away from

Standard trees

Despite the many types of trees available from plant nurseries, the most popular form for many gardens is still a standard tree, which has a clear, bare stem with no branches up to a height of about 6 feet above soil level.

A tree of this type can, of course, be readily bought from a nursery or garden center. But some gardeners relish the challenge and sense of achievement that comes from buying a young plant about 5 feet high and creating their own standard. This requires a different type of pruning, which must take place in stages over several years to build the stem of the tree and the framework of branches that forms the crown or head. The branches that develop on the trunk of the young tree must be reduced and then removed in stages to allow the trunk to thicken naturally so that it can support the crown. They shouldn't be allowed to become so large that they leave open wounds when removed.

FORMATIVE PRUNING

In the winter or early spring after planting, remove any shoots that are competing with the main stem. This will allow a strong, upright leading shoot to form.

In late spring, remove all the sideshoots from the bottom third of the stem. Cut these off as close to the stem (trunk) as possible.

At the same time, cut back by half all the sideshoots on the central third of the tree, leaving the top third to develop naturally.

In the second winter after planting, remove completely all the sideshoots from the central third of the tree—these are the shoots that were shortened by half during the previous spring.

In spring, cut back by half all the sideshoots on the upper third of the tree.

Cut back by half any new branches that have developed in the upper section of the tree. Leave the top section to develop naturally.

This process of removing the lower branches can be repeated each year until a clear stem of 6 feet has formed.

Standard stems (above) *are not naturally produced and must be created by careful pruning while the tree is quite young.*

Half and quarter standards (right) *may be produced in contrast to the true 6-foot standard stem.*

Formative pruning of standard trees After planting a young tree, remove the lowest branches and cut out damaged shoots from the crown.

As the tree develops, remove the lower branches and cut the branches immediately above this area back to about 4 inches in length.

In the following years, systematically remove the lowest branches and reduce the branches immediately above in stages to strengthen the trunk of the tree.

Conifers

Conifers of all types are among the mainstays of gardens because they provide color and shape throughout the year and, most importantly, require little specialist care. However, as with all plants, they will repay careful pruning, especially in the early years.

We tend to think of conifers as evergreen plants with narrow or needlelike leaves. There are, however, exceptions, and several conifers actually shed their leaves in fall. *Ginkgo biloba* (maidenhair tree), *Larix* spp. (larch), *Metasequoia glyptostroboides* (dawn redwood), and *Taxodium* spp. (swamp cypress) are sometimes referred to as deciduous conifers because they shed their leaves or needles in fall and produce new foliage the following spring.

Most true conifers go through two surges of growth each year: one in spring (the main growth period) and a second (lesser) one in late summer. Pruning just before these growth periods allows the plant to respond quickly to any training and shaping. If they are pruned while they are actively growing, many conifers bleed for long periods, producing large quantities of resin from the open pruning wounds.

Some erect and fastigiate conifers naturally develop a multistemmed habit yet maintain their shape. However, as they age, these plants may spread or splay, getting an open center and losing their attractive profile. Such plants will need remedial pruning.

Shape conifers by trimming new growth back lightly and cutting any shoots back which compete with the main stem.

FORMATIVE PRUNING

The basic growth pattern of conifers such as *Abies* spp. (fir), *Picea* spp. (spruce), and *Pinus* spp. (pine) is a single, central shoot with intermittent clusters of leafy shoots along its length. The central shoot usually becomes the main stem, and the leafy shoots become branches. Some conifers develop a stiff and erect central shoot at an early age, but on others the shoot tip is curved and drooping, becoming erect

lower down the stem only as the woody tissue develops. Such plants should be left to grow naturally. Pruning or training is necessary only if the shoots are damaged.

Some conifers develop a second strong shoot close to the top of the plant, and this may compete with the main stem. It's important to remove the growing tip of a competing leader to prevent it from forming a forked stem, which may split and damage the structure of the tree.

In late spring, remove any strong shoots competing with the growing point. If necessary, train a strong vertical shoot against a cane to establish a definite main stem.

Remove or cut back by two-thirds any shoots that are capable of competing with the main stem.

Minimal pruning is required for those conifers that naturally form a conical or pyramidal habit. Often the only work required is to trim back any shoots which splay out from the main branches.

ROUTINE PRUNING

Conifers grow best with minimal pruning. All shapes and sizes are available, so if the plant selected has an appropriate growth habit, there is little need for much routine pruning as the plant matures. Certainly, most pruning on mature conifers is to repair damage or irregular growth that could affect the plant's shape, balance, or stability. However, there are times when the leading shoot, which eventually forms the main stem or even just the growing point, is damaged or dies, and one or more shoots from the top cluster of branches will naturally begin to replace it. A problem arises if two or more branches compete to become the main shoot. When this happens, a forked head may develop. The fork is a weak point, and the tree may split when it is older.

As soon as you see the need for a replacement main stem, select the best-placed strong shoot from the upper cluster of branches and start training it to grow vertically to replace the damaged one. Any competing shoots should be reduced by a third of their length or cut out altogether to establish natural dominance in the replacement main stem.

Pruning of mature conifers should be restricted to removing badly damaged, dying, or dead branches or lower

A wide range of shapes (right) *and a huge variety of foliage colors are available. Pruning of most mature conifers can be restricted to removing dead, dying, or damaged growth.*

Slow-growing conifers (left) *with a spreading, prostrate pattern of growth have been very popular in recent years and require little pruning.*

branches that trail on the floor or spoil the plant's natural shape. Attempts to reduce or restrict the height of a mature conifer with an upright habit are usually unsatisfactory and often result in an ugly, mutilated plant—several of the upper branches may grow out at odd angles from the main stem. When this happens, it is better to remove the plant and replace it with a new specimen.

In early spring, remove any dead, dying, diseased, or damaged branches.

Lightly trim the tips of vigorous shoots to encourage branching and keep the growth balanced. On *Pinus* spp. (pine) pruning is seldom necessary, but by snapping up to two-thirds of the length of the soft new extension growths—candles—by hand, you will promote denser growth.

REMEDIAL PRUNING

Few conifers can produce new growth from old, bare wood, and they will not respond to remedial pruning. You should dig out any old, damaged, or neglected conifers and replace them. However, *Taxus* spp. (yew) responds positively to severe pruning and can be successfully renovated. *Thuja* spp. (arborvitae) can also be severely pruned, but it will not resprout from bare wood.

Conifers are available in a wide range of shapes and habit and can be slow growing or quite vigorous. But in recent years, the most popular types have been shrubby with a spreading or prostrate pattern of growth. Many slow-growing conifers need little pruning unless the plant has been damaged and foliage or branches have to be removed. However, these plants, as with all evergreens, shed some of their old leaves in summer, and the dead leaves often accumulate within the existing foliage and branches. As this dead foliage builds up, it can start to ferment and rot, killing nearby younger leaves and branches and causing sections of the plant to turn brown and die. At least once each summer, inspect the plants and remove the discarded foliage to prevent this type of damage and reduce the need for remedial pruning. Always prune dead branches when the foliage is dry to avoid spreading fungal diseases.

Sometimes a dwarf conifer attempts to revert to a standard-size plant by sending out a fast-growing or larger limb. These rogue shoots must be removed or the dwarf cultivar will quickly be overwhelmed by the faster-growing reversion.

Routine pruning of conifers generally consists of cutting the growing point of each side shoot back to encourage branching.

Hedges

Hedges play a vital role in our gardens. In addition to marking boundaries and keeping out intruders, they form a backdrop for other plants and features, help to frame a view, and even create screens to hide or divide different parts of the garden.

In many respects, a hedge is a natural-looking barrier created artificially. The individual plants are not allowed to develop their characteristic forms and habits of growth, but instead are treated collectively to fulfill a specific purpose. Trimming and clipping make what may be a disparate selection of plants work together as a unit; frequently cutting back soft, young growths instead of regularly pruning woody stems—as is done with most specimen plants—forces the plants to grow in a particular way. Fortunately for the gardener, many deciduous and evergreen trees and shrubs respond to this frequent cutting by producing an even covering of dense, compact growth.

Hedge clipping is simply a different type of pruning, done in a certain way to achieve a particular purpose. The same general principles that apply to pruning individual plants also govern hedge maintenance.

Hedges can be divided into two main groups: formal and informal. There is a third type—the tapestry or mixed hedge—that needs special attention.

FORMAL HEDGES

Hedges that require regular clipping or trimming for growth restriction and shape maintenance are known as formal hedges. They are often created from a single species—*Taxus* (yew) or *Fagus* (beech), for example—and they provide

A formal hedge can be an excellent and useful garden feature, but must be clipped regularly to maintain a neat shape.

the perfect backdrop for ornamental plants and features in a formal setting or in a garden with symmetrical or geometrically shaped beds and borders. In many respects, these hedges are but one step removed from topiary—in fact, topiary shapes are often combined into these hedges as points of interest.

INFORMAL HEDGES

An informal hedge may consist of a single species, and it is likely to be found in a country garden or in one with a relaxed planting style and irregularly shaped and

sited beds and borders. How and when informal hedges are pruned depends on the species that make up the hedge and when they flower. In general, informal hedges need less intensive management than formal ones because their pruning is limited to what will encourage flowering. They are usually pruned soon after flowering—removing the old, flower-bearing branches encourages the development of new shoots. Limited pruning means that there are times of the year when this type of hedge may look rather untidy. But this disadvantage is, for

Create a stepped effect with closely-clipped hedges of varying heights to provide interest in a formal garden.

many gardeners, outweighed by the reduced amount of work it takes to achieve and maintain an attractive hedge.

Some of the plants in both formal and informal hedges may produce fruits such as hips or berries; the timing of pruning may need slight adjustment so that colorful fruits are not cut off before their display has ended.

TAPESTRY HEDGES

Pruning the third type of hedge, the tapestry or mixed hedge, can be complicated. These hedges consist of more than one species of plant, selected to provide a range of visual interest as the plants change with the seasons. There may be a mixture of plants with different flowering times, leaf colors and textures, or a combination of evergreen and deciduous species. Wherever it is grown, this type of hedge becomes a feature in its own right as well as providing a colorful background.

Complications arise when it comes to pruning, because no two plants have exactly the same habit and rate of growth. You therefore have to adopt pruning techniques, methods, and timings that are slightly different from those used for single-species hedges.

To make life easier, if you are planting a new tapestry hedge, choose plants with similar growth rates. If you do not, the more vigorous plants will outgrow their weaker neighbors and eventually take over the hedge, spoiling the effect you want to achieve. Careful plant selection makes it possible to have both formal and informal tapestry hedges.

Low, formal hedges (left) *have traditionally been used to form divisions within a garden. They require regular maintenance, but the ornamental effect is well worth the effort.*

A hedge (right) *also makes an excellent boundary between garden borders and paths. The hedge gently links the soft plantings in the borders with the straight lines of paths and walkways.*

growth on the top and sides of the hedge. Most of the new growth will then form between the individual plants, forcing them to grow into one another.

Formative pruning

Year 1 Immediately after planting, cut deciduous plants back to between half and two-thirds of their original height. Remove at least 6 inches of the growing tip of evergreens and conifers.

In mid- to late summer, cut out the growing point of any overly vigorous plants as the new shoots develop. Trim back any shoots growing out at right angles to the hedge to create a thick, bushy habit and to keep the plants growing vertically.

Year 2 In the second winter, cut all new growth back by about a third and shorten any laterals growing out at right angles to the hedge.

As new shoots develop, lightly trim them back in late spring and early summer to keep the plants bushy and growing upright.

Cut back the growing points of any vigorous plants to prevent them from dominating neighboring plants.

FORMATIVE PRUNING AND TRAINING

The success of a hedge often depends on how it is treated in the first 2 or 3 years after planting. Early-stage pruning is critical for any hedge or windbreak so that growth is distributed evenly at the base and at the top. Plants that grow close together in such an unnatural way tend to grow upright fairly rapidly because they are competing with their immediate neighbors. Lack of early-stage formative pruning can lead to unattractive gaps at the base of the hedge that may prevent it from becoming an effective screen or barrier.

Most hedging plants benefit greatly from being cut back immediately after planting. This not only stimulates a dense, bushy habit but also encourages individual plants to grow into one another to form a single unit —the hedge.

Depending on the species used and its habit of growth, after planting it is usual to cut the plants down to about two-thirds of their original height. At the same time, cut back by about half any strong lateral branches that are growing out at right angles to the hedge. This process may be repeated annually for several years to check the amount of

Year 1 *Immediately after planting, cut the plants back hard.*

Year 1 (mid- to late summer) *As new shoots develop, trim those growing at right angles to the hedge.*

Year 2 (winter) *Cut new shoots back by about a third.*

Year 2 (spring and summer) *Trim new shoots and cut out the growing point of any overvigorous shoots.*

ROUTINE PRUNING

Frequently pruning young shoots creates a hedge that is covered with growth over its entire surface. If a hedge is well clipped—especially in the early stages—most species will stay no more than 3 feet wide at the base. The width of the hedge, particularly at the top, is important when it comes to clipping, simply because the wider the hedge the more difficult it is to cut neatly. Hedges that become too wide can also take up garden space valuable for other, more interesting species.

If you have a formal hedge, aim for one of two shapes. It should be either the same width from bottom to top, or, preferably, it should be narrower at the top than at the base. This sloping angle is known as the batter, and the slope has some practical applications as well as looking attractive. The sloping sides not only make hedge cutting easier, but they also expose the whole surface of the hedge to sunlight, which helps to keep it growing well.

In colder areas, snowfall may be a problem, especially when the hedge is created from evergreen plants. Snow and ice settling and accumulating on the top of the foliage can make the branches splay out or even break, causing considerable damage to the plants. A hedge with sloping sides is less likely to be affected.

When you clip a hedge, always start at the bottom and work upward, so that the clippings fall clear as they are cut rather than tangling up in the next area to be clipped. If you are using a mechanical hedge trimmer you will find it easier to cut upward in a series of sweeping, arc-like actions, holding the cutting edge parallel to the hedge as you work.

Clipping and shaping

Once the hedge has reached its required height, regularly prune the top to about 12 inches below this height. This will allow new, soft growth to hide any pruning cuts.

If you want a particular hedge shape or profile, use a pre-cut wooden template to help shape the plant. Draw your desired shape on the template, then cut it out with a saw. Place the template against or over the hedge so that you can easily shear or remove any growth that protrudes beyond the template. If you need to create a mirror image of the shape on the opposite side of the plant, flip the template over and use it to shape the other side. Once the profile has been established, you may find that you don't need to use the template every year.

Leveling the top of a hedge may be the most difficult task. The easiest way to do it is to stretch a length of brightly colored garden twine along the hedge, supporting it on two posts to hold it taut at the appropriate height.

Clipping the sides

In spring, starting at the bottom of the hedge, clip upward. Aim to cut the current season's growth back to a point just above the pruning cuts left by the previous trimming.

Use hand pruners to remove any dead or dying leaves of shoots as you come across them.

Clipping the top

Position two posts or stout canes about 12 feet apart and just touching the front of the hedge.

At the height desired for the top of the hedge stretch some garden twine between the posts. Use brightly colored string so that you can see it clearly.

Start clipping the top of the hedge, using hand pruners or long-handled pruners (loppers) for the thicker stems. Brush away any prunings and allow them to fall to the ground.

Shaping *Use a template while clipping and training to create a particular hedge profile.*

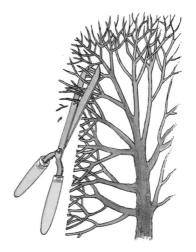

Prune upward *Always clip from the bottom up toward the top of the hedge so that the trimmings fall away from the area being pruned.*

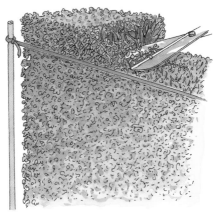

Level top *Use a post and a brightly colored line as a guide to produce an even hedge top.*

Hedges and topiary plants will help balance a garden vista, giving definition and contrast.

Even the best-kept hedges sometimes need to be reduced in size. An overgrown hedge should be pruned in stages over several seasons.

Topiary shapes can be created from popular hedge plants by trimming or clipping them in the same way as you would a hedge.

Remedial pruning to reduce width

Year I In spring, cut all the lateral growth on one side of the hedge back to within about 6 inches of the main stems.

Trim the growth on the other side of the hedge as usual.

Year 2 The following spring, cut the growth on the other side of the hedge back to within about 6 inches of the main stems. Lightly trim the new growth on the side of the hedge that was pruned severely in the previous year.

At the same time, keep the top of the hedge in check by trimming the new growth lightly to encourage the shoots to branch further down the main stems.

FEEDING

Hedges are usually clipped several times a year, which diminishes the food reserves within the plants, and thereby reduces their growth rate. Gardeners often forget about this loss of nutrients, but adding an annual mulch of well-rotted garden compost or manure or applying a general fertilizer will help compensate. Feeding is particularly important after renovation pruning.

TOOLS

Hand or power trimmers are normally used to trim hedges, but you may need to use hand pruners on larger-leaved evergreen plants, such as *Ilex* (holly) and *Aucuba* (Japanese laurel), even though it will take longer. On these types of hedges, mechanical trimmers will cut large leaves in half, causing unsightliness as they slowly turn yellow and die. You will need a stepladder or stable working platform to cut a hedge more than 5 feet high.

RENOVATION PRUNING

A hedge will eventually outgrow its intended space and may be damaged by strong winds or snow. Many plants used for hedging respond well to hard pruning for rejuvenation; when this succeeds it is often difficult to tell that the plants have actually been cut back hard. Don't forget that conifers, with the exception of *Taxus* spp. (yew) and *Thuja* spp. (arborvitae), cannot produce new growth from old wood and should never be renovation pruned.

When a hedge becomes seriously overgrown, staged remedial pruning, which is done over several seasons, is preferable to a single drastic pruning. If possible, always tackle the more sheltered side of the hedge first, because it will respond more quickly and help to protect the garden when the other side of the hedge is cut back.

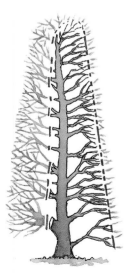

Remedial pruning to reduce width:
Year I Cut one side of the hedge back hard, but trim the opposite side only lightly.

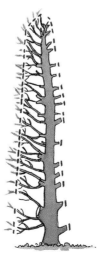

Year 2 Reverse the process, lightly trimming the new growth and cutting the older growth on the opposite side back hard.

Climbers

Climbers are usually grown as one-dimensional plants—that is, they are trained up and across a surface. They are pruned for the same reasons as other plants, but they may also need to be coaxed into growing toward and onto their supporting structure.

The aim is to achieve a well-spaced framework of shoots that grow close to their supports. This involves positioning and tying in the strongest stems.

When you're pruning climbing plants, you must bear in mind the plant's habit of growth, no matter what genus it belongs to. A true climber will be self-supporting to some degree, which can affect its pruning and training.

Climbers that can cling to other plants for objects for support are quite different from the artificial category of wall shrubs (such as *Pyracantha*), which are specially trained to grow against a vertical surface. Some of these plants can be extremely vigorous, with shoots growing many feet each year, which often means that some wall shrubs need pruning twice a year to regulate growth and train the shoots.

Formative pruning with climbers often goes on throughout the life of the plant, not just when it's young (which is the case for most trees and shrubs). Climbing plants may also need to be pruned to prevent property damage. Some are pruned in the summer to trim growth from around doors and windows. Climbers that attach themselves to supports with sucker pads or aerial roots

Campsis (above), *a clinging vine, is best grown in a warm, sunny position where the warmth of the sun will mature the shoots which will provide next year's flowers.*

Wisteria (right) *has twining stems that will attach themselves to any other plants or structures for support in order to reach bright sunlight.*

can do considerable structural damage if they are left unpruned.

Climbing plants fall into three broad categories according to their method of support.

CLINGERS

There are two main types of clinging vines. The first group includes natural clingers, such as the trumpet vine (*Campsis* spp.), English ivy (*Hedera helix*), and climbing hydrangea (*Hydrangea anomala* subsp. *petiolaris*), which support themselves by aerial roots. The second group is made up of plants such as Boston ivy (*Parthenocissus tricuspidata*) that cling with small sucker pads and usually need no additional support.

TWINERS

Twining plants are of three main types. Vines such as chocolate vine (*Akebia quinata*), climbing honeysuckles (*Lonicera* spp.), Russian vine (*Fallopia baldschuanica*), and wisteria support themselves by twining their stems around anything they can reach.

Plants with twining leaf stalks, including the clematis (*Clematis* spp.) and *Smilax aspera*, grip other plants and objects.

Plants with tendrils coil around any support they can reach and continue to coil to draw themselves closer to their supporting structure. This group includes grape vine (*Vitis* spp.) and passionflower (*Passiflora* spp.).

SCRAMBLERS

Some types of roses are called climbers but are in reality scramblers. They have rapidly growing stems that scramble through other plants and use hooked thorns to keep from sliding off their support. This is why the tip of each thorn usually angles back down the stem.

It's worth remembering that climbing sports of bush roses (that is, roses with the word "climbing" before the cultivar name—'Climbing Iceberg', for example) may revert to their original bush form if they are severely pruned in the first 2 years after planting.

Climbing roses are not true climbers, but scrambling plants which must be tied and trained into place to encourage them to grow in a particular way.

Groundcover

Planting low-growing, spreading plants to provide groundcover is a way of exploiting a plant's natural habit of growth to cover the soil. This has the dual advantages of looking attractive and suppressing weeds by preventing sunlight from reaching the soil.

Groundcover plants are usually those that grow no more than 18 inches high but that spread outward. Your goal is to create a multistemmed plant that covers the soil with a network of lateral and sublateral branches and spreads out to block out light. This means that formative pruning is important because it will create a plant that is pruned frequently to induce the maximum number of sideshoots.

FORMATIVE PRUNING

Prune to encourage the development of a multistemmed plant with a framework of low, spreading, evenly spaced shoots close to ground level.

In the first spring after planting, remove any dead or damaged shoots. Cut the remaining stems back to 6 to 8 inches in length.

Because these stems produce lateral branches, allow them to reach a length of 6 to 8 inches before you cut out the tip of each shoot to encourage a more branching habit.

ROUTINE PRUNING

Established plants need little in the way of routine pruning and will continue to flower and fruit for many years without any pruning at all. However, as new growth forms on top of the old, plants gradually get higher and leave gaps beneath. As long as you are not dealing with a conifer (see page 184), pruning back to older wood every 5 or 6 years will reduce the height of the plants and stimulate new growth from the base, encouraging a dense carpet of growth.

Cut the plants down to within 6 to 8 inches of soil level. Old or nonproductive shoots can be cut down to 2 or 3 inches above ground level to encourage new shoots to grow as replacements.

REMEDIAL PRUNING

Plants sometimes grow beyond their allotted area. When this happens, avoid the common error of simply cutting the shoots back to a point along the edge of the bed or border. A better approach is to cut each encroaching stem back to a point where it will take the plant a full growing season to reach the edge of the bed again.

Cut the shoots back to a bud or pair of buds and trim back any untidy growths.

Remove any dead or damaged shoots.

Formative pruning (above) *is very important for groundcover plants, like this ivy, to encourage the development of a spreading, multistemmed plant.*

As groundcover plants grow higher (left), *they will leave gaps beneath. Stimulate new growth from the base by pruning the plants back every 5 or 6 years.*

A dense thicket of Erica carnea (far left). *Such an abundance of shoots has been created by frequent pruning.*

Low-maintenance pruning

It is possible to minimize the amount of pruning you do in your garden, but this should be part of a thorough garden and plant management policy rather than a form of benign neglect. Plants need some pruning even in extremely low-maintenance gardens.

The low-maintenance approach to gardening has been used for many years in continental Europe to prune shrubs in municipal plantings. For a number of years, gardeners at the Royal National Rose Society trial grounds at St. Albans in England have tried different pruning techniques on roses to see how the plants respond to different regimens. One of these schemes has been to move away from the usual and long-established technique of using hand pruners, long-handled pruners (loppers), and pruning saws and instead to use garden shears or even mechanical hedge trimmers to prune bush roses. This method of pruning involves cutting back all the plant stems to a predetermined height, regardless of the thickness of the stems or their position on the plants. It has been found to produce larger numbers of good-quality flowers, although they were, on average, slightly smaller than those produced on plants pruned by traditional methods. It also appears to be

particularly useful for plants growing in massed beds, where they can all be treated in the same way and retain some degree of uniformity.

It is important that all the prunings created from this method are removed and disposed of and that the cutting tools are particularly sharp to ensure good, clean cuts with no snags or tears. (This, of course, is true with any other form of pruning.) Perhaps the main drawback is that it produces large quantities of small, sappy shoots, and this type of growth is susceptible to attack from pests and diseases—especially where the growth becomes congested.

A better approach seems to be a combination of traditional methods and new techniques with power equipment. Prune plants with hedge trimmers for a period of 4 or 5 years and interrupt this with a year of hand pruning to thin out congested growth and dead wood.

For some plants, this method of pruning is not new at all but has been

practiced for many years. Plants that produce lots of small, thin stems—heathers and lavenders, for example—have always been pruned with shears or clippers to trim off dead flowers as well as a small amount of stem growth. Many groundcover roses are also pruned in this way, and the old, spent flowers can be trimmed off with shears or mechanical trimmers.

First decide on the height at which the pruning cuts are to be made. Then use shears or a mechanical trimmer to cut off all the shoots standing above the predetermined height.

Use a gloved hand to stroke over the tops of the plants and brush off any trimmed shoots.

Gather up and dispose of all the trimmings.

Another low-maintenance technique is to remove a set amount of growth. This normally involves removing complete shoots or branches every year or every other year to reduce the amount of

Low-maintenance pruning *It is possible to prune some bedding roses with a hedge trimmer, rather than with hand pruners.*

After pruning, brush off all of the trimmings so that they fall onto the soil.

Gather up the prunings and dispose of them to reduce the spread of pests and diseases.

Many shrub roses will produce greater numbers of flowers using new low-maintenance pruning methods.

Minimal pruning Remove only the oldest growths and allow the plant to develop naturally.

pruning necessary. Often the shoots to be removed are selected on the basis of health and age: Dead, damaged, diseased, or dying growths are cut out first, followed by two or three of the oldest shoots, which are often removed with long-handled pruners (loppers) or a saw. This pruning method does not involve trimming, only removal of whole sections of the plant to create space for new growth.

MINIMAL PRUNING
In early spring or immediately after flowering, cut back two or three of the oldest stems as close to the ground as possible. This will give the maximum period of growth for the next season.

Remove and dispose of the stems that have been pruned out. Take care that you do not damage the remaining growths when you remove the discarded stems.

Your choice of plants can also play a part in the amount of pruning that needs to be done. Some plants do not need much regular pruning once they become established, especially if you have worked hard at the formative pruning when the specimens were first planted. Magnolias, camellias, most conifers, hebes, lilacs, rhododendrons, and skimmias will all do well for many years with an occasional light trim or deadheading to keep them tidy.

Renovation pruning

Left to their own devices, many plants flower and grow well for many years. After all, they seem to manage just fine when they are growing in the wild without a gardener in sight.

We choose most plants based on how they will look in our gardens, not how they would grow in the wild. Gardeners like to use their available space as well as possible, which means managing plants so they'll perform in particular ways— produce flowers, fruit, or attractive foliage, or even, with a few plants, all of these things. However, most cultivated forms remain attractive only with regular attention. Untended plants often become tangled masses of old and new growth, and flowers gradually get smaller— especially after they start producing seeds regularly.

Plants may be neglected for a number of reasons. It may be that someone who has no interest in or aptitude for plants takes over a garden and finds the work too difficult or onerous. Or it may be that the gardener does not know how to prune the plants and decides to let them alone rather than risk harming them.

Whatever the reason, the result is the same. But a plant will eventually have to be pruned if it is to remain a living garden specimen. This is when remedial or renovation pruning is necessary. Perhaps the hardest decision is whether the plant is actually worth the effort. Can it be rejuvenated, or would it be better to simply dig it up and plant something new?

As you decide, remember that some plants respond well to severe pruning and get a new lease on life, but others, such as *Cytisus* spp. (broom), will not survive as the stems dry and die back from pruning cuts. Most conifers, too, cannot produce new growth from old, bare wood. However, many trees and shrubs will respond to carefully managed renovation pruning. Rather than pruning a plant severely in a single season and letting it take its chances, it is better to plan and apply a phased pruning program over 2 or 3 years so the plant gradually replaces the old shoots. This will give you time to select the best of the new growths to train as replacements for main stems and laterals.

Renovation pruning is best done in early spring.

GRAFTED PLANTS

Sometimes plants are budded or grafted—a named cultivar or variety is attached to a rootstock that has a quality, such as vigor or size, not found in the cultivar. Severe pruning to rejuvenate a grafted plant can lead to problems if a grafted plant is cut back too low. The cultivated variety on the top of the rootstock could be inadvertently removed altogether, or the rootstock may grow so vigorously that the sucker growths it produces deny the choice selection the chance to grow.

FEEDING

Every time a plant is pruned severely it should be fed. Apply a slow-release fertilizer or a mulch of well-rotted garden compost or manure to help the plant recover more quickly from the shock of the drastic pruning.

RECLAIMING AN OLD SHRUB

The first step in rejuvenating any plant is to remove all the dead, dying, diseased, and damaged wood. Do this while the plant is actively growing rather than during its

Neglected plants (above) *may become too large for their allocated space as they grow to their full size, requiring remedial pruning to contain them.*

Slower growth rates (left) *occur naturally in some plants as they mature, making them far less invasive.*

dormancy because it is much easier to tell what is healthy and what is not.

Next, completely remove about half of the remaining live stems, cutting them down to ground level.

Finally, on all the stems that are left, cut all the remaining sideshoots back to within three or four buds of these main stems.

The following year, begin the second phase by cutting down all the stems that were trimmed but not cut out the previous year.

You may need to thin new stems that have grown in the previous season to

Renovating old, straggly plants:
Step *1 Cut all the stems back close to ground level to stimulate new growth.*

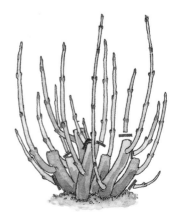

Step *2 Select the strongest of the new shoots and allow them to grow. Remove any weaker shoots.*

prevent overcrowding. Keep only the strongest, healthiest stems and make sure they are well placed to provide a good overall shape.

Completely remove the shoots you are not keeping, making sure that you cut out all thin, straggly, or damaged stems. Cut the unneeded stronger stems back to three or four buds, so that they can produce replacement growths if required.

With grafted plants, it is important to remove any suckering shoots emerging from the rootstock. If they originate from above soil level they can be ripped off the stem by hand to remove all the dormant buds around their bases. If suckers emerge through the soil, carefully dig the soil from around the base of the sucker and pull the sucker away by hand. Carefully replace the soil after removing the sucker.

If the plant responds well to the rejuvenation program, within 3 to 5 years

Large shrubs, such as this **Photinia** (**above**), *may need to be pruned in stages, rather than cutting all of the shoots back at the same time.*

Trees with a light canopy of branches (**above right**) *require little regular pruning. Simply remove any branches or shoots which are crossing each other or rubbing together.*

it should be impossible to tell how badly neglected the plant was before you started. After rejuvenation pruning, watch the plants carefully—they often produce large amounts of soft, sappy growth susceptible to pests and diseases. Don't forget to remove woody stumps that remain after the plant starts to regrow. They could become sites of fungal rots.

Crown lifting is a technique used to remove the lower branches from a tree in order to raise the crown.

Crown thinning reduces the density of the branches to allow more light into a garden or reduce the wind resistance of a large tree.

Specialized pruning

A number of pruning techniques are used only in special circumstances or to achieve a particular effect with, or result from, a plant. These special practices often replace routine pruning when it does not work as intended.

NICKING AND NOTCHING

Some plants naturally produce long sections of bare stem with hardly any branches, and you may occasionally need to correct the balance of the branch framework to improve its structure and overall appearance.

If you want to restrict the development of a bud or shoot, making a small, V-shaped nick with a sharp knife just below a bud can restrict the supply of growth-promoting chemicals and inhibit the growth of the shoot directly above it. Alternatively, if you want to encourage the development or growth of a particular bud, making a small V-shaped notch just above it can increase its vigor and stimulate new growth. Notching can also stimulate the production of sideshoots on sections of bare stem.

This type of formative pruning is most effective in spring just as the new growth starts and when plants are growing vigorously as the sap starts to rise.

POLLARDING

Pollarding is a traditional method of hard pruning that gives a constant and renewable supply of shoots. It's especially useful for getting a plant to produce plenty of relatively thin, 1-year-old shoots rather than allowing it to produce a heavy framework of thick branches.

Pollarding involves pruning in spring either annually or biannually. Cut the existing branches down to within 2 to 3 inches of the main stem, which can be up to 6 feet above ground. Vigorous plants— such as poplar or cottonwood (*Populus* spp.), Indian bean tree (*Catalpa* spp.),

linden (*Tilia* spp.), sycamore (*Platanus* spp.), redbud (*Cercis* spp.), and some willows (*Salix* cvs.)—can be pollarded to provide a display of attractive leaves or brightly colored young shoots in winter.

COPPICING

Coppicing—or stooling as it's also known—is one of the oldest pruning techniques. It was used as a method of woodland management for almost 700 years to produce young, straight stems for making fencing and material to supply charcoal burners. These days it's done to produce a particular type of growth and is restricted mainly to plants that can produce stems with brightly colored bark or those that bear attractive leaves.

The main aim is to produce vigorous stems with larger than normal leaves on

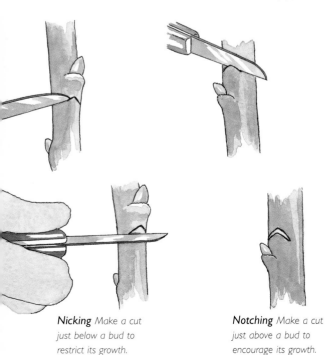

Nicking *Make a cut just below a bud to restrict its growth.*

Notching *Make a cut just above a bud to encourage its growth.*

Pollarding: Step 1
Cut all the stems back to small stubs of growth very close to the main stem.

Pollarding: Step 2
As new growth develops, thin the shoots out so that only the thickest and strongest remain.

plants such as princess tree (*Paulownia tomentosa*), smoke tree (*Cotinus coggygria*), elderberry (*Sambucus* spp.), gum tree (*Eucalyptus* spp.), hazel (*Corylus* spp.), and willow (*Salix* spp.). All these plants produce leaves that are brightly colored or otherwise decorative.

Alternatively, the technique can produce brightly colored stems on snakebark maples (*Acer davidii* and *A. pennsylvanicum*), dogwood (*Cornus* spp.), silver-stemmed bramble (*Rubus biflorus*), and white willow (*Salix alba*), all of which are most ornamental through winter after the leaves have fallen. The gum tree (*Eucalyptus* spp.) is also often coppiced to provide both stems and leaves for flower arrangers.

Many willows (right) *are grown for their brightly colored new bark and are therefore pollarded to encourage the development of fresh, new stems each spring.*

Coppicing trees *such as* Corylus **(below right)** *and* Sambucus *will stimulate the production of large, brightly colored leaves in the spring.*

Coppicing: Step 1
Cut all the stems back to small stubs of growth very close to ground level.

Coppicing: Step 2
As new growth develops, thin the shoots out so that only the thickest and strongest remain.

An avenue of pleached trees
(**right**) *is an attractive sight, particularly when
the lateral shoots start to intertwine.*

The hedge-on-stilts effect (**far
right**) *created by a row of pleached trees in
spring and summer is perfect for providing a
formal setting, while still allowing light to reach
the plants below.*

PLEACHING

At first glance, a row of pleached trees
looks like a hedge on legs or stilts. In
years gone by, avenues of pleached trees
were regarded as status symbols, and
landowners in Tudor England would boast
about how many gardeners they needed
to maintain their pleached trees. Gardens
in Europe, such as the royal gardens at
the Palace of Versailles in France,
originally contained numerous long
avenues flanked by pleached trees.
In recent years, the technique has
become popular again, especially in
formal gardens.

The process, which combines pruning
and training, is extremely labor intensive
and involved. Lateral shoots are trained
horizontally along wire supports, and any
shoots that branch out from these
laterals are pruned back to within one or
two buds of their point of origin. The
lateral shoots are intertwined as they
grow, so that they eventually form a
screen. Once this framework is
established, the shoots are clipped as they
would be on an ordinary hedge.

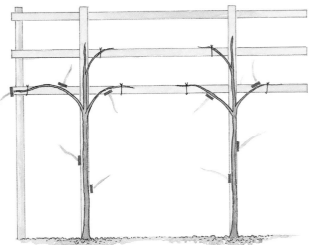

*Pleaching: Step 1 Train the main stem into the
supporting framework, remove any shoots forming on
the main stem, and remove any lateral shoots which
cannot be trained into the framework.*

Pleaching: Step 2 *As the leader reaches the top of the supporting framework, begin to train it horizontally (train all the leaders in the same direction). Shorten any very long lateral shoots and remove any shoots forming on the main stem.*

Pleaching: Step 3 *As the shoots from each tree reach each other, begin to weave them together. Cut back to a single bud any shoots growing at right angles to the main framework.*

FESTOONING

Many flowering plants tend to produce a greater number of flowers and, in some cases, more fruits when the shoots are growing horizontally or slightly below horizontal, so that the shoot tip is below the point where the lateral branch emerges from the main trunk. Some plants, such as crab apple (*Malus* spp.) and silver-leaved pear (*Pyrus salicifolia*), often produce long, flexible stems, which may take several years to produce flower-bearing spurs.

Rather than pruning back these long shoots and fighting against the natural growth habit of the plant—cutting them back will only stimulate the development of more, similar shoots to replace those you have removed—you can tie them down so that they form loops. Attach a length of string about 6 inches from the end of a long shoot and loosely fasten the other end of the string to the base of the main stem to keep the stems in place. Bending the stems like this causes a redistribution of growth-promoting chemicals in the shoots, and the buds along these curving stems will develop and produce lateral shoots that can be pruned back to three to five buds in summer. They will form flower-bearing spurs the following year and flower the next spring. If these branches become overcrowded, a complete branch or section of a branch can be removed, leaving room for a replacement to develop.

Root pruning: Step 1 Dig a trench around the tree, just outside the spread of the canopy of branches. The trench should be 1 spade's width wide and about 18 inches deep.

Root pruning: Step 2 Saw through any thick roots uncovered by the trench and remove the loose ends completely before refilling the trench with soil.

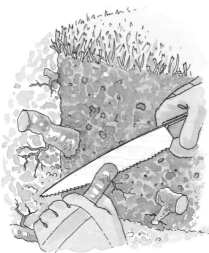

Festooning a tree involves training long, flexible shoots to curve inward toward the base of the plant to increase flower production.

ROOT PRUNING

This technique is rarely practiced these days, but it can be used as a last-ditch effort to control the vigor of plants or reduce root competition. It's also an excellent way of encouraging them to flower more frequently. If a plant is getting too big or producing too much shoot growth, you may be tempted to cut off the top of the plant, but this often simply makes it produce more vigorous shoots or creates a hopelessly misshapen plant.

If a plant is to produce healthy, balanced growth, there must be a physical and chemical balance between the shoots and the roots. Naturally occurring chemicals that originate in a plant's roots directly influence the rate of growth and the balance between shoot development and flower production. Root pruning works by removing sections of root that are responsible for producing these chemicals. Restricting their supply changes the balance of chemicals in a

plant, which limits the development and extension growth of the branches and reduces a plant's tendency to produce flowers rather than shoots. One advantage is that root pruning encourages the plant to produce a more branched root system with a higher proportion of small, fibrous roots.

Root pruning does have a number of disadvantages, however, and the timing must be precise. It must be done in spring when the windiest weather of the year is over. If you remove large sections of major supporting roots in fall, the plant is likely to blow over in strong winter winds. In spring the healing process and formation of new roots will be rapid, if the plant is healthy enough to survive root pruning. Remember, too, that some plants are propagated by root cuttings, and if plants such as some locusts (*Robinia* spp.), sassafras (*Sassafras albium*), glory flower (*Clerodendrum* spp.), and poplars (*Populus* spp.) are root pruned and the sections of severed root are left in the ground, they may start to produce shoots and quickly colonize large areas of the garden.

BARK RINGING

This is a simple but effective technique for restricting a plant's growth if other pruning methods have not had the desired effect. It can also be used when root pruning is impractical—if the main roots are located under a path or driveway, for example.

In midspring, remove a narrow strip of bark, ¼–½ inch wide, from around the main trunk. Take care that you don't form a complete ring around the trunk or you will kill the plant. The depth of the cut is important. You need to cut down to the cambium layer, the thin layer of cells on the surface of the wood, immediately below the bark. Removing this strip of bark forms a barrier that restricts the downward movement of the carbohydrates manufactured in the leaves and growth-promoting chemicals, and they will accumulate in the stem just above the ring. This starves the plant of food and growth-promoting chemicals in the area below the ring. The root system is below the ring, and root activity is slowed down, which checks the topgrowth.

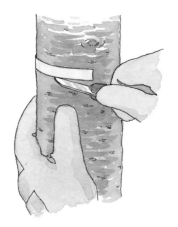

Bark ringing: Step 1 *Wrap a piece of tape around the stem of the tree as a guide.*

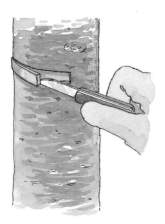

Bark ringing: Step 2 *Cut through the bark on each side of the tape, leaving a small segment of bark in place. Lift out the remaining strip of bark around the stem.*

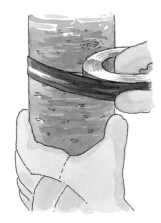

Bark ringing: Step 3 *Cover the cut surface with a strip of electrician's adhesive insulation tape.*

WHEN TO PRUNE MOST SPECIES

	Early spring (March)	Midspring (April)	Late spring (May)	Early summer (June)	Midsummer (July)
Abelia	■		■		
Actinidia					
Amelanchier			■		
Aronia					
Aucuba japonica		■			
Berberis (deciduous)				■	
Berberis (evergreen)				■	
Bignonia capreolata	■				
Bougainvillea					
Buddleja	■	■			
Callicarpa	■	■			
Callistemon					
Calluna	■				
Camellia		■			
Campsis	■				
Ceanothus (deciduous)					
Ceanothus (evergreen)					■
Cercis					
Chaenomeles			■	■	
Choisya			■	■	
Clematis (early-flowering)			■	■	
Clematis (midseason-flowering)	■				
Clematis (late-flowering)	■				
Cornus alba, Cornus sericea	■	■			
Cotinus					
Cotoneaster (deciduous)					
Cotoneaster (evergreen)		■			
Cytisus			■	■	■
Euonymus					
Ficus	■				
Forsythia			■	■	
Fremontodendron					■
Fuchsia	■				
Hedera					
Hibiscus					
Hydrangea (shrub)	■				
Hydrangea (climber)					
Ilex					■
Jasminum	■				
Lagerstroemia	■	■			
Lavandula	■	■			

Late summer (August)	Early fall (September)	Midfall (October)	Late fall (November)	Early winter (December)	Midwinter (January)	Late winter (February)

(continued)

WHEN TO PRUNE MOST SPECIES (cont'd)

	Early spring (March)	Midspring (April)	Late spring (May)	Early summer (June)	Midsummer (July)
Lonicera (climber)					
Lonicera (shrub)			■	■	
Magnolia					■
Mahonia	■	■			
Malus					■
Osmanthus			■		
Passiflora	■				
Philadelphus					
Photinia	■				
Potentilla		■			
Prunus (deciduous)			■		
Prunus (evergreen)					
Pyracantha			■		
Rhododendron					■
Rosa (large-flowered)	■				
Rosa (cluster-flowered)	■				
Rosa (shrub and species)	■				
Rosa (climbers)					
Rosa (ramblers)					
Rosmarinus					
Salix	■	■			
Sambucus					
Spiraea				■	
Syringa					■
Taxus		■	■		
Vaccinium					
Viburnum (deciduous)					
Viburnum (evergreen)				■	■
Vitis					
Weigela					■
Wisteria					■

Late summer (August)	Early fall (September)	Midfall (October)	Late fall (November)	Early winter (December)	Midwinter (January)	Late winter (February)

SUITABLE HEDGING PLANTS

FORMAL HEDGES (CLIPPED)

Plant	Evergreen/ deciduous	Best height	Hedge pruning times	Responds to remedial pruning
Buxus sempervirens	E	1 to 3 ft	Once in spring and twice in summer (but never in winter)	Yes
Carpinus betulus	D	5 to 20 ft	Once in late summer	Yes
Chamaecyparis lawsoniana	E	4 to 8 ft	Once in late spring, once in early fall	No
Crataegus monogyna	D	5 to 10 ft	Once in summer, once in fall	Yes
x Cupressocyparis leylandii	E	6½ to 20 ft	Once in spring and twice in summer (but never in winter)	No
Elaeagnus x ebbingei	E	5 to 10 ft	Once in mid- to late summer	Yes
Escallonia spp.	E	4 to 8 ft	Once immediately after flowering	Yes
Euonymus fortunei	E	4 to 6 ft	Once in summer	Yes
Fagus sylvatica	D	5 to 20 ft	Once in late summer	Yes
Griselinia littoralis	E	4 to 10 ft	Once in late spring, once in late summer	No
Ilex hybrids and cvs.	E	4 to 13 ft	Once in late summer	Yes
Ligustrum spp.	D	5 to 10 ft	Once in spring and twice in summer (but never in winter)	No
Lonicera nitida	E	3 to 4 ft	Once in spring and twice in summer (but never in winter)	No
Osmanthus spp.	E	6 to 10 ft	Once in spring	Yes
Prunus laurocerasus	E	4 to 10 ft	Once in late winter	Yes
Pyracantha spp.	E	6½ to 10 ft	Once after flowering, once in late summer (but avoid pruning berries)	No
Taxus baccata	E	4 to 20 ft	Once in summer, once in fall	No
Thuja spp.	E	5 to 20 ft	Once in late spring, once in early fall	No

INFORMAL HEDGES (UNCLIPPED)

Plant	Evergreen/ deciduous	Best height	Hedge pruning times	Responds to remedial pruning
Berberis darwinii	E	5 to 8 ft	Once after flowering	Yes
Berberis thunbergii	D	2 to 4 ft	Once after flowering	Yes
Choisya ternata	E	6 to 8 ft	Once after flowering	Yes
Cotoneaster lacteus	E	5 to 7 ft	Once after fruiting	Yes
Crataegus monogyna	D	5 to 10 ft	Once in winter	Yes
Escallonia spp.	E	4 to 8 ft	Once immediately after flowering	Yes
Forsythia x intermedia	D	5 to 8 ft	Once after flowering	Yes
Fuchsia magellanica	D	3 to 5 ft	Once in spring, to remove old stems	Yes
Garrya elliptica	E	5 to 7 ft	Once immediately after flowering	No
Hibiscus syriacus	D	6 to 10 ft	Once in spring	No
Ilex aquifolium and Ilex opaca	E	6½ to 20 ft	Once in late summer	Yes
Lavandula spp.	E	1 to 3 ft	Once in spring, once after flowering	No
Pyracantha spp.	E	6½ to 10 ft	Once after flowering, once in fall (but avoid pruning berries)	No
Rosa rugosa	D	3½ to 5 ft	Once in spring, to remove old stems	Yes
Viburnum spp.	E	3½ to 8 ft	Once after flowering	No

NO- OR LOW-PRUNE PLANTS

Some trees, shrubs, and climbers, if sited well, will grow for many years with little or no need for routine pruning. You can choose dwarf cultivars of both evergreen and deciduous shrubs to reduce the need for pruning. The plants on this list require little or no pruning, so try to incorporate them into your landscape as a low-maintenance alternative.

DECIDUOUS

Acer palmatum and cvs.

Cercis spp. and cvs.

Chaenomeles spp. and cvs.

Cotinus coggygria and cvs.

Cotoneaster upright spp. and cvs.

Daphne spp. and cvs.

Hibiscus syriacus and cvs.

Hydrangea anomala subsp. *petiolaris*

Ilex verticillata

Magnolia spp. and cvs.

Rhododendron spp. and cvs.

Syringa spp. and cvs.

EVERGREEN

Aucuba japonica and cvs.

Camellia spp. and cvs.

Choisya ternata and cvs.

Cistus × *corbariensis*

Cotoneaster upright spp. and cvs.

Euonymus spp. and cvs.

Gaultheria mucronata and cvs.

Ilex opaca and *Ilex aquifolium* and cvs.

Osmanthus spp. and cvs.

Photinia × *fraseri* and cvs.

Prunus spp. and cvs.

Rhododendron spp. and cvs.

Tsuga spp. and cvs.

Viburnum spp. and cvs.

GLOSSARY

Alternate (buds/leaves) Leaves that occur at different levels on opposite sides of the stem.

Apex The tip of a shoot, from which extension growth is made.

Apical bud The uppermost bud in the growing point of a stem (also known as the terminal bud).

Axil The angle at the point where the leaf or branch joins the main stem of a plant.

Axillary bud A bud which occurs in the leaf axil.

Bark A protective layer of cells on the outer surface of the roots and stems of woody plants.

Bark ringing The practice of removing a ring of bark from the trunk of a tree to help control vigor.

Biennial bearing A plant which slips into a habit of producing fruit on a 2-year cycle.

Bleeding The excessive flow of sap from spring-pruned plants.

Blind bud A bud that fails to produce a terminal bud.

Branch A shoot growing from a bud as a result of pruning.

Break A shoot growing from a bud as a result of pruning.

Broad-leaved Deciduous or evergreen plants with flat, broad leaves.

Bud A condensed shoot containing an embryonic shoot or flower.

Bud union The point where a cultivar is budded onto a rootstock.

Bush A multi-branched plant with a number of branches of similar size.

Callus The plant tissue that forms as a protective cover over a cut or wounded surface.

Climber A self-supporting plant capable of growing vertically.

Compound leaf A leaf consisting of a number of small segments (leaflets).

Conifer A classification of plants which have naked ovules often borne in cones, and narrow, needlelike foliage.

Coppicing The severe pruning of plants to ground level on an annual basis.

Cordon A tree trained to produce fruiting spurs from a main stem.

Crotch The place where two branches or stems join or where a branch meets a trunk.

Crown The upper branches and foliage of a tree.

Cultivar A plant form which originated in cultivation rather than having been found in the wild.

Deadheading The deliberate removal of dead flower-heads or seed-bearing fruits.

Deciduous Plants which produce new leaves in the spring and shed them in the fall.

Dieback The death of plant growth downward from the shoot tip.

Dormant period A period of reduced growth through the winter.

Espalier A tree trained to produce several horizontal tiers of branches from a vertical main stem.

Evergreen Plants which retain their actively growing leaves through the winter.

Framework The main permanent branch structure of a woody plant.

Fruit The seed-bearing vessel on a plant.

Graft union The point where a cultivar is grafted onto a rootstock.

Grafting A propagation method involving the joining of two or more separate plants together.

Hybrid A cross between two or more species or forms of a species.

Lateral A sideshoot arising from an axillary bud.

Leader The main dominant shoot or stem of the plant (usually the terminal shoot).

Leaf The main lateral organ of a green plant.

Leaflet One of the small segments of a compound leaf.

Loppers Long-handled pruners used for pruning thicker branches.

Maiden A young (1-year-old) budded or grafted tree.

Mulch A layer of material applied to cover the soil.

Opposite Where leaves, buds, or stems are arranged in pairs directly opposite one another.

Ornamentals Plants grown primarily for their decorative value rather than for their commercial usefulness or for the production of crops.

Perianth The two outer whorls (calyx and corolla or sepals and petals) which first protect and then display the generative parts. In general, perianth is used when the petals and sepals look alike, as in a tulip.

Pinching out The removal (usually with finger and thumb) of a shoot's growing point to encourage the development of lateral shoots.

Pollarding The severe pruning of a tree's main branches back to the main stem or trunk.

Rambler A vigorous trailing plant with a scrambling habit.

Renewal pruning A pruning system based on the systematic replacement of lateral fruiting branches.

Root The underground support system of a plant.

Root ball The combined root system and surrounding soil/compost of a plant.

Root pruning The cutting of live plant roots to control the vigor of a plant.

Rootstock The root system onto which a cultivar is budded or grafted.

Sap The juice or blood of a plant.

Scion The propagation material taken from a cultivar or variety to be used for budding or grafting.

Shoot A branch stem or twig.

Sideshoot A stem arising from a branch stem or twig.

Spur A short fruit/flower-bearing branch.

Standard A tree with a clear stem of at least 6 feet.

Stem The main shoot of a tree.

Stooling The severe pruning of plants to within 4 to 6 inches of ground level on an annual basis.

Stone fruits A term usually reserved for fruit-bearing members of the genus *Prunus*, e.g., apricot, cherry, damson, plum.

Sublateral A sideshoot arising from an axillary bud of a lateral shoot.

Sucker A shoot arising from below ground level.

Tap root The large main root of a plant.

Tendril A modified stem or leaf that twines around supports, enabling the plant to climb.

Tepal A division of a perianth.

Terminal bud The uppermost bud in the growing point of a stem (also known as the apical bud).

Thinning The removal of branches to improve the quality of those remaining.

Topiary The imposition of an artificial shape, geometric or representational, on a tree or shrub by trimming and training.

Tree A woody perennial plant usually consisting of a clear stem or trunk and a framework or head of branches.

Trunk The main stem of a mature tree.

Union (graft union) The point where a cultivar is grafted onto a rootstock.

Variegated Plant parts (usually leaves) marked with a blotched irregular pattern of colors such as gold or silver on a base color of green.

Vegetative growth Nonflowering stem growth.

Whip A young 1-year-old tree with no lateral branches.

Whorl The arrangement of three or more leaves, buds, or shoots arising from the same level.

Wood The lignified tissue of trees and shrubs but sometimes used as a synonym for growth.

Wound Any cut or damaged area on a plant.

INDEX

Page numbers in *italics* indicate captions.

ACKNOWLEDGMENTS

We would like to thank and acknowledge the following for supplying photographs reproduced in this book:

Key: l left, r right, t top, b bottom

2 Nick Wiseman/Science Photo Library; 4l Leigh Clapp/The Garden Picture Library; 8-9 GardenWorld Images; 10 Peter Stiles/Hortipix; 11r, 12l, 13t, 13b GardenWorld Images; 14 S. Orme/GardenWorld Images; 15tl T. Cooper/GardenWorld Images; 15tr D. Warner/ GardenWorld Images; 15b GardenWorld Images; 16 F. Davis/GardenWorld Images; 17 GardenWorld Images; 19b L. Kirton/GardenWorld Images; 23t, 24 GardenWorld Images; 25 Mark Bolton/The Garden Picture Library; 26 Ailsa M Allaby/Science Photo Library; 27b F.Davis/ GardenWorld Images; 28-29, 30 GardenWorld Images; 32t, 34t Peter Stiles/Hortipix; 36 GardenWorld Images; 38 Michael Comb/Flora-PIX; 42, 44 GardenWorld Images; 50 IPC Magazine/GardenWorld Images; 52 D.Gould/ GardenWorld Images; 54 Archie Young/Science Photo Library; 56, 60, 64 Peter Stiles/Hortipix; 66 Peter Etchells/Science Photo Library; 68 Peter Stiles/Hortipix; 70 Michael Comb/Flora-PIX; 72t Jane Sugarman/Science Photo Library; 76 Michael Comb/Flora-PIX; 78 Peter Stiles/Hortipix; 80, 82, 88 GardenWorld Images; 90 Patrick Johns/Corbis; 92 GardenWorld Images;100, 102 Peter Stiles/Hortipix; 104 Michael Comb/Flora-PIX; 108 GardenWorld Images; 120, 122 Peter Stiles/Hortipix; 134 Michael Comb/Flora-PIX; 140t M J Higginson/Science Photo Library; 144t Peter Stiles/Hortipix; 146t D.Gould/GardenWorld Images; 150, 152 GardenWorld Images; 154 Michael Comb/Flora-PIX; 156 Mrs W D Monks/ Science Photo Library; 158 Peter Stiles/Hortipix; 160 Michael Comb/Flora-PIX; 162, 166 GardenWorld Images; 164 Michael Comb/Flora-PIX; 168t, 170, 173t Peter Stiles/Hortipix; 176-7, 179t GardenWorld Images; 181t D. Gould/GardenWorld Images; 182t I. Anderson/GardenWorld Images; 183 GardenWorld Images; 184l Peter Etchells/Science Photo Library; 186t GardenWorld Images; 187 Peter Stiles/Hortipix; 188 F. Davis/GardenWorld Images; 189t Leigh Clapp/The Garden Picture Library; 190 Henk Dijkman/The Garden Picture Library; 191t C. Hawes/GardenWorld Images; 193 Jeremy Samuelson/Getty Images; 194 Elsa M Megson/Science Photo Library; 195 GardenWorld Images; 196l, 196r, 197 Peter Stiles/Hortipix; 198b Clive Nichols/The Garden Picture Library; 199t Mel Watson/ The Garden Picture Library; 199b K. Howchin/ GardenWorld Images; 201t A C Seinet/Science Photo Library; 202 GardenWorld Images; 203, 204r Peter Stiles/Hortipix; 205tr GardenWorld Images; 207t G.Connelly/GardenWorld Images; 207br Archie Young/Science Photo Library; 208t Paul Shoesmith/Science Photo Library; 209t GardenWorld Images; 210t D.Gould/GardenWorld Images; 217 Nick Wiseman/Science Photo Library.